PRAISE FOR VIKTOR SHKLOVSKY

"Shklovsky, who refers to own his style as 'serpentine,' employs digression, repetition, autobiography and occasional salutations to the reader, confounding one's expectations of how a book of literary criticism should unfold. In doing so, he crafts a true rarity: a superbly written, extended critical study that's capable of inducing a feeling of affection in the reader towards its author."

—*The Guardian*

"One of the most lively and irreverent minds of the last century"

—David Bellos (*Is That a Fish in Your Ear?*)

"Shklovsky is a disciple worthy of Sterne. He has appropriated the device of infinitely delayed event, of the digression helplessly promising to return to the point, and of disguising his superbly controlled art with a breezy nonchalance. But it is not really Sterne that Shklovsky sounds like: it is an intellectual and witty Hemingway."

—Guy Davenport

"A rambling, digressive stylist, Shklovsky throws off brilliant aperçus on every page. . . . Like an architect's blueprint, [he] lays bare the joists and studs that hold up the house of fiction."

—Michael Dirda, *Washington Post*

"A work of gossip, allusion and esoteric reference, with devices—some typographical—which Shklovsky borrowed from Sterne, whom he much admired."

—John Bayley, *Listener*

T0051664

Other Books by Viktor Shklovsky

Bowstring: On the Dissimilarity of the Similar
Energy of Delusion: A Book on Plot
The Hamburg Score
A Hunt for Optimism
Knight's Move
Leo Tolstoy
Life of a Bishop's Assistant
Literature and Cinematography
Mayakovsky and His Circle
A Sentimental Journey: Memoirs, 1917–1922
Third Factory
Zoo, or Letters Not About Love

Viktor Shklovsky

ON THE THEORY OF PROSE

Translated from the Russian by Shushan Avagyan

DALKEY ARCHIVE PRESS

Dallas / Dublin

Originally published by Federatsia, Moscow, as *O teorii prozy* (2nd edition) in 1929.

Copyright © 2021 by Varvara Shklovskaya-Kordi.

Translation copyright © 2021 by Shushan Avagyan.

Afterword copyright © 2021 by Lyn Hejinian.

First Dalkey Archive edition, 2021.

ISBN: 978-1-56478-769-9

www.dalkeyarchive.com

Dallas / Dublin

Printed on permanent/durable acid-free paper.

Table of Contents

Translator's Note.. vii

Acknowledgments xi

ON THE THEORY OF PROSE

Foreword..3

Art as Device 5

The Connection Between Devices of Plot Construction
and General Devices of Style......................................26
    On the Ethnographic School..................................27
    On Motifs..30
    Stepped Structure and Deferment 35
    Motivations for Deferment..................................52
    Framing as a Device of Deferment............................64

The Structure of the Story and the Novel..........................71
    I 71
    II...85
    III..90
    IV...94

How *Don Quixote* Is Made..99
    Don Quixote's Speeches 99
    Inset Stories in Don Quixote................................112

The Mystery Story..143

The Mystery Novel 168
    Story Built on a Mistake....................................171
    Story Built on a Parallelism.................................173
    The Mystery Novel..176
    Little Dorrit 179
        1. The Mystery of the Watch...........................180
        2. The Mystery of the Dreams 183
        3. The Mystery of the Inheritance 185

4. The Mystery of Mr. Merdle 187
5. The Mystery of the Noises in the House 189
6. Denouements 191
Connection Between Parallels as a Mystery 198

The Parody Novel 214
Sterne's *Tristram Shandy* 214

Ornamental Prose 252
Andrei Bely
I 252
II 256
III 260
IV 265
V 269
VI 273

Literature Without Plot 279
I 279
II 286
III 289
IV 296
V 298
VI 304

Sketch and Anecdote 306

Appendix I 312

Appendix II 315

Appendix III 325

Afterword: Destinations, by Lyn Hejinian 327

TRANSLATOR'S NOTE

O teorii prozy or *On the Theory of Prose* was first published in 1925 by the Moscow publishing house Krug. The second edition, with two additional chapters, "Ornamental Prose" and "Sketch and Anecdote," was issued in 1929 by the same publishing house, which, however, had been swallowed up by the Federation of Organizations of Soviet Writers and renamed Federatsia. As it was of critical importance to the Prague School and the development of Czech Structuralism, the book was first translated into Czech, by Bohumil Mathesius, in 1933. In his review of the translation, Jan Mukařovský of the Prague Linguistic Circle both stressed the significance of Shklovsky's work against traditional literary theory and criticized "pure" Formalism for recognizing only the internal and autonomous development of literature. Still, its influence was indisputable and far-reaching. A German translation by Gisela Drohla and an Italian translation by Maria Olsoufieva appeared simultaneously in 1966, followed by a Japanese translation by Tadao Mizuno in 1971, and a French translation by Guy Verret in 1973.[1] The first English translation of *O teorii prozy* did not appear until 1990, although two chapters from the book—"Art As Technique" and "Sterne's *Tristram Shandy*: Stylistic Commentary"—had come out earlier, in Lee T. Lemon's and Marion J. Reis's pioneering anthology *Russian Formalist Criticism: Four Essays* (University of Nebraska Press,

1965). Another representative chapter from the book, "Plotless Prose: Vasily Rozanov," was published in the first issue of *Poetics Journal* (1982) in Richard Sheldon's translation. The 1929 edition was translated into English in its entirety by Benjamin Sher (Dalkey Archive Press, 1990). The present translation is also based on the second edition.

The same as any retranslation, this one too has benefited and learned from its predecessors, and I am truly indebted to Lee T. Lemon and Marion J. Reis, Richard Sheldon, and Benjamin Sher for their meticulous work and extensive annotations that trace the often unapparent references made by Shklovsky. Being an exile in both Russian and English, "a person out of place," I have, in turn, tried to accentuate the strangeness of Shklovsky's language through the foreignness of the translating language (how else could one translate Shklovsky?). Translation, as Borges allegorically suggested in "Pierre Menard," is indeed the "hesitant and rudimentary art of reading."[2] And every translation, without exception, is a transcribed form of close reading interspersed with a range of idiosyncratic under- and over-readings. So there is no doubt that readers returning to these seminal articles on the theory of prose will find in my translation many stylistic and semantic divergences from the previous versions. "There is not a single form in the history of art that disappears, and neither are there pure repetitions. The old form returns anew in order to express something new," Shklovsky wrote in *Bowstring*. And it seems that divergences are inevitable in Shklovsky, as he himself found it necessary to revisit *O teorii prozy* after years of debates not only with the proponents of Socialist Realism, but also the Structuralists (particularly Roman Jakobson and the Prague Linguistic Circle).

In 1983, just a year before his death, Shklovsky published a totally rewritten *O teorii prozy*. In this new version he returns to some of his favorite themes such as Opoyaz, the formal method, the theory of collision, the texts of Sterne, Tolstoy, and Cervantes, but with a completely new reading of his earlier work. He writes in this regard:

The book *O teorii prozy* has been published twice—in 1925 and in 1929.

I have written a lot since then. They sent me new articles on the same subject from Czechoslovakia recently, something around five hundred pages.

Sorting through the archives, I found my letter to Eichenbaum dated March 27, 1955, in which I wrote: ". . . Art is certainly not a bookish enterprise, but it is not a verbal one either. It is a fight for a stepped (to make it more approachable) perception of the world."

Now, during the past few years, I have been working on *Teorii prozy* every day because it is the argument of the heart, a means for dealing with heartache.

The book that was written in 1925 has changed—as life continues to change.

I write every day.

I am in no hurry. I will turn ninety soon, and who will rewrite this book . . .[3]

This third version of *O teorii prozy* was submitted to the publishing house of the Soviet Writers' Union in Moscow for publication on April 19, 1983. It was cleared by the censor and signed for publication five months later on September 19, 1983. Who knows what was edited out of this version? Regardless of the editorial expurgations and changes, one is able to feel Shklovsky's jubilant desire to transform, to change, to catapult himself into the future. *O teorii prozy* is not only one of the twentieth century's most influential works of literary theory, but it is also the book that Shklovsky kept returning to, the book that he wanted to remake even after his life.

The new *O teorii prozy*, which has yet to be discovered, abandons the long paragraph completely and progresses in the short form, the one-sentence paragraph, which by then had become Shklovsky's inimitable signature style. In his new work Shklovsky places the words *otstranenie* (removal, dismissal, pushing away from self) and *ostrannenie* (making the familiar strange or unrecognizable) next to each other in a sentence. He clarifies, albeit ironically, that he had made an error and spelled the new word with only one "n"—*ostranenie*. The meanings of these words (*otstranenie* and *ostrannenie*) are different, but they have the same plot, he claims—"the plot about the strangeness of life."

---

1. "Art as Device" ("L'art comme procédé") and "The Structure of the Story and the Novel" ("La construction de la nouvelle et du roman") first appeared in Tzvetan Todorov's anthology *Théorie de la littérature: Textes des Formalistes russes*, trans. Tzvetan Todorov (T*el Quel*, Paris: Seuil, 1965).

2. Jorge Luis Borges, "Pierre Menard, Author of Don Quixote," trans. Anthony Bonner, in *Ficciones* (New York: Grove Press, 1962).

3. Viktor Shklovsky, *O teorii prozy* [On the Theory of Prose]. Moscow: Soviet Writer, 1983.

ACKNOWLEDGMENTS

I have used existing translations, when possible, for quotations from texts originally in other languages, while I have compared texts originally in Russian with existing translations and revised some of them (all revisions are indicated in the footnotes). Texts that began life in English have been restored to their original form.

For enabling me to see this work through, I am infinitely grateful to Rebecca Chase and Paula Ressler for their unconditional welcome and for turning their home into the most hospitable space for translational adventures. This project would not have come to fruition without their warmth, generosity, and friendship. I also wish to thank Rebecca Saunders for the long walks along the lake in Chicago, which sustained me with intellectual dialogue and new insights. I have benefited greatly from Milner Library at Illinois State University, and I am particularly thankful to the literature and languages librarian Jean MacDonald for providing me with access to the collections of the library and a work station. I would not have been able to complete this extraordinary project without the support of the American University of Armenia, which is my academic base, and the Calouste Gulbenkian Foundation. A large measure of my gratitude goes to my editors, Nathaniel Davis and Alistair Ian Blyth, who worked untiringly and with rigorous care on the final edits of the manuscript. Finally, I owe my greatest thanks to my partner, Arpi Adamyan, for being a constant source of inspiration, and to my parents for their infinite support.

S. Avagyan

On the Theory of Prose

FOREWORD

It is perfectly clear that language is influenced by social relations.

Gleb Uspensky has a sketch about how members of a fishing artel create their own way of life and come up with names for a constellation "because of the whitefish." They fish at night and need the stars for navigation.

In the language of cattle breeders, you can always find many terms for physical features, such as coat color variations, which cannot even be accurately translated.

Still, the word is not a shadow.

The word is an object. And it changes according to its linguistic laws related to the physiology of speech, etc.

If in some language the name for a breastplate becomes the name for the human chest itself, this, of course, can be understood historically. But the changes in the word will not occur parallel to the changes in the form of the breastplate, and, of course, the word may survive the phenomenon that created it.

I examine in literary theory the inner laws of literature. If I were to draw a parallel with the factory, I would say that I am neither interested in the international cotton market nor in the politics of trusts, but only in the types of thread and ways of weaving.

Therefore, this whole book is devoted to the question of change in literary forms.

ART AS DEVICE

"Art is thinking in images." This phrase, which you can hear even from a grammar school student, nevertheless appears to be a starting point for the philologist who is beginning to formulate something in literary theory. The notion has entered the consciousness of many, and according to Potebnya, who ought to be seen as one of its originators, "There is no art, and especially no poetry, without images" (83). Also: "Poetry, like prose, is first and foremost a mode of thought and cognition" (97).[1]

Poetry is a special mode of thought—to be exact, a mode of thought through images. This mode entails a certain economy of mental effort, "a sensation of a relative ease of the process," and this economy reflexively evokes an aesthetic feeling. Apparently, this is how the academician Ovsyaniko-Kulikovsky, who undoubtedly read the books of Potebnya, understood and summarized the ideas of his teacher.[2] Potebnya and his numerous followers consider poetry to be a special kind of thought—thought with the help of imagery—and the task of imagery, according to them, is to help organize different objects and actions into groups in order to explain the unknown by means of the known. Or, in Potebnya's words: "The relationship of the image to what is being explained is that: a) the image serves as a constant predicate for varying subjects—a

---

[1] Aleksandr Potebnya, *Iz zapisok po teorii slovesnosti* [From Notes on the Theory of Verbal Art], 1905.

[2] Dmitri Ovsyaniko-Kulikovsky, *Yazyk i iskusstvo* [Language and Art], 1895.

5

constant means for attracting variable apperceptives . . . b) the image is far simpler and clearer than what it explains" (314). In other words, "since the purpose of imagery is to bring the meaning of the image closer to our understanding, and since without it imagery has no meaning, the image ought to be better known to us than that which is explained by it" (291).

It would be interesting to apply this principle to Tyutchev's comparison of lightning to deaf and dumb demons, or Gogol's comparison of the sky to God's mantle.

"There is no art without an image." "Art is thinking in images." Monstrous stretches were made for the sake of these definitions: people strove to understand music, architecture, and lyric poetry as thinking in images. After a quarter century of effort, Ovsyaniko-Kulikovsky finally had to recognize music, architecture, and lyric poetry as a special class of imageless art, which he then defined as lyrical arts appealing directly to the emotions. And so, it turns out that a large sector of art is not a mode of thought. One of them, however, lyric poetry (in the narrow sense), is similar to "imagistic" art in its treatment of words, and, what is more important, imagistic art passes quite imperceptibly into imageless art, and yet our perceptions of them are similar.

But the definition "art is thinking in images," which means (I am omitting the intermediary links of the well-known equations) that art primarily creates symbols, still persists, having survived the collapse of the theory on which it was based. It mainly thrives in the Symbolist movement, especially among its theorists.

And so, many people still believe that the main characteristic of poetry is thinking in images ("roads and shadows," "furrows and ridges").[3] Thus, they should have expected the history of this so-called "imagistic" art to be a history of changes in the image. It turns out, however, that images are virtually fixed; they pass from century to century, from country to country, from poet to poet,

---

[3] A reference to Vyacheslav Ivanov's collection of critical essays *Borozdy i mezhi* [Furrows and Ridges], 1916. [—Trans.]

almost unchanged. Images "belong to no one," they "belong to God." The more you try to understand an epoch, the more convinced you become that the images you thought were created by a given poet were taken almost unchanged from others. Ultimately, the task of poetic schools comes down to collecting and revealing new devices for the arrangement and development of verbal material; poets are more concerned with arranging images than creating them. Images are given; poets do not think through images so much as remember them.

Imagistic thought is not, in any case, something that unites all types of art or even all types of verbal art. And a change in imagery is not essential to the dynamics of poetry.

We know that often an expression is perceived to be poetic, created for aesthetic pleasure, when, in fact, it was created with no such intention. Take, for example, Annensky's opinion that Slavonic is especially poetic, or Andrei Bely's delight in the way eighteenth-century Russian poets placed adjectives after nouns. Bely delights in this as in something inherently artistic, or rather as intended and therefore artistic. In reality, it is a general feature of the given language (the influence of Church Slavonic). Thus, a work may be: (1) intended to be prosaic and experienced as poetic, or (2) intended to be poetic and experienced as prosaic. This suggests that the artistic quality attributed to a given object results from the way we perceive it. By objects of art, in the narrow sense, we mean things created through special devices designed to make them as obviously artistic as possible.

Potebnya's conclusion, which may be formulated as "poetry = imagery," created the whole theory of "imagery = symbolism," the ability of the image to serve as the invariable predicate of various subjects. (This conclusion has attracted, by virtue of a kinship of ideas, such Symbolists as Andrei Bely and Dmitri Merezhkovsky, with his *Eternal Companions*, and underlies the foundation of Symbolist theory.) The conclusion stems partly from the fact that Potebnya did not distinguish between the language of poetry and the language of prose. Consequently, he failed to notice that there are two types of images: (a) the image as a practical means for thinking, a means for grouping objects into clusters, and (b) the poetic image as a means for intensifying an impression. Let me clarify with an example. I am walking down the street and see a man in a fedora, walking ahead of me, drop his packet. I call after him: "Hey fedora! You lost your packet!" This is a purely prosaic trope. Here is another example. Several men are standing to attention. The commander, noticing that one of them is slouching, shouts: "Hey fedora! Mind how you stand!" This is a poetic trope. (In the first case, the word "fedora" is a metonym; in the second case, it is a metaphor. But I am interested in something else.) The poetic image is a means for creating the strongest possible impression. It has the same task as other poetic devices such as positive and negative parallelism, comparison, repetition, symmetry, hyperbole, and any other figure of speech that amplifies the sensation of the object (these can be the words or even the sounds of a literary work). But the poetic image is only externally similar to the image-fable, the image-thought, for example, when a little girl calls a glass sphere a watermelon (in Ovsyaniko-Kulikovsky's *Language and Art*, 16-17). The poetic image is but one of the means of poetic language. The prosaic image is a means for abstraction: a watermelon in place of a round lampshade or a watermelon in place of a head is only the abstraction of one of the object's qualities and is not any different from "head = sphere" or "watermelon = sphere." This, too, is a mode of thought, but it has nothing in common with poetry.

———

The law governing the economy of creative effort belongs to a group of generally accepted laws. Herbert Spencer wrote in *The Philosophy of Style* (1852):

On seeking for some clue to the law underlying these current maxims, we may see shadowed forth in many of them, the importance of economizing the reader's or hearer's attention. To so present ideas that they may be apprehended with the least possible mental effort, is the desideratum towards which most of the rules above quoted point.[4]

And Richard Avenarius wrote:

If the soul possessed inexhaustible energies, it would be indifferent to how much might be spent from this inexhaustible source; the only thing that would matter would be, perhaps, the time expended. But since its energies are limited, one is led to expect that the soul hastens to carry out the apperceptive processes as expediently as possible—that is, with the least expenditure of energy possible or, which is the same, with the greatest result possible.[5]

With a mere reference to the general law governing the economy of mental effort, Leon Petrażycki refutes William James's theory of the physical basis of emotion, which happens to contradict his own theory. Aleksandr Veselovsky followed suit in acknowledging the principle of the economy of creative effort—an attractive theory, especially in the study of rhythm—and summed up Spencer's ideas in the following way: "The virtue of style depends precisely on the ability to deliver the greatest amount of ideas in the fewest possible words."[6] Even Andrei Bely, who in his best writings gave numerous examples of impeded, so-called "stumbling" rhythm (particularly in the examples from Baratynsky), and who showed the impediment of poetic epithets, deemed it necessary to speak of the law of economy in his book—a heroic attempt to create

---

[4] Herbert Spencer, *The Philosophy of Style* (New York: Pageant Press, 1959). All subsequent quotations from *The Philosophy of Style* are taken from this edition.

[5] Richard Avenarius, *Philosophie als Denken der Welt gemäß dem Prinzip des kleinsten Kraftmaßes* [Philosophy as Thinking of the World According to the Principle of Least Action], 1876.

[6] Aleksandr Veselovsky, *Tri glavy iz istoricheskoy poetiki* [Three Chapters from Historical Poetics], 1913.

a theory of art based on unverified facts from outdated books, his vast knowledge of poetic devices, and Kraevich's textbook of physics.

The idea of the economy of effort as the law and purpose of creativity is perhaps true for a particular case—"practical" language. However, due to the prevailing ignorance regarding the difference between the laws of practical language and the laws of poetic language, the idea was extended to poetic language as well. The fact that Japanese poetic language has sounds that do not exist in practical Japanese was perhaps the first factual indication that these two languages do not coincide. Lev Yakubinsky's article, in which he discusses the absence of the law of the dissimilation of liquids in poetic language and how poetic language admits such hard-to-pronounce sound clusters, is one of the first claims, withstanding scientific criticism, that factually indicates the opposition (for now applicable only to this case) between the laws of poetic and practical languages.[7]

We must speak, then, about the laws of expenditure and economy in poetic language not on the basis of prosaic language, but on the basis of the laws of poetic language.

If we study the general laws of perception, we will see that habitual actions become automatic. So, for example, all of our skills move into the realm of the unconscious-automatic; if one remembers the sensation of holding a pen in one's hand or speaking a foreign language for the first time and compares that with the sensation of performing the action for the ten thousandth time, then one will agree with us. This process of automatization explains the laws of our prosaic speech, with its unfinished phrases and half-articulated words. Algebra is the ideal manifestation of this process whereby objects are replaced with symbols. Words are not fully articulated in rapid practical speech; the mind barely registers

---

[7] Lev Yakubinsky's article "On the Sounds of Poetic Language" was published in the first volume of *Sborniki po teorii poeticheskovo yazyka* [Collected Works on the Theory of Poetic Language] in 1916; his second article, "The Accumulation of Identical Liquids in Practical and Poetic Languages," appeared in the second volume of *Sborniki* in 1917 along with Shklovsky's "Art as Device." [—Trans.]

the initial sounds of a name. Aleksandr Pogodin gives the example of a boy processing the phrase "Les montagnes de la Suisse sont belles" in the form of a series of letters: L, m, d, l, S, s, b.[8]

This kind of thinking prompted not only the logic of algebra, but also the choice of symbols (letters, and specifically initial letters). By means of this algebraic method of thinking, objects are grasped quantitatively and spatially—we do not see them but rather recognize them by their primary features. The object passes before us as if in a package; we know that it exists because of the space that it occupies, but we only see its surface. Perceived in this way, the object withers away, first losing its palpability, then its effect. This kind of prosaic perception explains why words are half-heard (Yakubinsky) and half-uttered (which also accounts for slips of the tongue). The algebraization process—the automatization of an object—permits the greatest economy of perceptual effort; objects are either presented by a single feature (for example, a number), or else performed by a formula without ever registering in our consciousness. Consider the following entry from Tolstoy's diary:

> I was dusting the room and, after making a circle, approached the sofa and couldn't remember whether or not I had dusted it. I couldn't and knew that it would be impossible to remember, since these movements are habitual and unconscious. If, in fact, I dusted it and forgot—that is, acted unconsciously— then it was the same as if I had not dusted it. If some conscious person had been watching, then the fact could have been established. Otherwise, it is as if nothing has ever transpired, nothing has ever been, just like the complex lives of many people who go on living unconsciously. (February 29, 1897, Nikolskoe)[9]

And so life is lost in oblivion. Automatization eats away at objects, clothes, furniture, one's wife, and the fear of war.

---

[8] Aleksandr Pogodin, *Yazyk, kak tvorchestvo* [Language as Creativity], 1913.

[9] Lev Tolstoy, "Dnevnik," *Letopis* (December 1915), 354.

"If nothing has ever transpired, then nothing has ever been, just like the complex lives of many people who go on living unconsciously."

And so in order to restore the sensation of life, in order to feel things—to make the stone stony—we have something called art. The purpose of art is to convey the sensation of an object as something visible, not as something recognizable. The devices of art—*ostranenie*, or the "estrangement" of objects, and the impeded form—magnify the difficulty and duration of perception, because the process of perception in art is an end in itself and must be prolonged. *Art is a means of experiencing the making of an object; the finished object is not important in art.*

The life of a poetic (artistic) work proceeds from being visible to being recognizable, from poetry to prose, from the concrete to the general, from Cervantes's Don Quixote—the scholar and impoverished nobleman, enduring half-consciously his humiliation in the court of the duke—to Turgenev's expansive but empty Don Quixote, from Charlemagne to the designation "king." As the work of art and its artfulness die, the work expands: a fable is more symbolic than a long poem, and a proverb is more symbolic than a fable. This is why Potebnya's theory was less self-contradictory in the analysis of the fable, which, in his view, he examined thoroughly. His theory didn't tackle artistic, "objectual" works, and this is why his book was unfinishable. As we know, *Notes on the Theory of Verbal Art* was published in 1905, thirteen years after his death. Potebnya managed fully to develop only the section on the fable.[10]

Objects become recognizable once they have been perceived several times: we know there is something in front of us, but we don't see it.[11] Hence we cannot say anything significant about it. The removal of an object from the automatism of perception is

[10] Aleksandr Potebnya, *Iz lektsij po teorii slovesnosti. Basnya. Poslovitsa. Pogovorka* [From Lectures on the Theory of Verbal Art: Fable, Proverb, Saying], 1914.

[11] From Shklovsky's article "The Resurrection of the Word," 1914.

accomplished through art in several ways. I want to highlight here one of the techniques used most often by Tolstoy—the writer who, at least for Merezhkovsky, seems to present things as he sees them, in their entirety, without changing them.

Tolstoy estranges a thing not by naming it, but by describing it as if he were seeing it for the first time, or describing an event as if it were happening for the first time. When describing something, he avoids the conventional names of its parts and instead names the corresponding parts of other things. For example, in the article "Shame!" (1895) Tolstoy estranges the idea of flogging in this way: ". . . that people who have violated the law, and sometimes old men, be undressed, thrown on the floor, and beaten with rods on their backsides," and a few lines later, "switched over their bare buttocks."[12] In a footnote to this passage, Tolstoy asks: "Why this particular stupid, savage method of causing pain, and no other? Why not stick pins into the shoulder or some other part of the body, compress the hands or feet in a vise, or something like that?" I apologize for this crude example, but it is typical of the way in which Tolstoy reaches our conscience. The familiar act of flogging is estranged both by the description and by the proposal to change its form without changing its essence. Tolstoy constantly draws on this method of estrangement. In one of his stories ("Strider"), the narrator is a horse and things are perceived not from a human, but an equine point of view.

Here is how the horse perceives the institution of property:

What they said about flogging and Christianity I understood well enough, but I was quite in the dark as to what they meant by the words "*his* colt," from which I perceived that people considered that there was some connection between me and the head groom. What the connection was I could not at all understand then. Only much later when they separated me from the other horses did I learn what it meant. At that time I could not at all understand what they meant by speaking of

[12] Lev Tolstoy, *Miscellaneous Letters and Essays*, trans. Leo Wiener (London: Dent, 1905).

me as being a man's property. The words "*my* horse" applied to me, a live horse, seemed to me as strange as to say "my land," "my air," or "my water."

But those words had an enormous effect on me. I thought of them constantly and only after long and varied relations with men did I at last understand the meaning they attach to these strange words, which indicate that men are guided in life not by deeds but by words. They like not so much to do or abstain from doing anything, as to be able to apply conventional words to different objects. Such words, considered very important among them, are *my* and *mine*, which they apply to various things, creatures or objects: even to land, people, and horses. They have agreed that of any given thing only one person may use the word *mine*, and he who in this game of theirs may use that conventional word about the greatest number of things is considered the happiest. Why this is so I do not know, but it is so. For a long time I tried to explain it by some direct advantage they derive from it, but this proved wrong.

For instance, many of those who called me their horse did not ride me, quite other people rode me; nor did they feed me—quite other people did that. Again it was not those who called me *their* horse who treated me kindly, but coachmen, veterinaries, and in general quite other people. Later on, having widened my field of observation, I became convinced that not only as applied to us horses, but in regard to other things, the idea of *mine* has no other basis than a low, mercenary instinct in men, which they call the feeling or right of property. A man who never lives in it says "my house" but only concerns himself with its building and maintenance; and a tradesman talks of "my cloth business," but has none of his clothes made of the best cloth that is in his shop.

There are people who call land theirs, though they have never seen that land and never walked on it. There are people who call other people theirs, but have never seen those others, and the whole relationship of the owners to the owned is that they do them harm.

There are men who call women their women or their wives; yet these women live with other men. And men strive in life not to do what they think right, but to call as many things as possible *their own*.

I am now convinced that in this lies the essential difference between men and us. Therefore, not to speak of other things in which we are superior to men, on this ground alone we may boldly say that in the scale of living creatures we stand higher than man. The activity of men, at any rate of those I have had to do with, is guided by *words*, while ours is guided by *deeds*.

The horse is killed toward the end of the story, but the mode of the narrative, its device, does not change:

The dead body of Serpukhovskoy, which had walked about the earth eating and drinking, was put under ground much later. Neither his skin, nor his flesh, nor his bones, were of any use.

Just as for the last twenty years his body that had walked the earth had been a great burden to everybody, so the putting away of that body was again an additional trouble to people. He had not been wanted by anybody for a long time and had only been a burden, yet the dead who bury their dead found it necessary to clothe that swollen body, which at once began to decompose, in a good uniform and good boots and put it into a new and expensive coffin with new tassels at its four corners, and then to place that coffin in another coffin of lead, to take it to Moscow and there dig up some long buried human bones, and to hide in that particular spot this decomposing body full of maggots in its new uniform and polished boots, and cover it all up with earth.[13]

Thus, as we see, Tolstoy continues to use the same device at the end of the story even when the motivation for it is gone.

Tolstoy used the same device in his description of all the battle

---

[13] Lev Tolstoy, "Strider: The Story of a Horse" in *Collected Shorter Fiction, Volume I*, trans. Louise and Aylmer Maude and Nigel J. Cooper (New York: Alfred A. Knopf, 2001). All subsequent quotations from "Strider" are taken from this translation.

scenes in *War and Peace*. He presented them, above all, as something strange. These descriptions are too long to be quoted here; I would have to copy out a considerable part of the four-volume novel. But Tolstoy also applied this method to describe the salons and the theater:

> The floor of the stage consisted of smooth boards, at the sides was some painted cardboard representing trees, and at the back was a cloth stretched over boards. In the center of the stage sat some girls in red bodices and white skirts. One very fat girl in a white silk dress sat apart on a low bench, to the back of which a piece of green cardboard was glued. They all sang something. When they had finished their song the girl in white went up to the prompter's box, and a man with tight silk trousers over his stout legs, and holding a plume and a dagger, went up to her and began singing, waving his arms about.
>
> First the man in the tight trousers sang alone, then she sang, then they both paused while the orchestra played and the man fingered the hand of the girl in white, obviously awaiting the beat to start singing with her. They sang together and everyone in the theater began clapping and shouting, while the man and woman on the stage—who represented lovers—began smiling, spreading out their arms, and bowing . . .
>
> In the second act there was scenery representing tombstones, and there was a round hole in the canvas to represent the moon, shades were raised over the footlights, and from horns and contrabass came deep notes while many people appeared from right and left wearing black cloaks and holding things like daggers in their hands. They began waving their arms. Then some other people ran in and began dragging away the maiden who had been in white and was now in light blue. They did not drag her away at once, but sang with her for a long time and then at last dragged her off, and behind the scenes something metallic was struck three times and everyone knelt down and sang a prayer. All these things were repeatedly interrupted by the enthusiastic shouts of the audience.

The third act is described similarly:

. . . But suddenly a storm came on, chromatic scales and diminished sevenths were heard in the orchestra, everyone ran off, again dragging one of their numbers away, and the curtain dropped. (Book II, Part V, Chapter 9)[14]

In the fourth act, "there was some sort of a devil who sang, waving his arm about, till the boards were withdrawn from under him and he disappeared down below."

Tolstoy described the city and the trial in the same way in *Resurrection*. He questioned marriage similarly in *The Kreutzer Sonata*: "'Spiritual affinity! Identity of ideals!' he repeated, emitting his peculiar sound. 'But in that case why go to bed together?'"[15] But he did not only use the device of estrangement to make visible the things that he criticized.

Pierre got up and left his new companions, crossing between the camp-fires to the other side of the road where he had been told the common soldier-prisoners were stationed. He wanted to talk to them. On the road he was stopped by a French sentinel who ordered him back.

Pierre turned back, not to his companions by the campfire but to an unharnessed cart where there was nobody. Tucking his legs under him and dropping his head he sat down on the cold ground by a wheel of the cart and remained motionless a long while sunk in thought. Suddenly he burst out into a fit of his broad, good-natured laughter, so loud that men from various sides turned with surprise to see what this strange and evidently solitary laughter could mean.

"Ha-ha-ha!" laughed Pierre. And he said aloud to himself: "The soldier did not let me pass. They took me and shut me

---

[14] Lev Tolstoy, *War and Peace*, trans. Louise and Aylmer Maude (New York: Alfred A. Knopf, 1992). All subsequent quotations from *War and Peace* are taken from this translation.

[15] Lev Tolstoy, *The Kreutzer Sonata* in *Collected Shorter Fiction, Volume II*, trans. Louise and Aylmer Maude and Nigel J. Cooper (New York: Alfred A. Knopf, 2001). All subsequent quotations from *The Kreutzer Sonata* are taken from this translation.

up. They hold me captive. What, me? Me? My immortal soul? Ha-ha-ha! Ha-ha-ha! . . ." and he laughed till tears started to his eyes. . . .

Pierre glanced up at the sky and the twinkling stars in its far-away depths. "And all that is me, all that is within me, and it is all I!" thought Pierre. "And they caught all that and put it into a shed boarded up with planks!" He smiled, and went and lay down to sleep beside his companions. (*War and Peace*, Book IV, Part II, Chapter 14)

Anyone who knows Tolstoy can find hundreds of such examples in his work. His way of seeing things out of context is evident in his late works too, where he applied the device of estrangement to the description of religious dogmas and rituals by replacing the customary religious terms used in church rituals with their literal meanings. The result was something strange, monstrous, and taken by many—quite sincerely—as blasphemy, wounding them to the core. And yet this was the same device whereby Tolstoy perceived and described the surrounding world. Tolstoy's perceptions unsettled his own faith, confronting him with things that he had long avoided.

————

The device of estrangement is not specifically Tolstoyan. I cited Tolstoy simply because his work is known to everyone.

Now, having explained the nature of this literary device, let us try to determine the limits of its application. In my opinion, estrangement can be found almost anywhere there is an image.

In other words, the difference between our point of view and Potebnya's can be formulated as follows: the image is not a constant subject modified by changing predicates. The purpose of the image is not to bring its meaning closer to our understanding, but rather to allow us to perceive the object in a special way, *to make the object "visible" rather than "recognizable."*

The aim of imagery may be traced more clearly in erotic art; an erotic object is usually presented as if it were seen for the first time. Consider, for example, Nikolai Gogol's "Christmas Eve":

Then he went closer to her and, with a cough and a smirk, touched her plump bare arm with his long fingers and said with an air expressive both of slyness and satisfaction:

"And what have you here, magnificent Solokha?" and saying this he stepped back a little.

"What do you mean? My arm, Osip Nikiforovich!" answered Solokha.

"Hm! your arm! He-he-he!" cried the sexton, highly delighted with his opening. And he paced up and down the room.

"And what have you here, incomparable Solokha . . . ?" he said with the same air, going up to her again, lightly touching her neck and skipping back again in the same way.

"As though you don't see, Osip Nikiforovich!" answered Solokha; "my neck and my necklace on my neck."

"Hm! A necklace on your neck! He-he-he!" and the sexton walked again up and down the room, rubbing his hands.

"And what have you here, incomparable Solokha . . . ?" There's no telling what the sexton might have touched next with his long fingers . . . [16]

Knut Hamsun has the following in *Hunger*: "Two white marvels showed through her lace."[17]

Or else erotic objects are depicted allegorically, where the author's intent is clearly not to bring its meaning "closer to our understanding."

This includes the depiction of sexual organs in the form of a lock and key, or parts of a loom, or in the form of a bow and arrow, or a game of rings and spikes as in the *bylina* about Staver

---

[16] Nikolai Gogol, *The Complete Tales of Nikolai Gogol, Volume I*, trans. Constance Garnett, ed. Leonard J. Kent (University of Chicago Press, 1985).

[17] Knut Hamsun, *Hunger*, trans. Robert Bly (Nobel Prize Library, 1971).

Godinovich.[18] The husband fails to recognize his wife dressed in the armor of a bogatyr. She poses the following riddle:

> "Do you remember, Staver, do you recall,
>> How we played as children in the yard?
>> We played rings and spikes—
>> Yours was the silver spike
>> And mine the gilded ring;
>> I hit the target only now and then
>> But you did every time."
> Staver, the son of Godinovich, replied:
>> "Surely I never played rings and spikes with you!"
> But Vasilisa Mikulichna went on:
>> "Do you remember, Staver, do you recall,
>> How we learned to write together?
>> Yours was the gilded pen
>> And mine the silver inkpot;
>> I inked the pen only now and then
>> But you did every time."

In another version of this *bylina*, the riddle is followed by the solution:

> Then the terrible ambassador Vasilyushka
> Lifted his robes all the way up to his navel.
> And behold, young Staver, the son of Godinovich,
> Recognized the gilded ring . . .

But the device of estrangement is not limited to the erotic riddle, which is a form of euphemism. It is the basis and meaning underlying all riddles. Every riddle either describes an object using words that establish and illustrate it, but which seem inapplicable to the object during the telling (for example, "two ends, two rings, a nail in the middle" for scissors), or it incorporates a

---

[18] The first two examples are from Dmitri Sadovnikov, *Zagadki russkovo naroda* [Riddles of the Russian People], 1901; the other two are from Pavel Rybnikov, *Pesni, sobrannye P. Rybnikovym* [Songs Collected by P. Rybnikov], 1910.

unique sound estrangement, a type of parroting game: "thloor and theiling" for floor and ceiling (Sadovnikov 51), and so on.

Erotic images that are not riddles may also be a type of estrangement. I mean, of course, the vocabulary of the *chansonette* with its "croquet mallets," "airplanes," "little dolls," "little brothers," and so on. These images are comparable to the folkloric images of trampling the grass and breaking the guelder rose.

The device of estrangement is perfectly obvious in the widespread image—the motif of the erotic pose, in which the bear and other animals (or the Devil) do not recognize the human being.[19]

Another typical example of non-recognition can be found in tale no. 70 in Dmitri Zelenin's collection of Russian tales from the Perm governorate:

A peasant was plowing a field with a piebald mare. A bear approached him and asked, "Uncle, who made this mare piebald for you?"

"I did the piebalding myself."

"But how?"

"If you let me, I'll do it to you."

The bear agreed. The peasant tied his feet with a rope, removed the plowshare from the plow, heated it on the fire, and applied it to his flanks. He made the bear piebald by scorching his fur down to the hide with the hot plowshare. The man untied the bear, who went off and lay down under a tree.

A magpie flew to the field to pick at the meat. The peasant caught her and broke one of her legs. The magpie flew off and perched on the same tree under which the bear was lying.

Then a giant horsefly flew over the field, landed on the mare, and started to bite the mare. The peasant caught the horsefly, shoved a stick up its rear, and let it go. The horsefly went to the tree where the bear and the magpie were. There all three sat.

---

[19] See "Besstrashnyy barin" [The Daring Barin] in Dmitri Zelenin's collection of Russian tales from the Vyatka governorate, and "Spravedlivyy soldat" [The Upright Soldier] (no. 84) in Yevdokim Romanov's collection of Belarusian tales.

The peasant's wife came to the field to bring him his dinner. The man and his wife finished their dinner in the fresh air, and he began to wrestle with her on the ground. The bear saw this and said to the magpie and the horsefly, "Holy Father! The peasant wants to piebald someone again!" The magpie said, "No, he wants to break someone's leg." And the horsefly said, "No, he wants to shove a stick up someone's rear."

The similarity between the device used in this tale and the one used in Tolstoy's "Strider" is obvious, I think.

Estrangement of the act itself is very frequent in literature. For example, Boccaccio uses images of "scraping the barrel," "catching the nightingale," or "merrily beating the wool" in *The Decameron* (the last image is not developed into a plot). Estrangement is also employed when depicting sexual organs.

A whole series of plots is built on this kind of "non-recognition"—for example, in "The Bashful Lady" in Aleksandr Afanasyev's *Cherished Tales*. The tale is constructed around the premise that an object is never called by its proper name; in other words, a game of non-recognition. The same can be seen in "The Bear and the Rabbit," where a bear and a rabbit are mending a "wound," and in "A Woman's Spot" (tale no. 252 in Nikolai Onchukov's *Northern Tales*).

Constructions such as "mortar and pestle" or "putting the devil back in hell" (*The Decameron*) also belong to this class of estrangement.

I will address estrangement in psychological parallelism in my next chapter on plot construction. However, let me reiterate here that the important thing in parallelism is the sensation of non-co-incidence in the similar.

The aim of parallelism, the same as that of imagery in general, is to transfer an object from its customary sphere of perception to a new sphere of perception; in other words, a unique semantic shift.

———

When studying poetic speech in its phonetic and lexical composition, as well as its syntactic and semantic construction, we encounter everywhere the same *sign of the artistic*: it is intentionally created to push perception beyond automatism, its visibility is the author's aim, and it is "artificially" created in such a way that it holds perception, raising it to its highest possible potential and duration, so that the work is perceived not in its spatiality but in its uninterruptedness. These are the conditions of "poetic language," which, according to Aristotle, must have the character of something outlandish and amazing. Practically speaking, such language is often literally foreign, like Sumerianisms in Assyrian, or Latinisms in medieval European languages, or Arabisms in Persian, or Old Bulgarian in literary Russian, or else like elevated, literary language in folk songs. To this category belong also the widespread archaisms of poetic language, the impediments of the *dolce stil nuovo* of the twelfth century, the language of Arnaut Daniel with its obscure style and impeded (*harte*) forms, which *anticipate difficulties in pronunciation*.[20] In his article, Lev Yakubinsky demonstrated the law of impediment in the phonetics of poetic language, particularly in the repetition of identical sounds. Therefore, the language of poetry may be said to be a difficult, impeded, decelerated form of language.

In some isolated cases, the language of poetry approaches the language of prose, but this does not violate the law of difficulty. Pushkin wrote:

> Her sister
> was called Tatyana.
> For the first time a novel's tender pages
> with such a name we willfully shall grace. (Chapter 2, XXIV)[21]

Pushkin's contemporaries considered poetic language to be the

---

[20] Friedrich Diez, *Leben und Werke der Troubadours* [The Lives and Works of the Troubadours], 1829.

[21] Aleksandr Pushkin, *Eugene Onegin, Volume I*, trans. Vladimir Nabokov (New York: Pantheon Books, 1964). All subsequent quotations from Eugene Onegin are taken from this translation.

elevated style of Derzhavin, and Pushkin's style, due to its "trivi-
ality" (as was thought at the time), seemed to them unexpectedly
difficult. We should remember the horror of Pushkin's contemporaries at the vulgarity of his expressions. He used folk speech
as a special device for arresting the reader's attention in the same
way that his contemporaries used *Russian* phrases in their typically
French speech (for examples, see Tolstoy's *War and Peace*).

An even more characteristic phenomenon occurs today. Literary
Russian, though foreign in its origin, has so permeated the vernacular of the people that it has raised much of popular speech to
its own level, while at the same time literature has developed an
affinity for dialects (Remizov, Klyuev, Yesenin, and others, who are
so unequal in their talents and yet so close in their intentionally
provincial language) and barbarisms (which made the emergence
of Igor Severyanin's school possible). Maxim Gorky is also making the transition from literary language to the Leskovian idiom.
Thus, vernacular speech and literary language have switched places
(Vyacheslav Ivanov and many others). We finally have a powerful
movement that aims to create a new, specifically poetic language.
At the head of this school, as we know, stands Velimir Khlebnikov.
Hence, we arrive at the definition of poetry as *decelerated, slanted*
speech. Poetic speech is *constructed* speech. Prose, on the other
hand, is ordinary speech: economical, easy, correct speech (*dea
prosae*—the goddess of correct, easy birth, the "straight" position
of the baby). I will write more about deceleration, deferral as a
general *law* of art in my next chapter, on plot construction.

The argument of those theorists who advance the economy
of effort as the defining feature of poetic language nonetheless
seems to be quite strong when it comes to the question of rhythm.
Spencer gives a seemingly indisputable interpretation of the role
of rhythm in his *Philosophy of Style*:

> Just as the body, in receiving a series of varying concussions,
> must keep the muscles ready to meet the most violent of them,

as not knowing when such may come; so, the mind in receiving unarranged articulations, must keep its perceptives active enough to recognize the least easily caught sounds. And as, if the concussions recur in a definite order, the body may husband its forces by adjusting the resistance needful for each concussion; so, if the syllables be rhythmically arranged, the mind may economize its energies by anticipating the attention required for each syllable. (IV: The Superiority of Poetry to Prose Explained)

This apparently convincing remark, however, suffers from a common flaw—the mixing of laws that govern poetic language with the laws of prosaic language. Spencer fails to differentiate between them in his book; meanwhile, there may be two types of rhythm. Prosaic rhythm, the rhythm of a work song such as "Dubinushka," can replace a command ("Hit it!") and at the same time ease and automatize work. And indeed, it is easier to walk to the beat of music than to no sound. The same goes for a conversation—it is much easier to walk engrossed in a lively conversation, as the act of walking recedes from our consciousness. So, prosaic rhythm is important as an *automatizing* factor. The rhythm of poetry is different. There is such a notion as "order" in art, yet not a single column of a Greek temple stands in perfect order, and artistic rhythm may be said to exist in prosaic rhythm as a disruption. Attempts have been made to systematize these disruptions. This is the task of current theories of rhythm. But one may assume that this systematization will not be successful because, in fact, the question is not about complex rhythmic patterns, but about the disruption of rhythm itself, which is unpredictable. If this disruption enters the canon, it will lose its power as an impeding device. But I will end my discussion of rhythm here, as I intend to devote a separate book to it later.

THE CONNECTION BETWEEN DEVICES OF PLOT CONSTRUCTION AND GENERAL DEVICES OF STYLE

"Why walk on a tightrope and, as if that were not enough, squat every four steps?" asked the Russian realist Saltykov-Shchedrin, speaking of poetry. The question is clear to anyone looking at art, except for those who have been poisoned by a defective theory of rhythm as an organizational factor. What calls for the slanted, difficult poetic speech that ties the poet's tongue? Why the strange, unusual lexicon, and the unusual arrangement of words? Why does King Lear fail to recognize Kent? Why do both Kent and Lear fail to recognize Edward?—asked Tolstoy, astonished by the laws of Shakespearean drama. And this was Tolstoy, who knew how to see things and how to be amazed by them. Why do the recognition scenes in the plays of Menander, Plautus, and Terence take place in the last act, when the spectators have already predicted the kinship between the antagonists (the author himself often hinting at it in the prologue)? Why does someone ask for the next dance even after consent has tacitly been given? What keeps Lieutenant Glahn and Edvarda apart in Hamsun's *Pan*, forcing them to wander through the world alone, despite their love for each other? Why is it that Ovid, in creating *The Art of Love* out of love, advised not to rush into the arms of pleasure?

The road of art is serpentine—it is a road on which the foot feels the stones, a road that turns back on itself. A word approaches another word; it feels the other word like a cheek feels another cheek. Then words fall apart and, instead of a single compound expression tossed out automatically like a chocolate bar from a vending machine, the word-sound is born—the word as an articulated movement. Dance is a way of walking that can be felt, or more precisely, a way of walking that is made to be felt. And so, we dance behind the plow. It is because we are plowing, but we don't need the tillage.[22]

In one of the old Greek books, a prince is so engrossed in dancing at his own wedding that he throws off his clothes and begins to dance naked while standing on his hands. When the exasperated king, the father of the bride, shouts at him, "Young man, you've just danced away your wedding!" he answers, "I couldn't care less!" and goes on kicking his legs in the air.

On the Ethnographic School

In developing a poetics of plot the Ethnographic school, the most prominent representative of which was Aleksandr Veselovsky, came to the conclusion that it is important to make a differentiation between plot and motif:

a) By motif I mean the simplest narrative *unit* that imaginally responds to the different inquiries of the primordial mind or to observation of everyday life. As a result of a similarity or concurrence of *everyday life and psychological* conditions existing at the early stages of human development, such motifs could have emerged independently from each other and at the same time still have represented similar features. The following can serve as examples: 1) the so-called *légendes des origines*, the representation of the sun as an eye, or

---

[22] An allusion to Tolstoy's statement in a letter to Afanasi Fet that writing poetry is the same as dancing behind the plow. [—Trans.]

the sun and moon as brother and sister or husband and
wife; the myths about sunrise and sunset, the dark spots
on the moon, eclipses, etc.; 2) everyday situations, such
as the abduction of a young maiden or someone's wife (a
scene from the folk wedding), the parting of the ways (in
fairy tales), etc.

b) By *plot* I mean a theme that weaves various situations—
motifs—together. For example: 1) tales about the sun (and
his mother, as in Greek and Malaysian legends about the
cannibal sun); 2) tales about abduction. The more complex and illogical the combination of motifs (as in songs,
with their combination of several stylistic motifs) and the
more motifs there are, the more difficult it is to suppose
(for example, in the case of two similar tales originating in
two different tribes) that they emerged by way of psychological autogenesis due to identical concepts and everyday
life factors. In such cases one may raise the possibility of
nations *borrowing* plot structures from each other *in historical time.*[23]

A few pages before this passage, in his introduction, Veselovsky
writes:

[I]f in different national settings we encounter a formula with
an identically arbitrary sequence of β ($\alpha + \beta$, β_1, β_2, etc.),[24]
such a similarity cannot be based on similar processes of the
psyche. If there are twelve repeating motifs (β), then, according to Joseph Jacobs (*Folk-lore*, III, 76), the probability of
it being independently formulated takes on the ratio of 1 :
479,001,599, and we can rightfully speak about borrowing.

---

[23] Aleksandr Veselovsky, *Poetika syuzhetov* [A Poetics of Plots] in *Sobranie sochinenii* [Collected Works],
Vol. II, 1913.

[24] The formula appears with a minus sign in Shklovsky's quotation: β ($\alpha - \beta$, β_1, β_2, etc.), which must
have been a typographical error. I have reverted here to Veselovsky's original formula. [—Trans.]

However, a coincidence of plots may occur even where there is no supposition of borrowing; for example, the Native American tale about the birds choosing a king for themselves—wherein, through cunning, the smallest bird is crowned—is surprisingly similar to a European fairy tale with the same subject (Klinger). Likewise, as Veselovsky points out in *Poetika syuzhetov*, a certain tale from Zanzibar is very similar to Grimm's fairy tale no. 15.

Especially remarkable is the parallel Grigori Potanin draws between the story of Bata and his brother Anpu's wife (the Egyptian tale of two brothers) and the Turkic epic of Edige.[25]

I should point out that the span between these two tales is four thousand years. Although the common hypothesis in such cases is that the second tale was introduced by colonists, this kind of explanation is reminiscent of Voltaire's supposition that fossil sea-shells found on the Alps were brought there by pilgrims. Besides, it is quite puzzling as to why the *arbitrary* sequence of motifs should be preserved in this borrowing. It is specifically the sequence of events that gets distorted in eyewitness accounts. Moreover, even when they remain within a single linguistic environment, tales do not stand out as being especially textually stable.

Let's listen to the *storyteller*. If he is a good one, his words will weave themselves into place like beads on a string, and you can even hear a rhythm, whole verses. But all of this is true for stories that are often retold, stories that the storyteller has *learned by heart*. The rhythm is accidental, the verse lines are obviously taken from *bylinas*. Force him to repeat and he will use other words to narrate the same thing. Ask him if anyone else knows the story and he will point to a *fellow villager*. The fellow villager heard the story along with him from an old man or a wanderer. If you ask the fellow villager to tell you the same story, you will hear the story told not only in a different language and different manner of speech, but often in a different

---

[25] Grigori Potanin, *Vostochnye motivy v srednevekovom evropeiskom epose* [Eastern Motifs in the Medieval European Epic], 1899.

tone as well. One storyteller introduces or preserves pathetic details, another inserts or maintains a derisive point of view in certain scenes, while a third storyteller adapts a denouement from another tale (or from the *general trove* available to all storytellers). He introduces new characters and new adventures. Then you ask him how he learned this tale. He says that he first heard it (and others) when he was fishing on the shores of Lake Ladoga or Lake Onega, or when he was in a shelter, or in a lodging, or sitting by a campfire. He heard some of these tales from the folk of Povenets, or from the folk of the Olonets region, or from the Karelians, or from the Swedes (Finns). He crammed as many of these tales into his memory as he could, yet all he had left were two or three tales. The well-known, popular representations had donned a familiar dress, attaining a familiar turn of phrase. As the saying goes, '*A tale—a turn*.'"[26]

The tale disintegrates and is assembled anew.

Let me conclude.

Random coincidences are impossible. Coincidences can be explained only by the existence of special laws of plot construction. Even the admission of borrowing does not explain the existence of identical stories separated by thousands of years and tens of thousands of versts. Hence, Joseph Jacobs is wrong when he presupposes the absence of any laws governing plot construction, instead positing an accidental arrangement of motifs into rows or axes. In reality, tales constantly disintegrate and re-turn in accordance with special laws of plot construction as yet unknown to us.

On Motifs

Many objections may be raised against the Ethnographic theory and the question of the origins of motifs. The representatives of this doctrine have explained the similarity of narrative motifs

---

[26] From Pavel Rybnikov's letter to O. Miller dated October 21, 1866. In *Pesni, sobrannye P. Rybnikovym* [Songs Collected by P. Rybnikov], Vol. III, 1910.

by the presence of identical forms of everyday life and religious beliefs. This doctrine has been concerned exclusively with motifs, while only cursorily addressing the question of the influence of one fairy-tale scheme on another, and completely ignoring the laws of plot construction. But besides that, the Ethnographic theory is flawed at its very core. According to this theory, fairy-tale motifs represent memories of real-life relationships. So, for example, incest in certain tales supposedly attests to primitive hetaerism, the animal helpers denote traces of totemism, while the abduction of the bride is a survival from the practice of elopement. The works of these scholars, and especially those of Veselovsky, are full of such explanations. I will analyze one classic study of the origins of a tale to show just where such an explanation of origins might lead: namely, the legend of Dido, who acquired land through cunning. I refer to Vsevolod Miller's analysis.

The plot is about acquiring land by means of a cowhide, which is cut into fine strips to encompass as much land as possible. Miller traces the plot of the tale to all of the following: the classical Greek legend of Dido as retold by Virgil; three Indian legends; an Indo-Chinese legend; a fifteenth-century Byzantine legend, along with a Turkish legend that coincides with the building of a fortress on the Bosphorus; a Serbian legend; an Icelandic saga concerning Ivar, son of Ragnar Lodbrok; the Danish chronicle written by twelfth-century historian Saxo Grammaticus; the *Rhymed Chronicle* of Gottfried Hagen; a Swedish chronicle; the legend of the founding of Riga, as recorded by Dionysius Fabricius; the legend of the founding of the Kirillo-Belozersky Monastery (with its tragic denouement); the folk legend from Pskov about the building of the walls of the Pechersky Monastery during the reign of Ivan the Terrible; the Chernigov Malorussian legend of Peter the Great; the Zyrian legend of the founding of Moscow; the Kabardian legend of the founding of Kudenetov village in the Caucasus (with a Jewish hero); and finally Native American stories about the deceitful seizure of land by European colonists.

Having thus exhaustively traced every version of this plot, Miller directs our attention to the peculiar fact that the deceived party in such narratives never protests against the other party's violent seizure of the land. This is possible, of course, due to the convention lying at the foundation of every work of art—namely, that the situations in question depart from their correlation with reality and influence one another in accordance with the laws of the given artistic composition. However, as Miller claims, "There seems to be a prevailing *conviction* in the story that the act of covering a piece of land with strips of cowhide was a juridical act that had the power of law."[27] The meaning of this act is apparently conveyed in a Vedic legend recorded in the oldest Indian religious work called *The Shatapatha Brahmana*. According to this legend, the Asuras—deities constantly at war with the Devas—measure out the land with cowhide and divide it amongst themselves. Correspondingly, the ancient Indian word *go* meant "land" or "cow." The word *gocarman* (cowhide) was used to describe a measured piece of land. According to Miller:

> The ancient Indian measurement (*gocarman*) can be compared with the Anglo-Saxon word *hyd*, or *hide* in English, which referred to skin (*Haut* in German) but also to a particular measurement of surface equivalent to forty-six morgens. It is very likely that the Indian term *gocarman* originally meant a piece of land that could be encompassed by strips of cowhide. And only later, when its ancient meaning was forgotten, did this word come to designate a measurement of surface that can hold one hundred cows, a bull, and their calves.

As one can see, the attempt to explain the origins based on everyday occurrences is carried not only to the bitter end but also to a certain level of absurdity. It turns out that the deceived party—and every version of the tale is based on an act of deception—didn't

---

[27] Vsevolod Miller, "Vsemirnaya skazka v kulturno-istoricheskom osveshchenii" [The Universal Tale in Cultural-Historical Light] in *Russkaya mysl* (November 1894).

protest against the seizure of land because land was generally measured by this means. This is, of course, complete nonsense. If at the time of the tale's supposed action the custom of measuring land was "as much as one can encircle with cowhide strips," and both seller and buyer knew this, then not only is there no deception but there is also no plot, since the seller knew what he was getting involved in from the outset.

Likewise, the abduction of brides in tales, which has been commonly seen as a depiction of a real custom, can hardly be regarded as a reproduction of an everyday phenomenon. There is every reason to believe that the wedding rites that survive as vestiges of this custom are really charms and spells against the evil spirit, lest it harm the bride. As Nikolai Derzhavin explains:

> We can be certain of this in part and by analogy with other particulars of the wedding ritual; for example, the wedding rooster that is usually an object of amusement, and which has an important role in Malorussian and Bulgarian weddings . . . . Therefore, we will not be mistaken if, in conclusion, we state that *the predatory abduction of women* practiced among some modern nationalities *is a degeneration of an original ritual abduction.* Wedding rites that are traditionally seen as simulations of abduction and are closely connected with primitive religious conceptions must be regarded as measures aimed at protecting the wedding procession from evil spirits.[28]

The same analogy is applied to the plot of "the husband at his wife's wedding." William Crooke and Veselovsky both explain its emergence through the custom of *levirate marriage*—the admission that the husband's relatives have a right to his wife. If this explanation is correct, then the wrath of Odysseus, who evidently was unaware of this custom, is incomprehensible.

Without denying the possibility of motifs being derived from

---

[28] Nikolai Derzhavin, *Sbornik statey, posvyashchyonnykh V. Lamanskomu* [Collected Articles, Dedicated to V. Lamansky], 1907.

aspects of everyday life, I would like to note that in creating such motifs storytellers make use of the collision of customs—their contradictions. Thus, the memory of a custom that no longer exists may be used for the construction of a conflict.

Maupassant has a whole series of stories ("An Old Man" and many others) that are based on the depiction of a simple, unsentimental attitude of a French peasant toward death. It might seem that the story is based on a simple depiction of everyday reality. But, in fact, the story is intended for a reader from a different milieu, someone who has a different attitude toward death.

The same can be seen in "The Return": a husband returns home after a shipwreck and discovers that his wife has remarried. The two husbands drink wine peacefully—even the tavern keeper is not surprised. This story is meant for a reader who is familiar with the plot of "the husband at his wife's wedding" and who has a more sophisticated attitude toward life. We see here the expression of the same law, according to which a custom is used as a basis for creating a motif when the custom is no longer customary.

Let me add the following as a general rule: a work of art is perceived against the background of and in association with other works of art. The form of the work of art is determined by its relationship with other preexisting forms. *The material of the artistic work is invariably accentuated, i.e., distinguished, "voiced."*[29] All works of art, not just parodies, are created as a parallel and contraposition to some model. *The new form makes its appearance not in order to express a new content, but rather to replace an old form that has already lost its artistic quality.*[30]

---

[29] *Vygolosit'* (verb) or *vygolashivanie* (noun), a term coined by Mikhail Bakhtin, meaning to hear and distinguish the voice and the tone behind the word, and to discern the gesture behind the tone as a plastic intonation accompanying and sometimes even forestalling the word. [—Trans.]

[30] See Appendix I.

Stepped Structure and Deferment

There are people who think that the purpose of art is to relieve, inspire, or generalize something. They don't have enough steam to drive in piles, so they recruit rhythm to do the job.[31] And yet, it is obvious for those who know how to look, just how alien art is to generalization and how close it is to particularization, and it is certainly not a march set to music, but rather a dance-walk that is palpable—or, more precisely, it is a movement built for the sole purpose of being felt.

The practical mind moves toward generalization, creating broad-ranging, all-encompassing formulas. Art, on the contrary, with its "desire for the concrete" (Thomas Carlyle), is based on a stepped construction and the particularization of even that which appears generalized and unified. The stepped construction includes repetition (with its special case of rhythm), tautology, tautological parallelism, psychological parallelism, deceleration, epic repetitions, fairy tale conventions, peripeteia, and many other devices of plot construction. The convergence of identical words such as "I order," "I command," etc., as Dickens pointed out in *David Copperfield*, are often encountered in high-level English business speech. They are also common in ancient oratorical prose (Tadeusz Zieliński). This phenomenon represents a general principle in Belarusian and Ukrainian folk poetry. Here are some examples from Mitrofan Dovnar-Zapolsky's *Songs of the Pinchuks* (1895): "Drums are beating-thumping," "tambourines-drums," "blows-breezes," "cherry-wild cherry," "I ordered-I said," "roaming-wandering," "warming-heating," "blazing-smoking," "querulous-quarrelsome," "badness-sadness," "living-being," "sees-knows," "spring-water," "I loved-I adored," "cries-sobs," "cries-weeps," "sown-planted," "drinking-carousing," "didn't come-didn't arrive," "chides-scolds," "to tap-to rap," "grass-moss," "bread-salt," "solid-thick," "rumbles-whistles," "I was sewing-stitching," and so on.

---

[31] See chiefly Karl Wilhelm Bücher's *Arbeit und Rhythmus* [Labor and Rhythm], 1896 (translated into Russian in 1899).

Here are some other examples from Professor Mikhail Speransky's analysis of Russian oral verbal art:

> Russian poetry is apparently quite enamored with this device and has arrived at a great diversity of forms. They consist of either a simple repetition of the same word or a repetition of homophones with identical meanings: *chudnym chudno, divnym divno* (miraculous miracle, marvelous marvel); *pryamoezzhaya dorozhenka, pryamoezzhaya* (the straight path, straight); *zagoralisya, zagoralisya dubovye drova* (the oak firewood was burning, burning), etc. Or (most often) they may consist of a repetition of prepositions: "In the glorious, in the city, in Kiev," or "Who would tell us about the old, about the old, about the past, about that very same Ilya, about Muromets?" Or (again most often) they may consist of a repetition of the same word or phrase in two consecutive lines, where the final word of the line reappears as the first word of the next line:
>
> The very sable brought from overseas,
>> From overseas, a sable with pointy ears,
> A pointy-eared sable with soft, downy fur.[32]
>
> Sometimes the repetition is achieved through a negation of the opposite: "take the straight road—not the roundabout way," "out of great frustration—not out of little," "a bachelor—not a married man." We could also add to this category synonymous expressions such as "without a battle, without a fight or bloodshed," "from grief, from sorrow," "an estate, a fortune," "then, at that time," and so on. Sometimes the expression consists of two words—one native, the other borrowed or in the vernacular; for example, "talent-fate" or "beauty-belle." Or else one of the words signifies species, the other class, for example, "pike-fish," "titmouse-bird," or "stipa-grass." A more developed form of repetition may involve entire episodes of a story that are especially effective or appealing. For example, the episodes

---

[32] From the *bylina* about Ilya Muromets and Nightingale the Robber. [—Trans.]

in the *bylina* about Dobrynya describing his fight with Dunai (the description of Dunai's tent, Dobrynya's arrival, Dobrynya and Alyosha Popovich, Dobrynya's injunction to his wife and its consequences). Another good example of repetition is the episode recounting Mikhailo Potyk's fight with the underground dragon. Finally, we should also include here the combination of two words with the same root, each belonging to a different lexical category: "bridging a bridge," "gilding with gold," "wintering the winter," "not heard by hearing nor seen by sight," etc.[33]

Gogol's favorite stylistic device was the use of synonyms. According to Professor Iosif Mandelshtam:

> The distinguishing feature of Gogol's style is the unusually frequent, nearly constant, use of two synonymous expressions in succession, which however does not necessarily contribute to a greater clarity or distinctness of thought. One of the expressions nearly always turns out to be completely redundant, being in every sense a full repetition of the other expression and only rarely serving to enhance the intensity of a trait. We do not need to look for long passages to be convinced—here is an example: "With firmness in the cause of life, with *invigoration* and *revival* of everything around you." Or the same, using verbs: "So that he may help his fellow man with good counsel . . . *invigorate, revive* him with wise words of parting." And finally, the same, using participles or adjectives: "You will therefore carry it out precisely as one should, and as required by the government, i.e., with *invigorating* and *reviving* effort . . ."[34]

Professor Mandelshtam goes on to cite numerous such examples. Pushkin also has something similar: "thunders with thunderstorms" and "locked with a lock" (see Osip Brik's article "Sound Repetitions").[35]

---

[33] Mikhail Speransky, *Russkaya ustnaya slovesnost'* [Russian Oral Verbal Art], 1917.

[34] Iosif Mandelshtam, *O kharaktere Gogolevskovo stilya* [On the Nature of Gogol's Style], 1902.

[35] Osip Brik, "Zvukovye povtory" [Sound Repetitions], *Sborniki*, II, 1917.

This phenomenon expresses the common rule whereby *form creates content for itself*. So whenever the corresponding word in the synonymous pair is missing, its place is taken by an arbitrary or derivative word—for example, shilly-shally, hurly-burly, etc. All of these instances of decelerated, stepped construction are not usually studied together, and each is explained separately. So, for example, theorists try to separate psychological and tautological parallelisms from each other completely. The following parallelism represents, in Veselovsky's opinion, an echo of totemism and a time when individual tribes regarded trees as their ancestors:

Yelinochka is happy all winter and summer long,
Our Malashka grows by the day—

Veselovsky thinks that if the singer compares a human being to a tree then either he is confusing the two with one another, or else his grandmother must have confused them. This (psychological) parallelism is, in his opinion, sharply different from the rhythmic parallelism employed in Jewish, Finnish, and Chinese poetry. He cites the following example from *The Poetic Edda*:

The sun knew not what seat he had,
The moon knew not what might she had.[36]

Psychological parallelism drastically differs from this musical-rhythmic tautology, which originates, in Veselovsky's opinion, from the method of performance—contesting choruses or amoebaean singing. But even the formulas of psychological parallelism occasionally cross over or, in Veselovsky's words, "lower themselves" to a tautological-musical type of parallelism. So, even Veselovsky admits that there is, if not a kinship between these two types of construction, then at least an attraction toward each other. They share a distinctive poetic gait. In both cases there is a

---

[36] *The Poetic Edda*, trans. Lee. M. Hollander (University of Texas Press, 1986).

need to slow down the imagistic mass and create unique steps out of it. One uses non-coinciding images for the creation of these steps, and the other employs verbal-formal non-coincidence. For example:

> How can I curse whom God
>   has not cursed?
> How can I denounce those
>   whom Jehovah has not denounced? (Numbers 23:8)[37]

Or here is an example illustrating a greater variety of steps:

> Ascribe to Jehovah, O heavenly beings,
>   ascribe to Jehovah glory and strength. (Psalm 29:1)

Or a move forward by seizing the next line with a repeated word:

> For Jehovah watches over the way of the righteous,
>   but the way of the wicked will perish. (Psalm 1:6)

Here we observe a common artistic phenomenon where a particular form seeks to complete itself by filling in words with specific sound patterns in a manner typical of lyrical poetry (see Veselovsky's "Three Chapters from Historical Poetics" and Jean-Marie Guyau's comments on filling in the spaces between rhymes). This is why in the Finnish epic, where synonymous parallelism is typical and the stanzas take the following form:

> Cease at last thine incantations,
> Only turn away thy magic—

numbers, which obviously have no synonyms, are given

---

37 *The New Oxford Annotated Bible* (New Revised Standard Version), ed. Bruce M. Metzger and Roland E. Murphy (Oxford UP, 1991). All subsequent quotations from the Bible are taken from this standard version.

consecutively despite the distortion of any possible quantitative meaning. For example:

Finds six seeds of golden barley,
Even seven ripened kernels.

Or consider the following:

Lo! thy blood fills seven sea-boats,
Eight of largest birchen vessels.[38]

The triolet, in my opinion, is quite close to tautological parallelism. Both the triolet and the rondeau have made the device canonical; it serves as the base of the "weave" and pervades the entire work. The effect of the triolet lies partly in the fact that the same line of verse appears in different contexts, which creates the required differential impression. Psychological parallelism has similar steps, and the development of negative parallelism alone indicates that there was never a confusion of a human being with a tree or a river. The song simply offers two unequal but partially overlapping figures; the effect rests on the premise that, despite the non-coincidence, the second line of the parallel construction formally echoes the first.

Further to refute a totemist interpretation, one may emphasize that a parallel is often established not between objects or the actions of two objects, but between similar relations between two objects taken as a pair. Here is an example from a marvelous *chastushka*:

The clouds glide not in the sky—
    but in the heavenly heights;
The lads pine not for the maidens—
    but for their maidenly beauty.

---

[38] *The Kalevala*, trans. John M. Crawford (New York: John B. Alden, 1888).

Synonymous (tautological) parallelism, with its transition and repetition from line to line, turns into what is called deceleration in the poetics of the Russian song. Here is an example from the *bylina* about Ilya Muromets, as recorded in the Simbirsk governorate for P. V. Kireevsky:

> Ilya rode up on a high hill,
> on a high, sloping hill,
> and pitched his white tent there,
> and after pitching his tent, he built a fire.
> After building a fire, he spread out the coals,
> and after spreading out the coals, he made some kasha,
> and after making the kasha, he ate it,
> and after eating the kasha, he lay down to rest . . .

We find the same device in a song recorded by Kireevsky in Moscow:

> Shall I go then, fair maiden,
> to roam in the clear field,
> to gather evil roots?
> Having gathered the evil roots,
> I will wash every root till white.
> And having washed the evil roots,
> I will dry every root till dry.
> And having dried the evil roots,
> I will grind to powder every root.
> And having ground the evil roots,
> I will make a honey potion.
> After making the honey potion,
> I will call the groomsman as a guest.
> And having called him as a guest,
> I will sit him down on my bed.
> After sitting him down on my bed . . .

There are numerous such examples of deceleration. But due to the negligence of scholars who search for reality, soul, and philosophy in these songs, many of the examples have been lost. All of the repetitions in Aleksei Sobolevsky's collection of Russian songs, for example, have been excised. The revered academician most likely shared the opinion that literature is of interest only insofar as it reflects the history of a culture.

We find unique instances of deceleration in the Old French *chanson de geste* about Renaud de Montauban. It includes a very long, almost endless episode in which Charles wishes to hang the imprisoned Richard and asks the knight Bérangier to carry out the sentence. Bérangier replies: "A curse on him who has shamefully plotted to seize the prisoner's estate for himself." Then Charles turns to Ogier and to six other knights, repeating his speech with minor changes, and receives the same response from each one of them. And each time Charles exclaims: "Scoundrel! May God punish you! But I swear by the beard of Charles, the prisoner will be hanged!" Finally, one of the knights agrees to carry out the charge.

Deceleration functions in the same way as parallelism: a certain form has to be filled, and if numerals are involved in the construction of its steps, then the storyteller or singer treats them uniquely by observing the laws of the given "weave":

> Young nightingale,
> don't you sing early in the spring,
> don't sing sweetly, don't sing loudly:
> then the brave young lad won't feel so wretched.
> He won't feel so wretched, he won't feel so bitter!
> I don't know why, I know only this—
> that I long for her, for my beloved,
> my beloved who has left me behind,
> left me behind—and moved four times a hundred,
> four times a hundred, five hundred, twelve cities away,
> twelve cities away, thirteen cities away,
> to the glorious city of Moscow.

In his article "Epic Repetitions as a Chronological Moment," Veselovsky tried to explain these unique repetitions that seize the next line through the mechanism of performance (Veselovsky's standard explanation): he assumed that these works (or prototypes of these works—a crucial factor insufficiently explained in his article) were originally performed as amoebaean songs and that the repetitions emerged when the song was passed back and forth between singers. Here are some of Veselovsky's examples of repetition (from *The Song of Roland*):

The Saracens have surrounded Charles's rear guard; Olivier tells his companion Roland that they are outnumbered by the enemy and that he should blow his horn, Charles will hear it and come to their rescue. But Roland refuses to blow his horn, and this is repeated three times in the following way:

1) "Therefore Roland, my companion, sound a blast on your horn. Charles will hear it, and he will return with his host." Roland answers: "That would be the act of a fool! I would forfeit the fame I have in sweet France. Soon I will be striking great blows with my sword Durendal, and blood will cover the blade up to the hilt. These villainous pagans will suffer for coming to this gateway through the mountains. I promise you, they are all marked out for death." (LXXXIII)

2) "Roland, my companion, sound your ivory horn, and Charles will hear it and command the army to return, and the King will come to our help with all his barons." Roland answers: "God forbid that my ancestry should be shamed by an act of mine, or that I should make sweet France an object of scorn! Instead I will attack unsparingly with my good sword Durendal, which I have girded on here at my side. You will see this weapon running with blood from one end to the other. These villainous pagans will suffer for massing against us. I promise you, they are all marked out for destruction." (LXXXIV)

3) "Roland, my companion, sound a blast on your ivory

horn. Charles will hear it as he marches through the pass, and I promise you the Franks will return." Roland answers: "God forbid that any man living should be able to say that because of the pagans I blew my ivory horn! No one will ever be able to shame my family with the mention of such a thing. When I have joined in the massed battle I will strike a thousand blows and follow them with seven hundred more, and you will see the steel of Durendal running with blood." (LXXXV)

Finally, wounded, Roland decides to blow his horn:

1) Roland has set his ivory horn to his mouth; he puts his lips hard against it and blows with all his strength. The mountains are high, and over them the voice of the horn rings long, and more than thirty leagues away its echo answers. Charles hears it, and all the knights in his company. The King says: "Our men are fighting!" And Ganelon, contradicting him, answers: "If anyone else had said so I would say he was lying." (CXXXIII)

2) Count Roland, in pain and anguish, and in great sorrow, blows a blast on his ivory horn, and the bright blood flows from his mouth, and the veins burst on his forehead, but the sound of the horn swells and mounts, and Charles hears it as he makes his way through the pass, and Duke Naimon hears it, and it comes to the ears of the Franks. Then the King says: "I hear the sound of Roland's horn, and he would not blow it unless there were a battle." Ganelon answers: "Battle? There is no battle! You are old and your beard and hair white and flowery, and when you speak like that you sound like a child. You are well aware of Roland's vast pride—it is a wonder that God has endured him for so long. . . . At the moment he is performing some kind of sport before his peers. Who under heaven would dare to take the field against him? Ride on! Why should you pause? The 'Land of the Fathers' is still a long way off." (CXXXIV)

3) Count Roland's mouth is streaming blood and the veins

on his forehead have burst. In sorrow and pain he blows his ivory horn. Charles hears it, and his Frenchmen hear it. Then the King says: "That horn has a long breath!" Duke Naimon answers: "Some knight is in anguish. There is a battle, I am sure of it, and he who has betrayed the knights in the rear guard is the same who now counsels you to fail them. Arm, sound your battle cry, and go to the help of your noble followers. You have heard enough. That horn is the sound of Roland's despair!" (CXXXV)

In the meantime, Roland, dying, tries to break his sword so that it should not fall into the hands of the pagans, and makes his confession. Each of these motifs is developed in three consecutive *laisses*:

1) Now Roland feels that the end of his life has come. He sees before him a gray stone. In sorrow and bitterness he strikes it ten blows with his sword, and the steel grates but will not break nor be blunted. [Then follows Roland's address to his sword with which he has won many battles.] (CLXXI)

2) Roland strikes the hard stone again, and the steel grates but will not break nor be blunted. [This is followed by Roland's laments and epically developed memories.] (CLXXII)

3) Roland, striking harder, brings the sword down on the gray stone, and it grates, but is neither chipped nor shattered. (CLXXIII)[39]

I can provide many examples that parallel the three strikes of Roland, although this device is not typical in other epics.

For example, Ilya strikes Svyatogor's coffin three times, or Thor strikes the giant three times. In pointing out these comparisons my purpose is not to underscore the similarity of motifs, which I consider to be of little significance, but the similarity of plot schemes.

The action does not stop with repetition but continues at a slower pace. The song about Marusya is constructed according to

---

[39] Quoted from *The Song of Roland*, trans. W. S. Merwin (New York: Modern Library, 2001).

the same scheme. Marusya, who has been poisoned in the factory, is visited first by her girlfriends, then by her mother, and finally by her sweetheart. The visitors find out about Marusya's condition first from the nurse, then from the doctor, and finally from the watchman: "Marusya is in delirium," "Marusya is unconscious," and eventually "Marusya is in the mortuary." The same device of three arrivals is used in the Malorussian ballad:

> Up on the Beskid Mountains,
> In the midst of guelder roses
> Stands a new tavern.
> A Turk sits drinking inside,
> And a girl bows before him:
> "O Turk, o Turk, o dear Turk!
> Spare my life, for I am young."

The girl says that her father is already bringing the ransom for her, but the father does not arrive and the girl cries. The next stanza repeats the same scene—the Beskid Mountains, the tavern, and the girl's plea. This time it is her mother who brings the ransom. This is followed again by the same description of the setting and finally it is her sweetheart who brings the ransom. Veselovsky cites another example, the young wife's call in the vernal *chansons de mal-mariée*, which is also broken up into three steps. Many Russian songs are based on the same device.

The stepped construction is also used in Charles Perrault's fairy tale "Blue Beard," in which the deceived wife waits to be rescued:

> When she was alone she called out to her sister, and said to her, "Sister Anne" (for that was her name), "go up, I beg you, to the top of the tower, and look if my brothers are not coming. They promised me that they would come today, and if you see them, give them a sign to make haste."
>
> Her sister Anne went up to the top of the tower, and the poor afflicted wife cried out from time to time, "Anne, sister Anne, do you see anyone coming?"

And sister Anne said, "I see nothing but a cloud of dust in the sun, and the green grass."

In the meanwhile Blue Beard, holding a great saber in his hand, cried out as loud as he could bawl to his wife, "Come down instantly, or I shall come up to you."

"One moment longer, if you please," said his wife; and then she cried out very softly, "Anne, sister Anne, do you see anybody coming?"

And sister Anne answered, "I see nothing but a cloud of dust in the sun, and the green grass."

"Come down quickly," cried Blue Beard, "or I will come up to you."

"I am coming," answered his wife; and then she cried, "Anne, sister Anne, do you not see anyone coming?"

"I see," replied sister Anne, "a great cloud of dust approaching us."

"Are they my brothers?"

"Alas, no my dear sister, I see a flock of sheep."

"Will you not come down?" cried Blue Beard.

"One moment longer," said his wife, and then she cried out, "Anne, sister Anne, do you see nobody coming?"

"I see," said she, "two horsemen, but they are still a great way off."

"God be praised," replied the poor wife joyfully. "They are my brothers. I will make them a sign, as well as I can for them to make haste."[40]

This scheme is widely popular in England, by the way, where it is mostly used in parodies. I will not cite further examples in order not to turn this chapter into a chrestomathy.

Constructions of the type $\alpha + (\alpha + \alpha) + [\alpha + (\alpha + \alpha)] + \ldots$ etc. follow an arithmetic progression with common difference.

There are tales constructed on a unique plot tautology of the following type: $\alpha + (\alpha + \alpha) + \{[\alpha + (\alpha + \alpha)] + \alpha_2\}$ etc. Let's look

---

[40] Charles Perrault, "Blue Beard," in *The Blue Fairy Book*, ed. Andrew Lang (London: Longmans, Green & Co., 1889).

at a couple of examples from Yevdokim Romanov's collection of Belarusian tales (1887):

The Speckled Hen

Once upon a time in a village there lived an old man and an old woman and they had a speckled hen. The hen laid a basketful of eggs. The old man tried to crack an egg but he couldn't. The old woman tried to crack it but she couldn't. A small mouse ran by, swung its tail, the egg fell on the floor and cracked. The old man cried, the old woman cried, the hen clucked, the gates creaked, the fish jumped up, the dogs barked, the geese honked, the people raised a ruckus.

A wolf came along and asked: "Why are you crying, old man?"

And the old man replied: "Why should I not be crying? The old woman and I led a peaceful life. We had a speckled hen and she laid a basketful of eggs. I tried to crack an egg but I couldn't. The old woman tried to crack it but she couldn't. A small mouse ran by, swung its tail, the egg fell on the floor and cracked. I cried, the old woman cried, the hen clucked, the gates creaked, the fish jumped up, the dogs barked, the geese honked, the people raised a ruckus."

The wolf howled.

Along came a bear and asked: "Why are you howling, wolf?"

And the wolf replied: "Why should I not be howling? The old man and the old woman led a peaceful life. They had a speckled hen and she laid a basketful of eggs. The old man tried to crack an egg but he couldn't. The old woman tried to crack it but she couldn't. A small mouse ran by, swung its tail, the egg fell on the floor and cracked. The old man cried, the old woman cried, the hen clucked, the gates creaked, the fish jumped out, the dogs barked, the geese honked, the people raised a ruckus, and I howled."

The bear roared.

Along came an elk and asked: "Why are you roaring, bear?"

And the bear replied: "Why should I not be roaring? The

old man and the old woman led a peaceful life. They had a speckled hen and she laid a basketful of eggs. The old man tried to crack an egg but he couldn't. The old woman tried to crack it but she couldn't. A small mouse ran by, swung its tail, the egg fell on the floor and cracked. The old man cried, the old woman cried, the hen clucked, the gates creaked, the fish jumped out, the dogs barked, the geese honked, the people raised a ruckus, the wolf howled, and I roared."

The elk lowered his horns. . . .

Next in line comes the priest's maid who breaks her buckets out of grief, followed by the deacon who tears up his books, and finally the priest who burns down the church. Here is another example:

The Rooster and the Hen

Once upon a time there lived an old man and an old woman, and they had a rooster and a hen. One day they were digging in the dirt. The hen found a pin and the rooster found a pea. The hen then said to the rooster: "Give me your pea, and I will give you my pin." The rooster agreed. The hen ate the pea, while the rooster swallowed the pin and started to choke.

The hen ran to the sea for water and said: "O sea, sea, give me water! The rooster is choking!"

"I will not give you water, unless you go down to the wild boar and ask him to give me his tusk."

The hen ran to the wild boar and said: "O wild boar, wild boar, give the sea your tusk! Then the sea will give me water, for the rooster is choking!"

"I will not give the sea my tusk, unless you go down to the oak and ask him to give me some acorns."

The hen ran to the oak and said: "O oak, oak, give the wild boar some acorns!"

"I will not give the wild boar my acorns, unless you go down to the cow and ask her to give me some milk."

The hen ran to the cow and said: "O cow, cow, give the oak some milk!"

"I will not give the oak my milk, unless you go down to the reaper and tell him to give me some hay."

The hen ran to the reaper and said: "O reaper, reaper, give the cow some hay!"

"I will not give the cow some hay, unless you go down to the linden tree and tell him to give me some bast for shoes."

The hen ran to the linden tree and said: "O linden tree, linden tree, give the reaper some bast for shoes!"

"I will not give the reaper my bast, unless you go down to the blacksmith and tell him to give me a knife."

The hen ran to the blacksmith and said: "O blacksmith, blacksmith, give the linden tree a knife!"

"I will not give the linden tree a knife, unless you bring me some coins."

The hen ran to the place where they made coins and brought some coins to the blacksmith, who gave her the knife. She then brought the knife to the linden tree, which gave her some bast. She brought the bast to the reaper, who gave her some hay. She brought the hay to the cow. The cow ate the hay and gave her some milk. She brought the milk to the oak, which gave her some acorns. She brought the acorns to the wild boar. The wild boar gave her a tusk, which she brought to the sea. The sea took the tusk and gave her some water. The hen finally brought the water to the rooster and poured some into his mouth, and the rooster called: Cock-a-doodle-doo!

It is interesting that the tale does not explain why the sea needs a wild boar's tusk as a form of payment. The motivation here is, of course, artistic—a requirement for the construction of a "step."

In some versions of the tale, the narrative becomes more realistic: when the rooster returns he finds the hen eaten by worms (in some versions it is the rooster who runs for help). I can cite another example of this type from Michal Federowski's collection: a little boy, miraculously born from a drop of water on a blade of grass, asks the blade of grass to rock him like a cradle. The blade of grass refuses and refers to the goat, the goat refers to the wolves, the wolves refer to the men, the men refer to the fire, etc. They all refuse to do something. Then finally the hens go to peck the worms, the worms go to sharpen the pin, and so on—until we return to the goat and the blade of grass.[41]

So, we see that whatever is signified in prose through "a" becomes "$A_1 A$" (as in a tautology) or "$A A_1$" (as in psychological parallelism) in art. This is the essence of all devices. Accordingly, if the realization of a certain task demands a degree of effort equal to A_n, it is represented as $A_{n-2} A_{n-1} A_n$. Thus, in the *bylina*, Alyosha Popovich goes to fight first, then Dobrynya Nikitich, and finally Ilya Muromets. This is also the order in which the fairy-tale heroes leave their home. The device was preserved and used in Tennyson's *Idylls of the King*. Similarly, Koshchei the Deathless's revelation about the source of his death is broken down into three parts. And in the Bible, too, Samson reveals the secret of his strength three times.

In Romanov's collection of Belarusian tales, as a "test of strength" Ivan is first bound with canvas, then with silk (or a strand of hair), and finally with wire. The obtaining of the ring or the princess's kiss through twelve panes of glass is constructed in a similar way. Ivan's horse jumps up and misses the first two times, but the third attempt is successful. While escaping from the Maiden-Tsar, Ivan finds a noble horse each time he reaches Baba Yaga's hut and each time the chase gets closer: first at a distance of fifteen versts, then ten, and finally five. Ivan saves himself by hiding in the grass and leaving behind a deceptive message.

Osip Brik ingeniously noted that dead water and living water are nothing other than the bifurcation of the singular notion of "healing water" (as we know, in fairy tales "dead water" joins and heals the severed parts of the quartered body); in other words, A is presented as $A_1 A_2$. Likewise, Bobchinsky and Dobchinsky in Gogol's *The Government Inspector* are undoubtedly one and the same "type" split into two. It is evident from their nearly identical surnames. Here, too, A is given as $A_1 A_2$.

---

[41] See Appendix II.

This is commonly called a "fairy-tale convention," but what goes unnoticed is that this is not just a convention of fairy tales, but is the convention and ordinance of all art. *The Song of Roland* is not a fairy tale, nor is cinematography. There are many films today that incorporate a chase sequence, with the enemy coming closer and closer, and the hero suddenly getting away in a car. Compare this with the chase sequence in Hugo's *Les Misérables*, where, as a final effect, Jean Valjean climbs over the wall and takes refuge in a convent.

Motivations for Deferment

Generally, the theme of "delayed help" is widely employed in fairy tales and adventure novels as a fitting subject for a stepped construction. The animal helpers chew through the twelve iron doors, but Ivan Tsarevich is close to death and asks Koshchei the Deathless for permission to wash in a steam bath. He takes his time warming up the bathhouse, thus gaining time for the greyhounds to break through the iron doors and rescue him. In another version, Ivan Zlatovus is permitted to play his pipe. He climbs up the birch tree and plays the pipe once, attracting a bird, then plays the pipe a second time, attracting flocks of birds, and when he plays a third time, all the wild beasts gather around him (from Romanov's collection of Belarusian tales). Similarly, in Veselovsky's version of "Solomon and Kitovras," Solomon blows the horn before his hanging, calling for help.

This convention has been generally accepted as something canonical for the fairy tale. Here are a few random examples out of the thousands that exist: the three underground kingdoms of honey, silver and gold; the three battles of the hero; and, most typically, the gradation of tasks, for example, the quest for the Firebird, the quest for the Humpbacked Horse, and the quest for Vasilisa the Beautiful. To these are appended expositions explaining the necessity of the tasks. This device (stringing tasks together) was then passed on to the adventure novel and chivalric romance.

The tasks themselves are incredibly interesting. They serve as a motivation for the creation of circumstances that require the elucidation of an apparently insoluble situation. Riddles often serve as the simplest means for creating an impossible situation. For example, in the tale of the seven-year-old girl ("The Wise Maiden" in Afanasyev's collection). The task is the following: come neither by foot nor on horseback, neither dressed nor undressed. The young maiden comes wrapped in a net on the back of a rabbit. The tale is constructed in reverse: the narrative is created to motivate the need for a successful resolution. This is similar to another tale, where the right person among twelve lookalikes is recognized with the help of a bee. "Wisdom" is more complex—for example, distinguishing the adolescent girl from the maidens, or recognizing the illegitimate son based on his "worthless thoughts," as in the case of the smith's son who had been switched with the young Solomon. When he sees a beautiful location, he says to King David: "We should build a smithy here."[42] Or here is another example from *The Arabian Nights*: a thief finds out, among other things, that the sultan is the son of the cook because he gives food as a reward. An echo of this theme is the discovery of nobility in "switched children" in adventure novels. For example, Destin in Paul Scarron's *Le Roman Comique* and the numerous heroes in children's stories. (Mark Twain has an interesting story called *Pudd'nhead Wilson* where a black child passes as white).

The part that precedes the tasks is what in the poetics of cinematography is called a "lead-in"—i.e. a scene that has no meaning on its own and only serves as preparation for what follows.

As I already noted, the resolution of tasks may often occupy the whole fairy tale. Looking at it not as an essential quality, but as a technical device, we can distinguish two types of resolution: by means of guessing the riddle and by means of some magical or non-magical helper, such as animal helpers. The classical type

---

[42] Nikolai Onchukov, *Severnye skazki* [Northern Tales], 1908.

of resolution in the latter case is when each animal carries out a task that it alone can do. In the story "Cupid and Psyche" from *The Golden Ass*, the ants sort the pile of grains into separate kinds. Sometimes the ants are given a more specific task, such as sorting and bringing the grain into or out of a locked granary. The fish or the crayfish finds and fetches a ring from the bottom of the sea. The mouse steals a ring from the mouth of the thief princess. The eagle or the falcon catches the duck. In cases when the tasks are similar, each animal is given a task based on a gradation of ability (for example, in the tale of Prince Larokopei). The animal helpers may be replaced by human helpers, magical objects, superhuman characters such as Oak-Feller and Mountain-Mover, or strongmen of progressively greater strength (compare the names of these characters with the names of the dogs from the fairy tale "Beast Milk," such as Mountain-Wrecker, Wall-Breaker, Iron-Breaker). Or else magical human helpers who possess specific traits: a parallel to the specific tasks given to animals. There are also types such as "the man who eats everything" or "the man who drinks everything," and "the man who trembles from cold in the fire." These assistants reappear in novels as strongmen—for example, Ursus in Henryk Sienkiewicz's *Quo Vadis*, Maciste in Gabriele d'Annunzio's film *Cabiria*, Porthos in Alexandre Dumas's *The Three Musketeers*, and others. Similarly, Rabelais employed the famous fairy-tale type of the acrobat helper in his *Pantagruel*. Contemporary "scientific" adventure novels have a similar type of the scientist helper. To this group belongs the fairy tale "The Seven Semyons" about seven brothers, each of whom has a special talent, such as stealing or building a ship (Afanasyev).

This whole set of fairy-tale devices allows one to construct a story in which the hero's fate, having seemingly reached a hopeless situation, unexpectedly changes course. A situation that is capable of creating such cruxes is chosen as a motif. For example, the motif of two keys to one lock (a Spanish drama), the secret door (*The Arabian Nights*), or the Egyptian tale about the cunning thief (in *The Histories* of Herodotus). Some motifs have become favorites—for example, the motif of the shipwreck or abduction of heroes in adventure novels. The hero is not killed immediately, since he is still needed for the recognition scene. If they want to get rid of him, they carry him off somewhere. Very often, such episodes involving re-abductions, escapes, and other futile attempts are complicated by the victims falling in love with each other and moving toward their goal by the longest route possible. The sequential episodes in adventure novels are nearly identical and serve the same function of deferral as the tasks or conventions in fairy tales, or the parallelism and deceleration in songs. The motifs of shipwreck or abduction by pirates were not introduced into a plot because of people's way of life, but for artistic-technical reasons. A way of life had as little influence on these episodes as the Indian way of life had on a chess king. According to Veselovsky, the adventure novel is still interrupted by the schemes and methods inherited from the fairy tale. Veselovsky himself considered "adventures" to be a stylistic device.[43]

The adventure novel, which is a kind of novel that takes a circuitous road, is very similar to the game called "Game of the Goose," which is played in the following way: the players roll the dice, each player takes his place on the board according to the number of points and, depending on the numbers on the dice, moves up or down in the labyrinth. This is exactly how an adventure novel is constructed. The similarity has been pointed out by the creators of adventure novels themselves, and in Jules Verne's *The Will of an Eccentric* the various mishaps and adventures of the heroes are determined by the throw of the dice: the map of the United States is divided into squares, just like the board game, and the novel's characters act as playing pieces in this version of the game.

The motivation for placing such impediments before the hero of the adventure novel is quite interesting. Let's take two examples

---

[43] Aleksandr Veselovsky, "Belletristika u drevnikh grekov" [The Belles-Lettres of Ancient Greeks], in *Vestnik Evropy* [Herald of Europe], Issue 12, 1876.

from Jules Verne again, as I have him to hand. The first novel is called *The Flight to France*. It is about a group of acrobats returning from the United States to their native France through Canada, Cape Dezhnev, and Siberia, having lost all their money. The other novel is called *Kéraban the Inflexible*, in which a stubborn Turk crosses the Bosphorus by a circuitous route, traveling seven hundred leagues around the Black Sea, to avoid paying a measly customs tax. These circuitous routes are, of course, called forth by specific conditions—the demands of plot. In order to understand the difference between prosaic and poetic solutions, I suggest that we look at Mark Twain's *Adventures of Huckleberry Finn*. The matter at hand concerns freeing a fugitive slave. Huck Finn represents the prosaic method:

> "My plan is this," I says. "We can easy find out if it's Jim in there. Then get up my canoe tomorrow night, and fetch my raft over from the island. Then the first dark night that comes, steal the key out of the old man's britches, after he goes to bed, and shove off down the river on the raft with Jim, hiding daytimes and running nights, the way me and Jim used to do before. Wouldn't that plan work?"
>
> "*Work?* Why cert'nly, it would work, like rats a-fighting. But it's too blame' simple; there ain't nothing to it. What's the good of a plan that ain't no more trouble than that? It's as mild as goose-milk. Why, Huck, it wouldn't make no more talk than breaking into a soap factory."[44]

Tom Sawyer then goes on to propose the impeded—poetic—plan. They must saw the bed-leg in two so as to get the slave's chain loose, even though they could simply lift up the bed-stead and slip the chain off. They must dig the foundations out from under the cabin, make a rope ladder and send it to the prisoner in a pie. Then they must send warnings to the people that something is up. In other words, everything is done in accordance with the rules of

---

[44] Mark Twain, *Adventures of Huckleberry Finn* (University of California Press, 2001).

art. In the end, it turns out that Jim is not a fugitive at all, but had been emancipated long ago. So, to Tolstoy's question "Why doesn't Lear recognize Kent and why doesn't Kent recognize Edward?" one might answer that this was necessary for the creation of drama, and that Shakespeare cared as little about the lack of realism as a chess player cares about the fact that the knight cannot move in a straight line.

I would like to come back to the plot of abduction and recognition. Zieliński presumes that it is based on everyday life occurrences. He writes about a play by Apollodorus of Carystus: "You couldn't find a better storyline. There is nothing superfluous in it, all the scenes hold together beautifully. And everything is lifelike and realistic, if we disregard the capricious workings of Fate. But people saw things differently in those restless times than they do now in the age of passports and telegraphs. Everything was unpredictable. Thus, it was permissible for the author to choose from a multitude of meaningless coincidences around him only those that offered some kind of a sensible plan and goodwill." First of all, Zieliński's explanation fails to clarify how this plot could have survived beyond the times of Alexander the Great to the times of Molière and even almost to our own day. Besides, his explanation is factually inaccurate. The plot of recognition (of abducted children) was not an everyday phenomenon, but had become a purely literary tradition by Menander's time. So, for example, in the play *Epitrepontes*, when the slave finds the child along with his tokens that indicate his birth, and he states that the tokens will help the parents recognize their child, he is referring not to social reality but to a play that he had seen in theater.[45] In the same way, Merezhkovsky laments the fall of moral values in Alexandria:

It is worth noting a similar moral trait in the frank and naïve confession made by Daphnis's father: he abandoned his young

---

[45] Grigori Tsereteli, *Novootkrytaya komedia Menandra* Epitrepontes [*Epitrepontes*, the Newly Discovered Comedy by Menander], 1908.

son to the whims of fate only because he thought that he already had enough children. Daphnis was an unwanted child, and his father threw him out of the house like a young pup. The same thing happens with Chloe, although her father apologizes for his poverty and inability to raise and marry off his daughter in a proper way. What we see here is the degradation of family values and the barbarism of late Byzantine culture, which is capriciously intertwined with a pathological refinement of mores, as it is in all ages of decadence. This is not the pagan patriarchal ruthlessness that we encounter in Homer and in the Greek tragedians—rather, it is a case of savagery, a coarsening of mores in a degenerating culture. Of course, it would be absurd to blame the author: he only took from life what he found in it, and his deep sense of artistic objectivity prevented him from embellishing it.[46]

As I have already said, the plot of abduction in this epoch was purely bookish. Let me say merely the following in order to set Merezhkovsky's mind at ease. In the epoch of *Sturm und Drang*, a great number of plays in Germany were written on the subject of fratricide in the span of five years. For instance, the three plays that were submitted to a contest hosted by the Hamburg Theater in 1776 dealt with fratricide.[47] It also played a part in Schiller's *The Robbers*. However, this does not serve as proof that that there were mass cases of fratricide in Germany during this historical period.

It took a long time for the device of abduction to grow stale. Its fate is an interesting one. As it began to degenerate, it started to appear in the secondary parts of plot—as something mentioned in passing, so to speak. Today it has descended to the level of children's literature. It had a brief resurgence in the so-called war stories of 1914–16. However, even before that, the device underwent an unusually curious transition. It should be mentioned

---

[46] Dmitri Merezhkovsky, *Vechnye sputniki: Portrety iz vsemirnoy literatury* [Eternal Companions: Portraits from World Literature], 1897.

[47] Johann Anton Leisewitz's *Julius von Tarent*, Friedrich Maximilian Klinger's *Die Zwillinge*, and *Die unglücklichen Brüder* by an anonymous author.

that a worn-out device can be used one more time as a parody of itself. For example, Pushkin made use of the banal rhyme "*morozy/rozy*" while at the same time pointing out its banality.[48] The plot of abduction had already been parodied by Boccaccio in the seventh story of the second day, where the "Sultan of Babylon sends one of his daughters to be married to the King of Algarve."[49] After suffering all kinds of adversities over the course of four years, she falls into the hands of several different men in different places. But finally she returns to her father as a virgin and goes to marry the King of Algarve as she had set out to do in the first place. The effect achieved in this classic adventure novella, with its young heroine, is due to the preservation of her innocence even in the hands of her abductors. Cervantes laughed at this virginity that was untouched for eighty years.

The ending of the novella for Veselovsky, with its assurances of chastity and the final couplet ("A mouth crushed with kisses loses no boon, / but ever reflourishes, as does the moon"), has the effect of dissonance that unexpectedly disrupts the music of fatalism.

The existence of several other parodic novellas by Boccaccio confirms that I am on the right track in my interpretation of this novella as a parody. I will cite only two of them. The eighth story of the fifth day:

Nastagio degli Onesti loves a lady of the Traversari family, and squanders his riches for her sake without having his love requited. At his friends' insistence, he goes to Chiassi, where he has a vision of a knight giving chase to a lady, slaying her, and throwing her body to be devoured by two hounds. Thereupon, he invites his family and the people of his beloved to a banquet, where the hard-hearted damsel sees the phantom lady torn to pieces. Fearing a similar fate, she takes Nastagio for

[48] In *Eugene Onegin*, Chapter Four: XLII: "And now the frosts already crackle / and silver 'mid the fields / (the reader now expects the rhyme "froze-rose"— / here, take it quick!)."

[49] Giovanni Boccaccio, *The Decameron*, trans. Frances Winwar (Random House, 1955). All subsequent quotations from *The Decameron* are taken from this translation.

her husband. . . . Nor was this the only good that came from that fearful spectacle, for indeed, all the women of Ravenna were so frightened because of it that from then on they were far more willing to yield themselves to men's pleasures than they had ever been before.

The effect here lies in the premise that the lady is punished so severely for her recalcitrance. In the legend that served as the prototype of the novella, however, such a punishment was reserved for adultery. In his analysis, Veselovsky cautiously suggests that Boccaccio didn't use this legend as a source, but another, less orthodox one. This is Veselovsky's usual point of view. He never fully recognizes the independent, deliberate changes and transformations employed by the author, which exemplify his creativity. We may suppose, in our own right, that Boccaccio intended to create a work based on the conflict between new and old interpretations of morality and punishment. There is another novella, the tenth story of the seventh day, which also concludes with reassurances regarding punishment in the other world.

But recognition is only a special case of peripeteia. The main law on which the peripeteia is based is the law of deferment—its deceleration. That which ought to have been revealed immediately and is already clear to the audience is only slowly made known to the hero. For example, how Oedipus finds out about his tragedy. Here the drama is slowed down, and there is no rush in the torment of deferred pleasure (see Zieliński's analysis of the peripeteia in Sophocles's *Oedipus*). But it is easier to study this question in rituals of everyday life than in a literary drama. Let's take Veselovsky's example of the groomsman's exchange at a Russian wedding (in *Historical Poetics*). The groomsman announces that he "has come neither by force nor coercion," but was sent by the bridegroom:

Our young prince, the bridegroom, came out of his high castle into the wide road, and then I, his groomsman, and my young attendant came out of the high castle into the wide road. I harnessed my noble horse, saddled and bridled him, and whipped him with a silk whip. My noble horse became angry and kicked the sodden ground. He leaped from mountain to mountain, over hills and rivers, leaving the mountains and dales behind his tail. He reached the blue sea, the white lake in the blue sea, where the gray geese and white swans swam and over which the falcons flew. I asked the geese and swans: "Where is the castle of our young bride?" And the geese answered me: "Go around the blue sea, to the eastern side of the blue sea. There you will see an oak with twelve roots." So I rode to the eastern shore, I reached the oak tree and a marten jumped out, not the kind that lives in the forest, but the kind that sits on a lattice chair in the high castle, embroidering a towel for our prince, the young bridegroom. I, the bridegroom's best man, and my young attendant followed the marten up to the high castle, the high castle on the wide road, to the young princess, the bride. The marten's tracks led to these gates and here they stopped. Take me to the marten's tracks or open the gates!" [Riddles by the gates.] "Who is it—a mosquito or a fly?" "I am neither a mosquito nor a fly. I am the same as a man sent by the Holy Spirit. Take me to the marten's tracks or open the gates!"

This is followed by an extremely important passage, which requires explanation. They argue by the gates. The groomsman is told from behind the gates: a) go stand under the corner window; b) crawl under the gates; c) the gates are locked, the keys are in the sea; d) you came through the wrong entrance; e) the gates are overgrown with trees and shrubs. To all these proposals the groomsman replies: "Take me to the marten's tracks or open the gates!" He repeats the phrase until they let him in. His response to (c) is the following: "Our young prince, the bridegroom, rode to the blue sea, where he hired some fine young fishermen, men of goodwill, who cast their silk net into the water and caught a white fish. They found the golden keys to the high castle in the stomach of the white fish." His response to (e) is the following: "Our young prince, the bridegroom, rode to some fine young blacksmiths, who made Damascus steel axes for him. He then hired some strong fellows, who cut down the trees and the shrubs and reached the gates."

We can see the device of deferment even more vividly in the extremely curious custom recorded by Roman Jakobson in Kostyushino village of the Rogachesky principality, in the Demidovsky district of the Moscow governorate. When the parents of a young woman go to town for the night, she invites several (typically two or three) girlfriends, then either notifies a few select young men about it, or she simply spreads a rumor (for instance, via a soldier's wife) among the young men that "so and so is having a house party." When the village goes to sleep, the young men (the invited, in the first case, and anyone who wants to go, in the second) go to the young woman's house. One of the young men knocks on the window, while the rest wait on the side. At first no one responds. He knocks again and the hostess responds:

"Who is it?"
    "It's me, (name)."
    "What do you want?"
    "Let me in."
    "So I let you in, then what happens? You have people with you, while I'm alone!"
    "I'm alone too."
    She exposes his lie, he justifies himself, then says:
    "You too are not alone. Aren't Nyushka, Manyushka, and the others in there with you?"
    She denies this, then says:
    "Sure, I'll let you in, but then I won't be able to let you out. Father will be back in an hour."

The young men say that they will only stay for half an hour. She finally lets them in through the window. They sit down, then they demand that she light the lamp. She says that she has run out of oil, that the wick is ruined, and that her mother hid the glass mantle. All of these arguments are refuted by the young men one by one. The lamp is lit. Then they demand that she light on the samovar. She replies that she has run out of coal and water, that the samovar needs soldering, and that her mother has hidden the tea. These, again, are refuted by the young men. The samovar is heated, they drink tea and the young men propose: "Now let's go to sleep." The young women refuse to go under all kinds of pretexts. The young men refute their arguments and finally they all go to bed in pairs. Every attempt at revelation, every immodest touch provokes a reasonable response, but the young men don't give up. They usually don't reach the point of possession, by the way. They all disperse by morning. Returning home, the parents pretend not to notice anything.

There was a similar custom in Germany that was called *Probenacht* (trial night). Nikolai Sumtsov has already written about the similarity of these two customs at the turn of the century.

In addition to borrowed elements, a work of art also contains an element of creativity, the will of the author who constructs his work by placing one piece next to the others.

The laws of this artistic will aimed at creating palpable works need to be elucidated. Let me quote from a letter that Tolstoy wrote on May 3, 1865:

To Princess V[olkonskaya]:

I am very glad, dear princess, of the occasion which made you think of me, and as proof of it I hasten to do the impossible for you—i.e., answer your question. Andrei Bolkonsky is nobody, like any character by a novelist, as opposed to a writer of personalities or memoirs. I would be ashamed to be published if all my work consisted of copying a portrait, trying to find things out, and memorizing things. . . . I will try to tell you what sort of a man my Andrei is.

I needed a brilliant young man to be killed at the battle

of Austerlitz, which will be described later, but with which
I began my novel. In the further course of the novel I only
needed the old Bolkonsky and his daughter, but since it was
awkward to describe a character not connected with the novel
in any way, I decided to make this brilliant young man the son
of the old Bolkonsky. Then he began to interest me; I imagined
a part of him to play in the further course of the novel and
I took pity on him, merely wounding him seriously instead
of killing him. So there you have, dear princess, a completely
truthful, although for that very reason unclear, explanation of
who Bolkonsky is.[50]

Pay attention to Tolstoy's motivation for kinship between characters. When comparing it to Hugo's novels (for example, *Les
Misérables*), it becomes clear just how conventional Tolstoy's motivation is for connecting the separate parts of the work by way of
the protagonists' kinship and common place of residence. We
used to see a greater audacity in this regard. If, for compositional
reasons, an author needed to connect two pieces, he did not necessarily turn that connection into a causal one. You can see such
motivations for connecting stories in Eastern tales. For instance,
the narrator of one such tale has a wheel whirling around his head
(Johannes Østrup). The unrealistic nature of this situation didn't
disturb the compiler at all, since the parts of a work don't necessarily have to influence or depend on each other based on any
non-compositional law.

Framing as a Device of Deferment

Note: The method of organizing a set of narratives wherein the
characters tell their stories in succession *ad infinitum* until the first
story is completely forgotten may be called specifically Indian.

———

---

[50] *Tolstoy's Letters*, ed. and trans. R. F. Christian (London: Athlone Press, 1978). All subsequent quotations from *Tolstoy's Letters* are taken from this translation.

The technique of the frame story can be seen everywhere in the *Panchatantra, Hitopadesha, Vetalapanchavimsati*, and all other similar works. Indians pay no particular attention to the improbability of situations in which the characters find themselves. So, amidst the most terrifying torments, on the brink between life and death, the characters narrate or listen to different fables with absolute calmness (for example, the fable about the Brahmin who tells his life story while a wheel is whirling around his head).

There is also the story of "The Seven Viziers," undoubtedly Indian in origin, where we encounter the same method of storytelling. *The Arabian Nights* has the same feature of a slow and continuous narration of different stories; the premise, in this case, is to defer the execution of a death sentence.

There is an analogous case in Indian literature, where the narrator relates a whole series of fables to draw out time and prevent an imprudent decision. *Sukasaptati*, or *Seventy Tales of the Parrot*, is about a lady who wants to visit her lover when her husband is away, but the parrot (a gift from her husband) narrates a different story each night in order to dissuade her from going out, and ends each story by saying: "I shall tell you the rest tomorrow, if you stay here tonight."

Let's compare this story with "The Lay of Alvis," a poem from *The Poetic Edda*, in which Thor must keep Alvis occupied until sunrise with questions about how various objects are called by the Æsir, Vanir, giants, dwarfs, and elves. Alvis succeeds in answering the questions, but is turned to stone when touched by the light of the rising sun.

It is interesting that in this case the device is easily perceived as a method of delay. Let me give another example. The king gives orders to kill the queen, but instead the vizier hides her. The king doesn't know this and mourns her death. The vizier responds to him, playing with his patience in the same way as a framing device does. So, for instance, the king says: "You have upset me and increased my pain by killing the *ûpâxn*." The *ûpâgh* replies: "Only two types of men ought to grieve—those who commit sins every day and those who never commit a good deed, because their joy in the world and their felicity are insignificant, while their repentance, after a long punishment, cannot be measured." The king says: "You are right. If I could only see the *ûpâxn* alive, I would never grieve about anything ever again." The *ûpâgh* replies: "Only two types of men should not grieve—those who commit good deeds . . ." and so on.

In one version of the story (from *Kalila and Dimna*), the vizier's responses, along with the parables, stretch to nine pages.

This device of Indian poetics plays the same role as the fairy-tale convention in fairy tales and the "delaying moments" in adventure novels.

But let us return to the question of artistic intent, and compare the following excerpt from Aristotle's *Poetics* with Tolstoy's letter quoted above:

> As for the story, whether the poet takes it ready-made or constructs it for himself, he should first sketch its general outline, and then fill in the episodes and amplify in detail. The general plan may be illustrated by *Iphigenia*. A young girl is sacrificed; she disappears mysteriously from the eyes of those who sacrificed her; she is transported to another country, where the custom is to offer up all strangers to the goddess. To this ministry she is appointed. Sometime later her own brother chances to arrive. The fact that the oracle for some reason ordered him to go there, is outside the general plan of the play. The purpose, again, of his coming is outside the action proper. However, he comes, he is seized, and, when on the point of being sacrificed, reveals who he is. The mode of recognition may be either that of Euripides or of Polyidus, in whose play he exclaims very naturally: "So it was not my sister only, but I too, who was doomed to be sacrificed"; and by that remark he is saved.
>
> After this, the names being once given, it remains to fill in the episodes. We must see that they are relevant to action. In

the case of Orestes, for example, there is the madness which led to his capture, and his deliverance by means of the purificatory rite. (Chapter 17)[51]

Hence, the battle between father and son is the result of artistic choice and not, as Veselovsky claims, the result of matriarchal memory (see the *bylina* about Ilya Muromets and Sokolnik, or the tragedy of Rostam and Sohrab).[52]

Notice how all of the versions speak of the father's "recognition" of his son, which means that the creator of the plot is convinced that the father ought to know his own son. Of interest to us are the different expositions that allow for patricide and incest. For instance, Julian the Hospitaller slays his slumbering mother and father, whom he mistakes for his wife and her lover. Compare this with the Russian tale "On Poverty and Want" from the Vyatka governorate (tale no. 5 in Zelenin's collection): "Returning home after a period of absence, the merchant saw two young boys lying in his wife's bed. He wanted to kill them. They were his sons." Compare this with the tale "A Kind Word" (tale no. 92 in Afanasyev's collection), tales no. 12 and no. 82 in Onchukov's collection, tale no. 16 in Erlenvein's collection, as well as "The Source of A. N. Maikov's Tale 'Three Truths'" by Vladimir Peretz.

What we are seeing here is the will of the artist striving to motivate a crime that his work requires. And I quote again from Aristotle:

> Let us then determine what are the circumstances which strike us as terrible or pitiful.
>
> Actions capable of this effect must happen between persons who are either friends or enemies or indifferent to one another. If an enemy kills an enemy, there is nothing to excite pity either in the act or the intention—except so far as the suffering

---

[51] Aristotle, *Poetics*, trans. S. H. Butcher (New York: Hill and Wang, 1961). All subsequent quotations from *Poetics* are taken from this translation.

[52] See Appendix III.

in itself is pitiful. So again with indifferent persons. But when the tragic incident occurs between those who are near or dear to one another—if, for example, a brother kills, or intends to kill, a brother, a son his father, a mother her son, a son his mother, or any other deed of the kind is done—these are the situations to be looked for by the poet. (*Poetics*, Chapter 14)

The poet could not destroy the framework of the received legends—the fact, for instance, that Clytemnestra was slain by Orestes and Eriphyle by Alcmaeon. There was a characteristic way in which myths could be changed, if at all. According to the legend and in Aeschylus's *Libation Bearers*, Orestes alone informs Clytemnestra of her son's death. Sophocles, on the other hand, splits this role, giving Talthybius the role of the messenger, while Orestes delivers the ashes of the supposedly dead son. In other words, Sophocles uses the common device of expressing A through $A_1 A_2$.

But the poet ought to show invention of his own, and skillfully handle the traditional material. Let us explain more clearly what is meant by skillful handling.

The action may be done consciously and with knowledge of the persons, in the manner of the older poets. It is thus too that Euripides makes Medea slay her children. Or, again, the deed of horror may be done, but done in ignorance, and the tie of kinship or friendship be discovered afterwards. The *Oedipus* of Sophocles is an example. Here, indeed, the incident is outside the drama proper; but cases occur where it falls within the action of the play: one may cite the Alcmaeon of Astydamas, or Telegonus in the *Wounded Odysseus*. Again, there is a third case—when someone is about to do an irreparable deed through ignorance, and makes the discovery before it is done. These are the only possible ways. For the deed must either be done or not done—and that wittingly or unwittingly. But of all these ways, to be about to act knowing the persons, and then not to act, is the worst. It is shocking without being tragic, for no disaster follows. It is, therefore, never, or very rarely, found in poetry. One instance, however, is in the *Antigone*, where Haemon threatens to kill Creon. The next and better way is that the deed should be perpetrated. Still better, that it should be perpetrated in ignorance, and the discovery made afterwards. There is then nothing to shock us, while the discovery produces a startling effect. The last case is the best, as when in the *Cresphontes* Merope is about to slay her son, but, recognizing who he is, spares his life. So in the *Iphigenia*, the sister recognizes the brother just in time. Again in the *Helle*, the son recognizes the mother when on the point of giving her up. This, then, is why a few families only, as has already been observed, furnish the subjects of tragedy. It was not art, but happy chance, that led the poets in search of subjects to impress the tragic quality upon their plots. They are compelled, therefore, to have recourse to those houses whose history contains moving incidents like these. (*Poetics*, Chapter 14)

Compare this with the descriptions of incest in Maupassant: father-daughter in "The Hermit" (recognition by means of a photograph), and brother-sister in "The Port" (recognition by means of a conversation).

I am trying to find the right comparison. The action of a literary work unfolds on a specific field: the types—the masks, the *emploi* of contemporary theater—correspond to chess pieces. The plots correspond to the gambits, that is, to the classical tricks of the game that the players employ in their own way. The obstacles and the peripeteias correspond to the moves made by the opponent.

The methods and devices of plot construction are similar to and, in principle, identical with the devices of musical orchestration. Works of literature represent a *weaving* of sounds, articulated movements and thoughts.

Thought in a literary work is either the same kind of material as the pronunciation and sound of a morpheme, or it is a foreign body. And I quote from Tolstoy's letter to Nikolai Strakhov (Yasnaya Polyana, April 26, 1876):

> If I were to try to say in words everything that I intended to express through my novel, then I would have to write that same novel again. And if the critics already understand and can express in a feuilleton article what I wanted to say, I congratulate them and can boldly assure them that *qu'ils en savent plus long que moi.* And if the shortsighted critics think that I only wanted to describe the things that I like, what Oblonsky has for dinner or what Karenina's shoulders are like, they are mistaken.
>
> In everything, or nearly everything, that I have written, I have been guided by the need to gather together thoughts interlinked for the purpose of expressing myself; but every thought expressed separately in words loses its meaning and is terribly impoverished when taken by itself and out of the linkage in which it occurs. The linkage itself is not formed by thought (I think), but by something else, and it is impossible to express the basis of this linkage directly through words. It can only be expressed indirectly—by describing characters, actions, and situations.
>
> . . . But now, indeed, when the nine-tenth of everything printed is criticism, we need people who could show the pointlessness of looking for separate thoughts in a work of art and can steadfastly guide readers through that endless labyrinth of linkages, which is the essence of art, and through those laws that serve as the basis for those linkages.

The fairy tale, the story, and the novel are all combinations of motifs. The song is a combination of stylistic motifs. Hence, plot and plottedness represent form in the same way that rhyme does. The notion of "content" is irrelevant when analyzing a work of art from the point of view of plot. Form should here be understood as the law of construction.

THE STRUCTURE OF THE STORY
AND THE NOVEL

I.

Before starting this chapter, I ought to say that I don't have a definition for the novella. In other words, I don't know what properties its motif should have, or how the motifs should be arranged to form a plot. A simple image and a simple parallel or even a simple description of an event do not readily produce the sense of a novella.

I tried to show in the previous chapter the connection between the devices of plot construction and the general devices of style. I discussed in particular the stepped accretion of motifs. Such accretions are by their nature never-ending, just like the adventure novels that are based on them—we can think of the countless volumes about Rocambole, as well as *Ten Years Later* and *Twenty Years After* by Alexandre Dumas. That is why such novels require an epilogue. It is possible to end them only by changing the scale of narrative time, by "crunching" it.

But usually the conglomeration of novellas is held together by a framing novella. Besides abduction and recognition, authors most often use the motif of an impeded wedding that nevertheless takes place as a frame for the adventure novel. This is why Mark

71

Twain concludes at the end of *Tom Sawyer* that "when one writes a novel about grown people, he knows exactly where to stop—that is, with a marriage; but when he writes of juveniles, he must stop where he best can." As we know, the story of Tom Sawyer had its sequel—the story of Huckleberry Finn (who takes center stage after having played a secondary role in the first book), and even after that it carried on as a detective novel, before finally adopting the devices of Jules Verne's *Five Weeks in a Balloon*.

But what does a novella require in order to be perceived as something complete in and of itself?

Through analysis it may easily be seen that, in addition to the stepped construction, there is also the circular or loop construction. The description of a happy, reciprocal love cannot produce a novella or, even if it does, then only perceived against the traditional background of descriptions of love full of obstacles. A novella requires a love story with obstacles. For example, A loves B, but B doesn't love A; and when B falls in love with A, A has already ceased to love B. This is the plot scheme of Eugene Onegin and Tatyana Larina's affair, where the causes of the non-simultaneity of their attraction for each other are motivated by complex psychological factors. Boiardo uses the same device in *Orlando Innamorato*, however, motivated by magic spells. Rinaldo is in love with Angelica, but he accidentally drinks from an enchanted spring and forgets his love for her. Meanwhile, Angelica drinks from another spring, which has the reverse effect and makes her fall in love with Rinaldo, whom she hated before. As a result, Rinaldo is running away from Angelica, while she pursues him from country to country. After wandering all over the world, Rinaldo, followed by Angelica, ends up in the same forest of enchanted springs. They drink from the same springs and their roles are reversed once again: Angelica conceives a hatred for Rinaldo, while he falls in love with her again. The motivation here is almost laid bare.

So, to structure a novella, one needs not only action but also counteraction—or, some kind of non-coincidence. This links the motif to the trope and the pun. As I have already noted in the chapter on erotic estrangement, the plots of erotic tales are extended metaphors—for example, male and female sexual organs are compared to a pestle and a mortar in Boccaccio. The comparison has motivated an entire story and turned into a motif. We see something similar in the novella about "putting the devil back into hell," only here the unfolding is shown more clearly, as there is a direct statement at the end about the existence of such an expression among the folk. Apparently, the novella is an unfolding of this expression.

Many novellas appear to be the unfolding of puns—for instance, stories about the origins of names. I had occasion to hear from the lips of an old man who lived by the Okhta River that the river's name originated from Peter the Great's exclamation: "*Okh! Ta!*" (Oh! That!). When a name does not lend itself to wordplay, then it is broken up into nonexistent proper names, for example, the name Moskva comes from "*Mos*" and "*Kva*," the name of the river Yauza comes from "*Ya*" and "*Uza*" (from the legend of the founding of Moscow).

A motif is not always the unfolding of linguistic material. Contradictions in customs can also serve as a basis for the development of a motif. Here is an interesting detail from military folklore (of course, it is not without the influence of linguistic elements): the ring mount of the bayonet is called a "socket" (which is basically a hole), and young soldiers often complained: "I have lost the socket." A similar motif was based on the concept of smokeless fire (electricity)—the story is about a non-commissioned officer who was being persuaded by the soldiers, who had been smoking in the barracks, that the "smoke was coming from the light bulbs."

The motif of a false impossibility is also based on a contradiction. A prophecy, for instance, represents a contradiction between the intention of the main character, who seeks to avoid the prophecy, and the fact that it is nevertheless fulfilled (as with Oedipus). In other words, the prophecy that seemed impossible occurs after all, but in the manner of a play on words. Examples: the Witch's promise to Macbeth that he "shall never vanquish'd be" until Birnam wood marches to fight him, and that "none of woman born" can harm him. When assaulting Macbeth's castle, the soldiers camouflage themselves with branches of trees in order to conceal their numbers, and Macbeth's killer was not born naturally, but ripped prematurely from his mother's womb. Or take the Alexander romance: Alexander is told that he will die in an iron land under a sky of bone. In the end, he dies on a shield under a ceiling made of ivory. And another example from Shakespeare's *Henry IV*: the king, who is told that he will die in Jerusalem, dies in an abbey in England, in a room called the "Jerusalem Chamber."

Motifs such as "a battle between father and son," "a brother marries his sister" (in the folk song adapted by Pushkin, the motif is complicated further), and "the husband at his wife's wedding" are all built on a contrast. The same goes for the motif of the "uncapturable thief" in the tale inserted into the history of Herodotus, where what appears to be an impossible situation is subsequently resolved by means of trickery. Also belonging to this class are fairy tales with the motif of posing and solving riddles, or the extended version that combines riddle solving with heroic deeds. The motif of the false or innocent criminal became popular in the literature of later periods. In this type of motif, we have the preparation for a possible accusation of an innocent person, then the actual accusation, and finally the acquittal. Sometimes the acquittal is attained through a juxtaposition of the false testimonies (as in the story of Susanna and the Elders) or the intervention of a conscientious witness.

If we don't have a denouement, we don't get a sense of a plot either. A good example of this is Le Sage's *The Devil upon Two Sticks*, which is comprised of snapshots that seem to have no structure at all. Here is a passage from the novel:

You observe that new building, which is divided into two wings. One is occupied by the proprietor, the old gentleman whom you see, now pacing the apartment, now throwing himself into an easy chair. He is evidently immersed in some grand project, said Zambullo: who is he? If one may judge by the splendor which is displayed in his mansion, he is a grandee of the first order. Nevertheless, said Asmodeus, he is but an ancient clerk of the treasury, who has grown old in such lucrative employment as to enable him to amass four millions of reals. As he has some compunctions of conscience for the means by which all this wealth has been acquired, and as he expects shortly to be called upon to render his account in another world, where bribery is impracticable, he is about to compound for his sins in this, by building a monastery; which done, he flatters himself that peace will revisit his heart. He has already obtained the necessary permission; but, as he has resolved that the establishment shall consist of monks who are extremely chaste, sober, and of the most Christian humility, he is much embarrassed in the selection. He need not build a very extensive convent.

The other wing is inhabited by a fair lady, who has just retired to rest after the luxury of a milk bath. This voluptuary is widow of a knight of the order of Saint James, who left her at his death her title only; but fortunately her charms have secured for her valuable friends in the persons of two members of the council of Castile, who generously divide her favors and the expenses of her household.

Hark! cried the Student; surely I hear the cries of distress. What dreadful misfortune has occurred? A very common one, said the Demon: two young cavaliers have been gambling in a hell (the name is a scandal on the infernal regions), which you perceive so brilliantly illuminated. They quarreled upon an interesting point of the game, and naturally drew their swords to settle it: unluckily they were equally skillful with their weapons, and are both mortally wounded. The elder is married, which is unfortunate; and the younger an only son.

The wife and father have just come in time to receive their last sighs; and it is their lamentations that you hear. Unhappy boy, cries the fond parent over the still breathing body of his son, how often have I conjured thee to renounce this dreadful vice!—how often have I warned thee it would one day cost thee thy life. Heaven is my witness, that the fault is none of mine! Men, added the Demon, are always selfish, even in their griefs. Meanwhile the wife is in despair. Although her husband has dissipated the fortune she brought him on their marriage; although he has sold, to maintain his shameful excesses, her jewels, and even her clothes, not a word of reproach escapes her lips. She is inconsolable for her loss. Her grief is vented in frantic exclamations, mixed with curses on the cards, and the devil who invented them; on the place in which her husband fell, and on the people who surround her, and to whom she fondly attributes his ruin. (Chapter 3)[53]

The fragments in this passage cannot be considered as novellas, and it is not because of their length. The following short scene, however, which interrupts the novella told by Asmodeus, brings the sense of completion:

Asmodeus was at this moment interrupted in his recital by the Student, who thus addressed him: My dear Devil, interesting as is the history you are relating to me, my eyes have wandered to an object which prevents my listening to you as attentively as I could wish. I see a lady, who is rather good-looking, seated between a young man and a gentleman old enough to be his grandfather. They seem to enjoy the liqueurs which are on the table near them, but what amuses me is, that, as from time to time the amorous old dotard embraces his mistress, the deceiver conveys her hand to the lips of the other, who covers it with silent kisses. He is doubtless her gallant. On the contrary, replied the cripple, he is her husband, and the old fool is her

---

[53] Alain-René Le Sage, *Asmodeus; or, The Devil upon Two Sticks*, trans. Joseph Thomas (London: William Tegg & Co, 1877).

lover. He is a man of consequence,—no less than a comman-
dant of the military order of Calatrava; and is ruining himself
for the lady, whose complaisant husband holds some inferior
place at court. She bestows her caresses on the sighing knight,
for the sake of his gold, and is unfaithful to him in favor of
her husband from inclination. (Chapter 4)

The sense of completion comes from the fact that the narrative first
offers a false recognition, then reveals the true state of affairs—i.e.
the formula is carried through.

Nevertheless, vast passages of the book read as long, unfinished
novellas in which many things are left unsaid. Such a quasi-novella
can be found at the end of Chapter 10. It begins with a description of a serenade and a citation of couplets sung by two voices:

. . . but enough of these couplets, continued he, you will hear
music of another kind.

Follow with your eyes those four men who have suddenly
appeared in the street. See! they pounce upon the serenaders:
the latter raise their instruments to defend their heads, but
their frail bucklers yield to the blows which fall on them, and
are shattered into a thousand pieces. And now see, coming
to their assistance, two cavaliers; one of whom is the gallant
donor of the serenade. With what fury they charge on the
four aggressors! Again, with what skill and valor do these latter
receive them. What fire sparkles from their swords! See! one
of the defenders of the serenade has fallen,—it is he who gave
it,—he is mortally wounded. His companion, perceiving his
fall, flies to preserve his own life; the aggressors, having effected
their object, fly also; the musicians have disappeared during
the combat; and there remains upon the spot the unfortunate
cavalier alone, who has paid for his gallantry with his life. In
the meanwhile, observe the alcade's daughter: she is at her window, whence she has observed all that has passed. This lady is
so vain of her beauty,—although that is nothing extraordinary
either,—that instead of deploring its fatal effect, she rejoices

in the force of her attractions, of which she now thinks more than ever.

This will not be the end of it. You see another cavalier, who has this moment stopped in the street to assist, were it possible, the unfortunate being who is swimming in his blood. While occupied in this charitable office, see! he is surprised by the watch. They are taking him to prison, where he will remain many months: and he will almost pay as dearly for this transaction as though he were the murderer himself.

This is, indeed, a night of misfortunes! said Zambullo.

The novella is perceived as something incomplete. Sometimes appended to such "vignettes" is what I shall call a "false ending," usually comprising a description of nature or the weather, in the manner of the Christmas story, made famous by the journal *Satirikon*, which ends with the words "the frost was becoming even more vicious."[54] For the sake of diversion, I suggest that the reader compose a description of Seville at night or of an "indifferent sky" and append it to the passage from Le Sage above.

In terms of a false ending, it is very typical to use a description of autumn followed by an exclamation: "It's a dreary world, gentlemen!"—as Gogol does at the end of "How Ivan Ivanovich Quarreled with Ivan Nikiforovich."[55]

This new motif is formed parallel to the preceding material, and the novella appears to have ended.

There is yet another, entirely unique type of novella with a "negative ending." First, let me explain what I mean by this term. In words like *stola* and *stolu*, the letters *a* and *u* are added as suffixes to the root word *stol* (table). The word *stol* does not have a suffix in the nominative singular case, but compared to other case inflections this absence is perceived as a special feature and can be

---

[54] A reference to Dickens's *A Christmas Carol* and Arkadi Averchenko's parodistic short story "Tysyacha pervaya istoriya o zamerzayushchem malchike" [The Thousand and First Story about a Freezing Boy], 1914. [—Trans.]

[55] Nikolai Gogol, *The Diary of a Madman, The Government Inspector and Selected Stories*, trans. Ronald Wilks (Penguin Classics, 2005).

called a "negative form" (Filip Fortunatov's term) or "zero affix" (Jan Baudouin de Courtenay's term). We encounter such negative forms most frequently in novellas, particularly in the novellas of Maupassant.

For example, a mother travels to see her illegitimate son, who had been sent to a country village for his upbringing. He has turned into a boorish peasant. His mother runs away in grief and falls into a river. The son, knowing nothing about her, searches the bottom of the river with a pole and finally pulls her out by the dress. The novella ends here. By the way (and this is more of an opinion, rather than an assertion), the French novel of everyday life from Flaubert's period widely employed the device of unrealized action (see *Sentimental Education*).

Typically, a novella represents a combination of circular and stepped constructions, complicated by an explication.

Among all of Chekhov's works, his book of short stories is always the one that gets worn out the most. His most popular works are the early stories, the stories that he used to call "mottled." If you read them and then retell them to yourself, it will be obvious that Chekhov's themes are rather ordinary. He tells stories about petty officials and merchants—themes that were introduced into literature long ago. These were the themes of Leikin and Gorbunov. In fact, these social realities are rather antiquated for the modern day.

The success of Chekhov's stories lies in the construction of plot. Russian literature had paid little attention to novelistic plot. Gogol spent years waiting for the right anecdote that could be unfolded into a story or a tale.

The structure of Goncharov's plotting is rather feeble. For the exposition of *Oblomov*, Goncharov has various types of people visit Oblomov over the course of one day, and the reader is supposed to infer from this that Oblomov leads a restless life.

Turgenev's *Rudin* is based on a novella, an episode, and Rudin's confession.

Pushkin's novellas have particularly dynamic plots. However, the rest of the novelistic tradition is replete with the monotonous high-society tales of Marlinsky, Kalashnikov, Vonlyarlyarsky, Sologub, and Lermontov.

Chekhov's novellas abruptly interrupted this tradition. Simple in terms of their material, these novellas differ from the countless physiological sketches, which at one time competed with the high-society tale, in the sense that the Chekhovian novella is constructed around a precise plot with an unexpected resolution.

The main device of construction in Chekhov is the mistake—the mix-up. The first story, "At the Bathhouse," is based on the fact that both nihilists and clergymen in old Russia wore their hair long. All other secondary features had to be eliminated in order for the "mistake" to work. Hence, the action takes place in the bathhouse. In order to amplify the impact of the conflict, Chekhov sets the story during Lent, when the question of the clergy is topical. The remarks of the deacon who is mistaken for a nihilist are constructed in such a way that, when the reader finds out that he is actually a deacon and not a nihilist, the moment of recognition is unexpected but legitimate, as it explains the meaning of his obscure words. It is crucial to involve the characters in the denouement in order for it to work. In this case, the barber is upset, because he is fasting and thinks that he can't go to confession now, since he has insulted a member of the clergy by accusing the latter of "having ideas in his head."

We have in front of us a correctly constructed equation, all of whose parts are functionally connected to each other.

The novella titled "Fat and Thin" is only two pages long. It is based on the social inequality between two former schoolmates. The situation is rather elementary, but it is explicated with unexpected and precise inventiveness. At first the old friends kiss each other and gaze at each other with eyes full of tears, both of them pleasantly surprised. The thin man hastens to tell his friend about his family; the words pour out uncontrollably, in a friendly manner. In the middle of the novella, that is, at the end of the first page, the thin man finds out that the fat man is a member of the Privy Council. Suddenly, the chasm of class difference opens up between them—which is made quite clear, because prior to this revelation the friends were presented as completely unencumbered by the social reality of the day. Stuttering his words, the thin man repeats the phrases about his family, but now with a reporting tone. The repetition of the phrases reveals a difference in their coincidence and exposes the structure of the novella.

The work is brought to an end by way of its parallel construction. It has a double denouement based on the different reactions of the two friends. The Privy Councilor is almost sickened by the reverences of his former friend; he turns away from the thin man, giving him his hand at parting. The thin man presses three fingers, bows his whole body and sniggers like a Chinese man: "He-he-he!" His wife smiles. His son, Nafanil, bows and scrapes with his foot, and drops his cap. All three are agreeably overwhelmed.

Very often Chekhov bases his work on a violation of some traditional plot convention. Let us take a look at another story called "A Dreadful Night," which concerns a man who finds coffins in every apartment that he visits at night, including his own. The story begins in a primitive-mystical way. The storyteller's name is Ivan Petrovich Panikhidin.[56] He lives in Moscow, near the Church of Eternal Sleep by the Graves, in a house belonging to the civil servant Trupov.[57] To soften the effect of the bared device, Chekhov adds—"apparently in one of the remotest parts of the Arbat district."

Through such an accumulation of referential inner rational horrors, Chekhov builds up to a completely unexpected ending, which is based on the contradiction between the coffin as a mystical object and central element of a horror story, and the coffin

---

[56] A play on the word *panikhida*, a liturgical memorial service for the repose of departed in the Eastern Orthodox Church. [—Trans.]

[57] A wordplay on *trup*, which means a corpse in Russian. [—Trans.]

as a valuable item in the inventory of a coffin-maker. To avoid his creditors, the coffin-maker hides the coffins in the apartments of his friends.

"An Enigmatic Nature" is a novella that ironizes the epigones of the high-society tale. To bare the device completely, the heroine tells her story directly to a writer. The action is set in a first-class railway carriage—a setting that was often used at the time to introduce a high society heroine. "On the seat opposite sits the Provincial Secretary of Special Commissions, a budding young author, who from time to time publishes short stories of high life, or 'novellas' as he calls them, in the leading paper of the province."[58] The beginning of the novella, narrated by the woman, is completely traditional. She tells how she once was poor: "the monstrous education at a boarding-school, foolish novel-reading, the errors of early youth, the first timid flutter of love." She falls in love with a young man, she wants to be happy. This is followed by another parody thread, this time on the epigones of the psychological novel. "'Exquisite creature!' murmured the author, kissing her hand close to the bracelet. 'It's not you I am kissing, but the suffering of humanity.'" The woman then recounts her marriage to an old general, and this is followed by a parody of her life in a few lines. The old man dies, leaving her a fortune. Happiness comes tapping at her window, but again there is an obstacle in her path. "'But what—what stands in your way? I implore you tell me! What is it?' 'Another old general, very well off—' . . ."

The doubling of the motif completely deprives it of its original motivation and transfers the material of a high-society tale into a novella about an ordinary sale.

The novella "Who Was She?" is a work of lesser quality, but it is also based on parody. It operates on the inertia of the Christmastide story—an encounter with an unknown woman, whose mysteriousness is not asserted by the narrator, but implied

---

[58] Anton Chekhov, *The Horse Stealers & Other Stories*, trans. Constance Garnett (New York: Ecco Press, 1986).

by the young ladies listening to the story (or the reader). In the end, the mysterious woman turns out to be the wife of the narrator, the young ladies listening to the story protest, and the narrator reverts to a traditional ending.

The brilliant story "A Gentleman Friend" is again based on the duality of relations to the same subject but without employing the inertia of another genre. A prostitute is released from the hospital. Without her professional costume—her fashionable short jacket, big hat, and bronze-colored shoes—she feels naked. She no longer thinks of herself as the charming Vanda, but as the plain Nastasya Kanavkina, as it says in her passport. She needs money. Vanda-Nastasya is a dual character who pawns her ring, her only piece of jewelry, for a ruble and goes to see her gentleman friend Finkel, a dentist. She thinks out her plan of action before reaching the dentist's door: she will run laughing up the stairs, dash into the dentist's room and demand twenty-five rubles. But she is wearing a plain dress. She enters timidly and asks the porter: "Is the doctor at home?" The staircase seems luxurious to her, and there is a mirror above the staircase. Vanda sees herself again without her big hat, without her fashionable jacket, and without her bronze-colored shoes. She enters the doctor's consulting-room and out of shyness says that she has a toothache. Finkel soils Vanda's lips and gums with his tobacco-stained fingers and pulls out her tooth. She ends up giving him her last ruble.

The structure of this story is based on the duality of a person's station in life. Here we have two people of different professions—a prostitute and a dentist; she comes to him now as a non-professional to a professional. The change of situation is repeatedly emphasized through the reminders of Vanda's "disguise." The underlying premise here is the idea of shame, the shame of revealing who you are, which leads to pain—and this is the theme that glues the piece together.

When she got out into the street she felt more overwhelmed

with shame than before, but now it was not her poverty she
was ashamed of. She was unconscious now of not having a big
hat and a fashionable jacket. She walked along the street, spit-
ting blood, and brooding on her life, her ugly, wretched life,
and the insults she had endured, and would have to endure
tomorrow, and next week, and all her life, up to the very day
of her death.[59]

Chekhov rarely used unmediated oral speech (*skaz*) in his work,
but he has one remarkable novella called "Polinka" in which he
employs this oral form of narrative for compositional purposes.

A salesman talks with a dressmaker, whom he has been courting
for a while, about her infatuation with a university student and
suggests that the latter will someday deceive her. The conversation takes place in a shop, as the dressmaker is purchasing trim-
mings, and the voices in the fashionable shop contradict the drama
between the couple. The sale is intentionally prolonged, as one of
them is in love and the other feels guilty. "The most fashionable
now are real bird feathers. If you want the most fashionable color,
it's heliotrope or *kanak*—that is, claret with a yellow shade in it.
We have an immense choice. And what all this affair is going to
lead to, I really don't understand."[60] The woman is pale and there
are tears in her eyes as she picks out buttons:

> "I mustn't forget some buttons for a dressing-gown . . . It's for
> a shopkeeper's wife, so give me something rather striking."
>
> "Yes, if it's for a shopkeeper's wife, you'd better have some-
> thing bright. Here are some buttons. A combination of col-
> ors—red, blue, and the fashionable gold shade. Very glaring.
> The more refined prefer dull black with a bright border. But
> I don't understand. Can't you see for yourself? What these . . .
> walks lead to?"

---

[59] Anton Chekhov, *Early Short Stories, 1883-1888*, trans. Constance Garnett (New York: Modern Library, 1999).

[60] Anton Chekhov, *Short Story Collection*, trans. Constance Garnett (Sovereign, 2010).

"I don't know," whispers Polinka, and she bends over the buttons; "I don't know myself what's come to me, Nikolai Timofeich."

The novella ends with an almost meaningless list of haberdashery items and tears:

Nikolai Timofeich screens Polinka, and, trying to conceal her emotion and his own, wrinkles his face into a smile and says aloud: "There are two kinds of lace, madam: cotton and silk! Oriental, English, Valenciennes, crochet, torchon, are cotton. And rococo, soutache, Cambray, are silk . . . For God's sake, wipe your eyes! They're coming this way!" And seeing that her tears are still gushing he goes on louder than ever: "Spanish, Rococo, soutache, Cambray . . . stockings, thread, cotton, silk . . ."

Chekhov's novellas first appeared in publications of "low" literature—they were published in humoristic journals. His literary reputation rose when he started to write plays and short novels. Chekhov ought not only to be reprinted but also reexamined, as this will lead everyone to admit that his most popular and frequently read works are the ones that are formally the most perfect.

II.

Parallelism is a special device for composing a novella. Let us analyze it in the works of Tolstoy.

In order to turn an object into a fact of art, one must extract it from the facts of life. To do so, it is necessary, first and foremost, to "budge the thing" as Ivan the Terrible "plucked up" men. It is necessary to wrest the object from its row of common associations. It is necessary to turn the object over like a log in the fireplace. Chekhov has the following example in his notebook: Someone who had passed down the same street for either fifteen or thirty years kept seeing the sign "A large selection of GARS" every day and thought: "Who needs a large selection of gars?" Finally, one day the sign was taken down and leaned against the wall sideways. And then he read: "A large selection of CIGARS."

The poet removes all the signs from their usual places. The artist always incites things to revolt. Things run riot in the hands of poets, throwing off their old names and adopting new ones—adopting new guises. The poet uses figures of speech—tropes, similes; for example, he may refer to fire as a red flower, or he may use a new epithet with an antiquated word, or else, like Baudelaire, he may describe a carcass that raises its legs in the air "like a lustful woman."[61] Thus, the poet creates a semantic shift (*sdvig*) by wresting the concept from its "natural" semantic axis and moving it, with the help of a word (trope), onto another semantic axis. We perceive the innovation when we find the object on the new axis. The new word fits the object like a new dress. The sign has been removed. This is one of the ways of transforming an object into something palpable, something capable of becoming material for a work of art. Another way is by creating a stepped form. The thing splits and its reflections and contrapositions are rearranged.

> Oh, little apple, where are you rolling to?
> Oh, mama dear, I want to get married—

sings the tramp in Rostov, most likely continuing the tradition of the following song type:

> The apple was rolling down the bridge,
> Katichka was asking if she could leave the feast.

There are two completely different, non-coinciding themes here, but each displaces the other from its respective system of ordinary associations.

---

[61] Charles Baudelaire, "A Carcass," in *The Flowers of Evil*, trans. William Aggeler (Fresno, CA: Academy Library Guild, 1954).

Sometimes a thing doubles or decomposes. In Aleksandr Blok, for example, the word "railroad" (used as an adjective) is broken down into "iron road ennui." Tolstoy, in works as formal as music, created structures using the principle of estrangement (giving a thing an unusual name) as well as stepped construction.

I have already written about Tolstoy's method of estrangement. One of the varieties of this device is that the writer focuses on and emphasizes a certain detail in the picture, which changes the standard proportions. For example, in his depiction of the battle scene, Tolstoy expands the detail of the moist, chewing mouth. This attention to detail creates a unique shift. Konstantin Leontyev failed to understand this device in his book about Tolstoy.

But Tolstoy's most common device is when he refuses to recognize objects and describes them as though he were seeing them for the first time, calling the stage decorations in *War and Peace* "painted cardboard," or the communion bread "a bun," or asserting that Christians eat their God. I believe that this Tolstoyan device comes from French literature, perhaps from Voltaire's *L'Ingénu* or the descriptions of the French court made by Chateaubriand's *indigène* in *Atala*. In any case, Tolstoy "estranged" Wagnerian things, describing them precisely from the viewpoint of an intelligent peasant, i.e. someone who had not been corrupted by customary associations, in the manner of the French "noble savages." In fact, according to Veselovsky, a similar device of describing the city from a villager's perspective was first used in the ancient Greek novel.

The second device, the device of stepped construction, was developed by Tolstoy in the most original way.

I will not attempt to give a concise outline of the evolution of this device in Tolstoy's development of his own unique poetics, but I will mention a few examples to show what I mean. The young Tolstoy constructed parallels rather naïvely. For example, in order fully to explicate the theme of death, Tolstoy felt the need to illustrate it through three narratives: the death of a lady, the death of a peasant, and the death of a tree. I am talking about the story "Three Deaths." The separate parts of this story are connected through a concrete motivation: the peasant is the lady's coachman, while the tree is cut down to serve as a cross on the peasant's grave.

Parallelism is also occasionally motivated in late Russian folk lyric poetry. So, for instance, the common parallel between love and trampling the grass is motivated by the fact that lovers trample the grass while strolling.

Tolstoy supports the horse/man parallelism in the last chapter of "Strider" with the following statement: "The dead body of Serpukhovskoy, which had walked about the earth eating and drinking, was put under ground much later. Neither his skin, nor his flesh, nor his bones, were of any use." The connection of the parallel threads is motivated by the fact that Serpukhovskoy had once been Strider's owner.

In *Two Hussars*, the parallel structure is obvious from the title itself and is also implemented through the details of love, card games, and friend relations. The motivation that links the threads is the bond of kinship between the characters.

If we compare the devices of Tolstoy's craftsmanship with those of Maupassant, we will notice that the French master omits the second part of the parallel. In his novellas Maupassant usually silences the second parallel thread, which is often either the traditional ending (which he violates—for example, by eliminating it), or else the common, let's say, conventional French bourgeois attitude toward life. So, for example, in many of his novellas Maupassant depicts the death of a peasant, which he describes in a simple, but surprisingly "estranged" way, where the implied contrast of the comparison is, of course, the literary depiction of the death of a city dweller, which is, however, omitted. Sometimes this contrast is introduced into the novella as the emotional evaluation of the narrator. In this respect, Tolstoy is arguably more primitive than Maupassant, since he feels the need to expose the complete parallel structure—as, for example, in his play *The Fruits of Enlightenment*, where he juxtaposes the kitchen with the drawing room. I suppose that this can be explained by the difference between the French and Russian literary traditions. The French reader feels the violation of conventions more intensely, or otherwise picks up the parallel thread more easily than the Russian reader, who has only a vague conception of what is normal.

I would like to mention in passing that by literary tradition I don't mean borrowing from another writer. By tradition, I mean a writer's dependence on a collective repository of literary norms, which, like the tradition inherited by an inventor, consists of the sum of the technical possibilities of his time.

More complex instances of parallelism can be found in the Tolstoy novels that juxtapose one protagonist or a group of protagonists with another. For example, in *War and Peace* we distinctly perceive the following juxtapositions: Napoleon against Kutuzov, Pierre Bezukhov against Andrei Bolkonsky (and simultaneously against Nikolai Rostov, who functions as a measure (a gauge) for one or the other). In *Anna Karenina*, the Karenina-Vronsky group is set against the Levin-Shcherbatskaya group; the connection between these groups is motivated by kinship. This is a common motivation in Tolstoy and, perhaps, among novelists in general. Tolstoy himself wrote that "since it was awkward to describe a character not connected with the novel in any way, I decided to make this brilliant young man the son of the old Bolkonsky."[62] Tolstoy hardly ever employed the other method—the method of using the same character in various combinations (favored by the English novelists), with the exception, perhaps, of the episode with Petrushka and Napoleon, where he employed it for the purposes of estrangement. In any case, the two parallel threads in *Anna Karenina* are so loosely connected in terms of motivation that it seems to have been constructed solely out of artistic necessity.

On the other hand, Tolstoy made use of "kinship" in a rather interesting way for his stepped constructions. For instance, the two

---

[62] See the longer excerpt from Tolstoy's letter to Princess Volkonskaya in the previous chapter. [—Trans.]

brothers and one of the sisters in the Rostov family represent the explication of a single type. Sometimes Tolstoy compares them, for example, in the scene before Petya's death. Nikolai is the simplified, "cruder" version of Natasha. Stiva Oblonsky exposes one side of Anna Karenina's soul; the link is given through the word "very little," which Anna utters in Stiva's voice (Part I, Chapter 29).[63] Stiva serves as a step toward his sister. Here the connection between the characters is not explained by kinship—Tolstoy certainly did not shy away from linking the separately conceived heroes in the novel. In this case, the kinship bond was needed for constructing the steps.

The traditional device of describing a noble brother and a criminal brother born into the same family shows that in the literary tradition, the depiction of relatives bears no connection to the author's duty to show the refractions of a single character. However, some writers might here introduce a motivation: illegitimacy (Fielding).

Everything here, as always in art, depends on the motivation for mastery.

III.

The short story collection was a precursor of the modern novel. I am stating this as a chronological fact, without implying any causal relationship between them.

Collections of stories were usually put together in such a way that the separate parts were connected, even if only by formal considerations. This was achieved through a frame story that tied the separate stories together.

We may distinguish several types of frame story, or, more precisely, methods of nesting a story within a story. The most widely used method is *storytelling*, which defers the fulfillment of an action. For example, the premise in "The Seven Viziers" is

---

[63] Lev Tolstoy, *Anna Karenina*, trans. Louise and Aylmer Maude (New York: Norton, 1970).

to restrain the king from executing his own son, whereas in *The Arabian Nights* Scheherazade tells stories to defer her own execution. In *Arji Borji Khan*, a Mongolian collection of narratives of Buddhist origin, the wooden statues tell tales, serving as steps that prevent the king from ascending to the throne. Here, the third and fourth stories are nested within the second story. In the same way, the parrot in *Śukasaptati* holds a lady back from betraying her husband by telling stories and keeping her at home until he returns.

We may consider *the storytelling contest* as a second method of embedding a story within a story, wherein stories are introduced to prove a certain idea, and one serves as a refutation of another. This method is interesting to us because it extends to other materials of development. Poems and aphorisms, for instance, can be inserted in this way.

It is important to note that the devices we are discussing here are bookish devices; the bulkiness of the material does not allow for the use of such methods in the oral tradition. The connection between the parts is so formal that it can be perceived only by a reader, not by a listener. The methods of connecting stories in the so-called *folk* (i.e., anonymous, unconscious, non-individual) creativity were developed only in the embryonic stage. The novel, from the day of its birth, and even before that, gravitated toward the book form.

Story collections *framed* as a whole by another story began to appear rather early in European literature.

The Eastern collections, which reached Europe through Arabs and Jews, introduced into the lives of Europeans many foreign stories that undoubtedly encountered local, similar versions of stories.

At the same time, the *European type* of framing was created, with a motivation of *storytelling for the sake of storytelling*.

I am speaking here of *The Decameron*.

The Decameron, along with its successors, differs greatly from the European novel of the eighteenth and nineteenth centuries in that the individual parts of the collection are *not linked* together by their characters. Moreover, we don't yet see the development of a main character here; the focus is on the action—the agent of the action serves merely as a playing card that aids the formation of the plot.

I will venture to say that this state of affairs went on for a very long time; even in Le Sage's *Gil Blas*, the main protagonist is so characterless that critics wonder if the author was trying to depict the most mediocre person. But this is not so. Gil Blas is not a person, but a *thread*—a gray thread—that stitches the episodes of the novel together.

The action and the agent are much more unified in *The Canterbury Tales*.

Most picaresque novels used a framing device.

The fate of this device is quite interesting in the works of Cervantes, Le Sage, Fielding, and Sterne, who refracts it in the new European novel.

Very curious indeed is the tale of Qamar al-Zaman and Princess Budur, which extends from the hundred seventieth night to the two hundred forty-ninth night in *The Arabian Nights*. It breaks up into several tales: the tale of Qamar al-Zaman (the son of Shahraman)—a story with a very complex structure that ends with a wedding and Princess Budur leaving her father—and the tale of the two princes, Prince Amjad and Prince As'ad. The second tale is connected with the first only by the fact that the princes are King Qamar's sons from two different wives. The King wants to punish them, but they escape and undergo all sorts of adventures. Queen Marjanah falls in love with Prince As'ad who is brought to her as a slave. He goes through many other adventures, always falling into the hands of Bahram the magician. Finally, the two brothers are united. On this occasion, the magician, who had repented and converted to Islam, tells the story of Ni'amah and Naomi. The story is long and intricate. "Now when Amjad and As'ad heard from Bahram this story, they marveled with extreme marvel and said, 'By Allah, this is indeed a rare tale!'" By this time Queen Marjanah arrives with her armies and demands the return of her beardless slave who had earlier been abducted from her. Then the armies of King Ghayur arrive—he is the father of Princess Budur and the grandfather of Prince Amjad. Soon thereafter, King Qamar's armies arrive—Qamar had been searching for his sons after having learned of their innocence. And finally, King Shahriman appears with his armies (the reader has long forgotten about him)—he too is looking for his son.[64] As you can see, several stories have been welded together by artificial means.

Another interesting example is the plot development of the Russian folk play *Tsar Maximilian*. It has a fairly simple plot: the son of Maximilian, who is married to Venus, refuses to worship idols and is killed for it by his father. The father and the entire court are then struck down by Death. This text was later converted into a play; motifs developed elsewhere (using different motivations) were interpolated into its different parts. Take, for example, the folk plays *The Ship* and *The Gang of Robbers*. Sometimes they are inserted into *Tsar Maximilian* without any sort of motivation, just like the shepherd scenes in *Don Quixote* or the verses in *The Arabian Nights*. Sometimes—and I take this to be a later historical development—they are inserted in the following way: Maximilian's disobedient son, Adolf, refuses to submit to his father and joins a gang of robbers. At some point, the play also incorporated the episode "Anika and Death." It was probably inserted into the version of the text that first appeared in the village, and which we may, for the sake of simplicity, but quite erroneously, call the original text. The episode with the mock requiem mass, which is also well known beyond this comedy, was inserted into the text much later. In many cases, new episodes, especially those that include wordplay, that is an accumulation of homonyms motivated by deafness, sprouted with such abundance that they pushed Maximilian out of the play. He became a mere

---

[64] *The Arabian Nights' Entertainments, or the Book of a Thousand Nights and a Night*, trans. Richard Burton (New York: The Modern Library, 1932).

pretext for initiating the comedy. The path from the original *Tsar Maximilian*, which bears some affinity to the school of South Russian theater, to the later text, which became loaded with puns and evolved according to a completely different principle, was not shorter than the path from Gavrila Derzhavin to Andrei Bely. Incidentally, Derzhavin's verse occasionally finds its way into the texts of the play. This, more or less, is the history of the changes in the device of plot development in *Tsar Maximilian*. The text basically changed with every performance, adapting to local material.

IV.

As I already said, a typical anecdote story or novella represents something that has been resolved. If our material is a successful answer that gets a person out of a difficult situation, then we have a motivation for a difficult situation, the answer, and a certain resolution. This is the general structure of stories involving "cunning." For example, if, after committing a crime, a character has been marked by his rival (say, by cutting off a lock of his hair), he does the same to his companions and thus saves himself. A similar strategy is used in an analogous tale about the house marked with chalk (in *The Arabian Nights* and Andersen's fairy tales). These are narratives with a resolved plot, which is sometimes extended with descriptions or characterizations, but which in itself represents something complete and finished. As I mentioned previously, some of these stories may form a more complex structure by being framed; or, in other words, combined within a single plot cluster.

There is also another more widely used device of plot composition that is known as stringing. In this case, resolved novella-motifs are placed one after the other; they are connected by the unity of the protagonist. The conventional many-layered fairy tale, where the hero is faced with several problems, is based on this kind of structure. Stringing makes it possible for one story to assimilate the motifs of another story. So we get fairy tales that are made up of two or even four motifs. We can delineate two types of stringing. The first type is when the hero is neutral and the adventures merely happen to him—he is not the one who causes them to happen. This often occurs in the adventure novel, where the pirates steal a captive from each other and their ships cannot reach the appointed destination, thus giving rise to endless adventures. The second type is when there is an attempt to connect the action with the agent. The adventures of Odysseus are motivated, though rather externally, by the wrath of the gods who thwart the hero at every turn. The Arabic brother of Odysseus, Sinbad the Sailor, has a more concrete explanation for his numerous adventures: he has a passion for voyaging, and thus his seven voyages allow for the stringing together of the entire travel folklore of his time.

In Apuleius's *The Golden Ass*, the motivation for the stringing device resides in the curiosity of Lucius, who is always either eavesdropping or observing. I should note here that *The Golden Ass* incorporates both framing and stringing devices. By means of stringing, Apuleius inserted the episode of the battle with the wineskins, the transformation stories, the adventures of the robbers, the anecdote about the ass in the attic, and other episodes. The device of framing helped introduce the stories about the sorceress, the famous tale of "Cupid and Psyche," and many minor stories. The parts that are based on the stringing device convey a feeling that they once had a life of their own. For instance, in *The Golden Ass*, after the episode in which the ass is hidden in the attic and found by his shadow, there is a suggestion that the incident lies at the origin of a popular saying, in other words, it is presumed that the audience is familiar with the story or its source (Book IX: 39-42).

Still, by far the most popular motivation for stringing has been the journey, and especially the journey in search of a place of employment. We can see such a construction in *The Life of Lazarillo de Tormes*, one of the oldest of the Spanish picaresque novels, which depicts a variety of adventures experienced by a boy in search of employment. It has been suggested that certain episodes and expressions that appear in the text later entered into the bawdy vernacular of the Spanish bazaar. However, I believe that they were probably to have been found there even before their inclusion in the novel. The novel ends strangely with fantastic adventures involving transformations—a rather common phenomenon, since the organizing idea that informs the first part of any such novel nearly always exhausts itself by the second part. These second parts are usually constructed on a completely new principle, as happened with Cervantes's *Don Quixote* and Swift's *Gulliver's Travels*.

Sometimes the stringing device is employed using material unrelated to the plot. In *The Glass Graduate*, a short novel about a peasant who becomes a scholar and then goes insane after having been affected by a love potion, Cervantes inserts, or rather strings to it, the madman's proclamations for paragraphs and even pages.

> He bitterly attacked puppeteers, saying that they were tramps, who treated sacred things most inappropriately, because they turned devotion into mockery with the figures they showed in their theaters, and they would throw all their figures, or most of them, from the Old and New Testament, into a bag and would sit on it to eat and drink in taverns and pubs. Finally he said that he was surprised that the authorities did not order them to keep silent during their performances, or exile them from the kingdom.
>
> There once happened to pass by where he was an actor, dressed like a prince, and when he saw him, he said:
>
> "I remember seeing that man coming on stage with a shepherd's sheepskin jacket on back to front, and with his face covered with flour, and despite all that, when he is off the stage, he swears by 'his word as a gentleman' at every step."
>
> "He must be one," said someone, "because there are many actors who are well-born and of good family."
>
> "That may be true," replied Glass, "but the last thing the

theater needs is well-born people; good-looking, yes, gentlemanly and with facile tongues. I would also say of them that by the sweat of their brow they earn their bread, and with unbearable labor, learning by heart all the time, perpetual gypsies moving from place to place, from inn to inn, ever vigilant to please others, because their good lies in the pleasure of others. Furthermore, they do not deceive anyone with their trade, because each time they exhibit their wares in public, to the eye and inspection of everyone. The work of actor-managers is incredible, and their responsibility immense, and they need to earn a great deal so as not to be so much in debt at the end of the year that they are sued by their creditors; and yet they are necessary in society, as indeed are parks, walks, and pleasant views, and other things which give pleasure in a decent way."

He said that it had been the opinion of a friend of his that a man who was courting an actress was courting many people in one person, a queen for instance, and a nymph, and a goddess, and a chambermaid, and a shepherdess, and sometimes it might happen that he might find he was courting a page or a lackey, because an actress might play all these parts and many more.[65]

These proclamations supplant the action from the short novel. The scholar recovers at the end of the novel, but he continues to make similar proclamations, despite the fact that he is no longer mad: his speech about the court is of the same type as his previous pronouncements. This is a common phenomenon in art: the device does not change despite the fact that the motivation for it has disappeared.

Similarly, in Tolstoy's "Strider," the description of life from a horse's point of view continues even after the horse's death; the horse's point of view is passed on to the narrator. While in Andrei Bely's *Kotik Letaev*, the punning language, motivated by a child's perception of the world, functions according to its own

---

[65]   Miguel de Cervantes, *The Glass Graduate* in *The Complete Exemplary Novels*, ed. Barry Ife and Jonathan Thacker, trans. R.M. Price (Oxford: Oxbow Books, 2013).

development of a material that is obviously unknown to the child.

To return to my topic, I can generally say that in the history of the novel, both the framing device and the stringing device have evolved in such a way that the interpolated material gradually becomes more tightly integrated into the body of the novel. This can be very easily traced in *Don Quixote*, a work familiar to everyone.

HOW *DON QUIXOTE* IS MADE

Don Quixote's Speeches

Monologues in ancient drama often ended with a *gnōmē* or aphorism—the memorable punch line of the speech. The ancients made a distinction between the aphorisms of Sophocles and Euripides. The aphorisms of Sophocles always tended toward moralistic *sententiae* regardless of the character of the speaker, while the ending in Euripides, depending on the speaker, was either moral or amoral.

The ancients explained this difference rather naively, saying that Sophocles didn't want anyone to remember a supposedly blasphemous statement as the words of Sophocles. There is possibly another explanation. The speeches of the characters were used as a means of developing the plot; they were interpolated with new material. In other words, the speech originally served only as a motivation for interpolation. The connection between the speech and the speaker, as between the action and the agent, has never been constant in the history of literary form. "Speech" in Sophocles is always the speech of the author. The author is yet unwilling to diversify the speeches of his masks.

Cervantes's Don Quixote was conceived as not being very intelligent: "The sun . . . was sufficient to have melted his brains, if he had had any."[66] Yet, already in the first pages of the novel—or actually, even before that, in the author's preface—Cervantes laments, half-ironically, of course, that his book is "without quotations in the margin, or annotations at the end":

> All this my book is likely to want; for I have nothing to quote in the margin, nor to make notes on at the end; nor do I know what authors I have followed in it, to put them at the beginning, as all others do, by the letters A, B, C, beginning with Aristotle, and ending at Xenophon, Zoilus, or Zeuxis: though the one was a railer, and the other a painter.

Later in the same preface, the author's friend advises him: "'You have no business to go begging sentences of philosophers, passages of holy writ, poetical fables, rhetorical orations, or miracles of saints; but only to endeavor, with plainness, and significant, decent, and well-ordered words, to give your periods a pleasing and harmonious turn.'" Despite this advice, Cervantes goes on to write an encyclopedic novel, a novel-iconostasis.

But we should also take into consideration the fact that the novel's scope evidently exceeded Cervantes's original conception. The novel unfolded and extended like a dining table.

Let's return to Don Quixote.

At first, Don Quixote is presented as someone "without brains." But later Cervantes uses him as the connecting thread of several wise speeches. Cervantes nourishes him with his own ideas and ennobles the poor knight just as he ennobles the madness of the Glass Graduate.

The first of many speeches that alter his character over the course of the novel appears in Part I, Chapter 11, when Don Quixote invokes the Golden Age:

> "Happy times, and happy ages! those, to which the ancients

---

[66] Miguel de Cervantes. *Don Quixote de la Mancha*, trans. Charles Jarvis (Oxford University Press, 1999). All subsequent quotations from *Don Quixote* are taken from this translation.

gave the name of golden, not because gold (which in this our iron age, is so much esteemed) was to be had in that fortunate period without toil and labor; but because they who then lived were ignorant of these two words, *meum* and *tuum*. In that age of innocence all things were in common: no one needed to take any other pains for his ordinary sustenance, than to lift up his hand and take it from the sturdy oaks, which stood inviting him liberally to taste of their sweet and relishing fruit. The limpid fountains, and running streams, offered them in magnificent abundance their delicious and transparent waters. In the clefts of rocks, and in the hollow of trees, did the industrious and provident bees form their commonwealths, offering to every hand, without usury, the fertile produce of their most delicious toil. . . ."

As you may have guessed, this is an almost verbatim translation of Ovid's Golden Age. The motivation for this speech is rather interesting. "Our knight made this tedious discourse (which might very well have been spared), because the acorns they had given him put him in mind of the golden age, and inspired him with an eager desire to make that impertinent harangue to the goatherds; who stood in amaze, gaping and listening, without answering him a word." In other words, the author here suggests that the speech is completely out of place. This reminds me of Chichikov's monologue on Plyushkin's list of runaway serfs: in its form and content, the speech is most certainly not Chichikov's, but Gogol's. Equally interesting is Tolstoy's hesitancy in regard to ascribing some of his own ideas to his hero. For instance, the views on war in *War and Peace* were initially presented as Andrei Bolkonsky's thoughts, but later appeared as the thoughts of the author.

I am skipping over Don Quixote's speech on procuring (in Part I, Chapter 22) and some of his chivalric speeches. After a series of recognitions at the inn, Don Quixote delivers a speech on the warrior and the scholar. Curiously, right before this speech, Cervantes mentions Don Quixote's speech to the goatherds: "Don

Quixote, who, moved by such another spirit, as that which had moved him to talk so much when he supped with the goatherds, instead of eating, spoke as follows . . ." (Part I, Chapter 37). This echoing from one typical episode of the novel to another is quite interesting. In similar vein, the critical passages interpolated into *Don Quixote* (the scrutiny of Don Quixote's library, the conversation with the innkeeper, etc.) mention the housekeeper, who is instructed to burn the knight's books (Part I, Chapters 6 and 7), i.e., the first episode of criticism.

In the complex novelistic schemes of the new age, the link between similar episodes is achieved by means of a repetition of certain words in the manner of Wagnerian leitmotifs (see, for example, Andrei Bely's *The Silver Dove*, or the works of Aleksandra Veksler).

The speech delivered by Don Quixote at the inn is, once again, out of place. He is supposed to speak about the vagaries of fate and instead praises the profession of arms. It is interesting how Cervantes switches to his own topic:

> "In truth, gentlemen, if it be well considered, great and unheard-of things do they see, who profess the order of knight-errantry. If one thinks otherwise, let me ask him what man living, that should now enter at this castle gate, and see us sitting in this manner, could judge or believe us to be the persons we really are? Who could say, that this lady, sitting here by my side, is that great queen that we all know her to be, and that I am that Knight of the Sorrowful Figure, so blazoned abroad by the mouth of fame?
>
> "There is no doubt, but that this art and profession exceeds all that have ever been invented by men; and so much the more honorable is it, by how much it is exposed to more dangers. Away with those who say, that letters have the advantage over arms: I will tell them, be they who they will, that they know not what they say. For the reason they usually give, and which they lay the greatest stress upon, is, that the labors of the brain

exceed those of the body, and that arms are exercised by the body alone; as if the use of them were the business of porters, for which nothing is necessary but downright strength; or as if in this, which we who profess it call chivalry, were not included the acts of fortitude, which require a very good understanding to execute them; or as if the mind of the warrior, who has an army, or the defense of a besieged city, committed to his charge, does not labor with his understanding as well as his body. If not, let us see how, by mere bodily strength, he will be able to penetrate into the designs of the enemy, to form stratagems, overcome difficulties, and prevent dangers which threaten: for all these things are acts of the understanding, in which the body has no share at all. It being so then, that arms employ the mind as well as letters, let us next see whose mind labors most, the scholar's or the warrior's." (Part I, Chapter 37)

This is followed by a lengthy and, in its own way, brilliant speech comparing the fates of the scholar and the warrior. The speech, of course, is interpolated into the text the same as the verses or tales within a tale in *The Arabian Nights*, but at the end of the long speech (it continues from Chapter 37 to Chapter 38) Cervantes finally remembers the speaker:

Don Quixote made this long harangue while the rest were eating, forgetting to reach a bit to his mouth, though Sancho Panza ever and anon desired him to mind his victuals, telling him, he would have time enough afterwards to talk as much as he pleased. Those who heard him were moved with fresh compassion, to see a man, who to everybody's thinking had so good an understanding, and could talk so well upon every other subject . . . (Part I, Chapter 38)

By this point the wisdom of the "brainless knight" has been fully confirmed. This is analogous to how Pickwick's image and function change in Dickens's construction of *The Pickwick Papers*.

From this point on Cervantes begins to exploit the effect of the contrast between the madness and wisdom of Don Quixote. So, for example, during Don Quixote's conversation with his niece, his speech begins with the madness of the knight errant, then switches to moralizing *sententiae*, making his niece exclaim:

"Bless me! uncle . . . that your worship should be so knowing, that, if need were, you might mount a pulpit, and hold forth anywhere in the streets, and yet should give in to so blind a vagary, and so exploded a piece of folly, as to think to persuade the world, that you are valiant now you are old; that you are strong, when alas! you are infirm; and that you are able to make crooked things straight; though stooping yourself under the weight of years; above all, that you are a knight, when you are really none: for, though gentlemen may be such, yet poor ones hardly can."

"You are much in the right, niece, in what you say," answered Don Quixote, "and I could tell you such things concerning lineages as would surprise you: but because I would not mix things divine with human, I forbear.

"Hear me, friends, with attention. All the genealogies in the world may be reduced to four sorts, which are these. First, of those, who, having had low beginnings, have gone on extending and dilating themselves till they have arrived at a prodigious grandeur. Secondly, of those, who, having had great beginnings, have preserved, and continue to preserve them in the same condition they were in at first. Thirdly, of those, who, though they have had great beginnings, have ended in a small point like a pyramid, having gone on diminishing and decreasing continually, till they have come almost to nothing; like the point of the pyramid, which, in respect of its base or pedestal, is next to nothing. Lastly, of those (and they are the most numerous) who, having had neither a good beginning, nor a tolerable middle, will therefore end without a name, like the families of common and ordinary people."

Don Quixote concludes his speech with the following quatrain:

> "Through these rough paths, to gain a glorious name,
> We climb the steep ascent that leads to fame.
> They miss the road, who quit the rugged way,
> And in the smoother tracks of pleasure stray."
> "Ah, woe is me!" quoth the niece; "what! my uncle a poet
> too! he knows everything; nothing comes amiss to him. I will
> lay a wager, that, if he had a mind to turn mason, he would
> build a house with as much ease as a bird-cage."
> "I assure you, niece," answered Don Quixote, "that if these
> knightly thoughts did not employ all my senses, there is noth-
> ing I could not do, nor any curious art, but what I could turn
> my hand to, especially bird-cages, and tooth-picks." (Part II,
> Chapter 6)

The reference to the birdcage brings us back to Alonso Quixano
the Good—i.e. Don Quixote before his madness. It is worth noting here that Cervantes himself didn't realize that before his madness Don Quixote, with all his birdcages and toothpicks, could
have never been as wise as the mad Knight of the Sorrowful Figure.
The author did not provide Don Quixote with wisdom either at
the beginning or in the middle of the novel. Alonso was merely
good. Don Quixote's speech on fame is a mixture of quotations
and recollections, a kind of a chrestomathy, from which I excerpt
below. The whole speech is stitched together from external material, in the manner of Denis Fonvizin's comedy *The Young Oaf* (the
conversation between Starodum and Mitrofan comprises excerpts
from a dictionary of synonyms).

> "That, Sancho," quoth Don Quixote, "is just like what hap-
> pened to a famous poet of our times, who having wrote an
> ill-natured satire upon the court-ladies, a certain lady, who was
> not expressly named in it, so that it was doubtful whether she
> was implied in it or not, complained to the poet, asking him

what he had seen in her, that he had not inserted her among the rest, telling him he must enlarge his satire, and put her in the supplement, or woe be to him. The poet did as he was bid, and set her down for such as duennas will not name. As for the lady, she was satisfied to find herself infamously famous. Of the same kind is the story they tell of that shepherd, who set fire to, and burnt down, the famous temple of Diana, reckoned one of the seven wonders of the world, only that his name might live in future ages; and though it was ordered by public edict, that nobody should name or mention him either by word or writing, that he might not attain to the end he proposed, yet still it is known he was called Erostratus.

"To the same purpose may be alleged what happened to the great emperor Charles the Fifth, with a Roman knight. The emperor had a mind to see the famous church of the Rotunda, which by the ancients was called the Pantheon, or Temple of all the gods, and now, by a better name, the Church of All Saints, and is one of the most entire edifices remaining of heathen Rome, and which most preserves the fame of the greatness and magnificence of its founders. It is made in the shape of a half-orange, very spacious, and very lightsome, though it has but one window, or rather a round opening at top: from whence the emperor having surveyed the inside of the structure, a Roman knight, who stood by his side, showing him the beauty and ingenious contrivance of that vast machine and memorable piece of architecture, when they were come down from the skylight, said to the emperor.

"'Sacred sir, a thousand times it came into my head to clasp your majesty in my arms, and cast myself down with you from the top to the bottom of the church, merely to leave an eternal name behind me.'

"'I thank you,' answered the emperor, 'for not putting so wicked a thought in execution, and henceforward I will never give you an opportunity of making the like proof of your loyalty, and therefore commend you never to speak to me more, or come into my presence.'

"And after these words he bestowed some great favor upon him. What I mean, Sancho, is, that the desire of fame is a very active principle in us. What, think you, cast Horatius down from the bridge, armed at all points, into the depth of the Tiber? What burnt the arm and hand of Mutius? What impelled Curtius to throw himself into the flaming gulf, that opened itself in the midst of Rome? What made Caesar pass the Rubicon in opposition to all presages? And, in more modern examples, what bored the ships, and stranded those valiant Spaniards, conducted by the most courteous Cortés in the New World! All these, and other great and very different exploits, are, were, and shall be, the works of fame, which mortals desire as the reward and earnest of that immortality their noble deeds deserve: though we Christian and Catholic knights-errant ought to be more intent upon the glory of the world to come, which is eternal in the ethereal and celestial regions, that upon the vanity of fame, acquired in this present and transitory world; for, let it last never so long, it must end with the world itself, which has its appointed period." (Part II, Chapter 8)

It is interesting to note that as Don Quixote becomes wiser, the same thing happens to Sancho Panza: "'Sancho,' said Don Quixote, 'you are every day growing less simple and more discreet'" (Part II, Chapter 12).

The fact is that Sancho serves as a stringing device—he strings together all the folk wisdoms, while Don Quixote strings together all the bookish and high-society wisdoms. The highest point of Panza's wisdom is his governorship; his judgments as a governor represent the novel's appropriation of existing stories about wise judgments.

Here is an example from the list of Panza's countless proverbs; such strings are typical of the second part of the novel in particular:

"Heaven will order it better," quoth Sancho; "for God that gives the wound, sends the cure: nobody knows what is to come: there are a great many hours between this and tomorrow: and in one hour, yea, in one moment, down falls the house: I have seen it rain, and the sun shine, both at the same time: such an one goes to bed sound at night, and is not able to stir next morning: and tell me, can anybody brag of having driven a nail in Fortune's wheel? no, certainly; and, between the Yes and the No of a woman, I would not venture to thrust the point of a pin; for there would not be room enough for it. Grant me but that Quiteria loves Basilius with all her heart, and I will give him a bagful of good fortune: for love, as I have heard say, looks through spectacles, which make copper appear to be gold, poverty to be riches, and specks in the eyes pearls." (Part II, Chapter 19)

By the beginning of the second part of the novel, Sancho takes center stage and even overshadows Don Quixote. This is a rather common phenomenon in the history of the novel; in Rabelais, for instance, Panurge comes to the fore toward the end of the novel. This merely signals the fact that, in essence, the old novel has come to an end and a new novel has begun, often based on new devices.

It would be very interesting to trace the alternation between wisdom and madness in Don Quixote, now used by the author as a device, in the episode where the knight meets Don Diego. The episode begins with Don Quixote's "chivalric speech," after which he quickly turns to the subject of literature, astounding the reader (or, at least, those who read without omitting anything) with his professional knowledge of literature. The speech is motivated by the fact that Don Diego's son is a poet. At first the mad knight speaks of the duty of parents to their children, and then moves on to literary criticism. Unfortunately, there is not enough room here for me to quote the entire speech, which occupies nearly half of the sixteenth chapter of Part II. While declaiming his wise speeches, Don Quixote nevertheless remains true to his own madness and continues to wear the barber's basin as a helmet and, what is more, puts it on his head with Sancho's curds still in it.

But the next adventure with the lions, which Don Quixote challenges to combat, somehow stands out from the adventures that usually end with monotonous battles, and Don Quixote's speech, which serves as a measure for gauging the diversion of his real action from its imagined form, carries no signs of parody:

"But, above all these, a much finer appearance makes the knight-errant, who, through deserts and solitudes, through crossways, through woods, and over mountains, goes in quest of perilous adventures, with design to bring them to a happy and fortunate conclusion, only to obtain a glorious and immortal fame. A knight-errant, I say, makes a finer appearance in the act of succoring some widow in a desert place, than a knight-courtier in addressing some damsel in a city.

"All cavaliers have their proper and peculiar exercises. Let the courtier wait upon the ladies; adorn his prince's court with rich liveries; entertain the poorer cavaliers at his splendid table; order jousts; manage tournaments, and show himself great, liberal, and magnificent, and above all, a good Christian: and in this manner will he precisely comply with the obligations of his duty. But let the knight-errant search the remotest corners of the world; enter the most intricate labyrinths; at every step assail impossibilities; in the wild uncultivated deserts brave the burning rays of the summer's sun, and the keen inclemency of the winter's frost: let not lions daunt him, spectres affright him, or dragons terrify him: for in seeking these, encountering those, and conquering them all, consists his principal and true employment.

"It being then my lot to be one of the number of knights-errant, I cannot decline undertaking whatever I imagine to come within the verge of my profession; and, therefore, encountering the lions, as I just now did, belonged to me directly, though I knew it to be a most extravagant rashness. I very well know, that fortitude is a virtue placed between the two vicious extremes of cowardice and rashness . . ." (Part II, Chapter 17)

In the following chapter, the professional literary knowledge of Don Quixote—a poor nobleman from the remote village of La Mancha, Alonso Quixano the Good, known for his rare talent for making birdcages—continues to grow and expand. He gives Don Diego's son advice on his poems:

> "If they are designed for a poetical prize, endeavor to obtain the second; for the first is always carried by favor, or by the great quality of the person: the second is bestowed according to merit; so that the third becomes the second, and the first, in this account, is but the third, according to the liberty commonly taken in your universities. But, for all that, the name of the first makes a great figure."
>
> "Hitherto," said Don Lorenzo to himself, "I cannot judge thee to be mad: let us proceed." (Part II, Chapter 18)

Or here is another example from the same chapter:

> "A friend of mine, a very ingenious person," answered Don Quixote, "was of opinion that nobody should give themselves the trouble of glossing on verses: and the reason, he said, was, because the gloss could never come up to the text, and very often the gloss mistakes the intention and design of the author. Besides, the rules of glossing are too strict, suffering no interrogations, nor 'said he's,' nor 'shall I say's,' nor making nouns of verbs, nor changing the sense, with other ties and restrictions, which cramp the glossers, as your worship must needs know."

Further on, Don Quixote's speeches unfold with more specific material. Here Cervantes equips him with knowledge in linguistics.

> "Albogues," answered Don Quixote, "are certain plates of brass like candlesticks, which, being hollow, and struck against each other, give a sound, if not very agreeable, or harmonious, yet not offensive, and agreeing well enough with the rusticity of the tabor and pipe. And this name *albogue* is Moorish, as are

all those in Spanish that begin with *al*: as *almohaza, almorzar, alhombra, alguazil, alhucema, almacen, alcancia*, and the like, with very few more: and our language has only three Moorish words ending in *í*, namely *borceguí, zaquizamí*, and *maravedí*: *alhelí* and *alfaquí*, as well for the beginning with *al*, as ending in *í*, are known to be Arabic. This I have told you by the by, the occasion of naming albogues having brought it into my mind." (Part II, Chapter 67)

Or here is an even more specialized conversation, where Don Quixote delves into the theory of translation:

"What title has the book?" demanded Don Quixote.

To which the author answered:

"Sir, the book in Italian is called, *Le Bagatelle*."

"And what answers to *Bagatelle* in our Castilian?" quoth Don Quixote.

"*Le Bagatelle*," said the author, "is as if we should say, *Trifles*. But, though its title be mean, it contains many very good and substantial things."

Quoth Don Quixote:

"I know a little of the Tuscan language, and value myself upon singing some stanzas of Ariosto. But, good sir, pray, tell me (and I do not say this with design to examine your skill, but out of curiosity, and nothing else), in the course of your writing have you ever met with the word *pignata*?"

"Yes, often," replied the author.

"And how do you translate it in Castilian?" quoth Don Quixote.

"How should I translate it," replied the author, "but by the world *olla*?"

"Body of me," said Don Quixote, "what a progress has your worship made in the Tuscan language! I would venture a good wager, that, where the Tuscan says *piace*, you say, in Castilian, *place*; and where it says *più*, you say *mas*; and *sù* you translate *arriba*, and *giù* by *abaxo*."

"I do so, most certainly," quoth the author; "for these are their proper renderings." (Part II, Chapter 62)

Generally speaking, the speeches from the second part are more fragmentary and episodic than those from the first. The second part, as I have already mentioned, is constructed more in the manner of a mosaic, and if it does not include interpolated stories that tend to push Don Quixote temporarily to the side, it nonetheless includes short episodic anecdotes that seem to have been rather hastily inserted into the novel.

Here are some concluding remarks, although I do not like making them: it is the reader who ought to draw his own conclusions.

Firstly, the character of Don Quixote, so glorified by Heine and sensationalized by Turgenev, was very different from what the author originally intended. This character type appeared in the process of the novel's construction, in the same way that the mechanism of performance often created new forms of poetry.

And secondly, toward the middle of the novel Cervantes realized that he had created a duality in Don Quixote by imposing his own (the author's) ideas on his protagonist. He then employed or started to employ this duality for his own artistic purposes.

Inset Stories in *Don Quixote*

. . . [W]e, in these our times, barren and unfruitful of amusing entertainments, enjoy not only the sweets of his true history, but also the stories and episodes of it, which are, in some sort, no less pleasing, artificial, and true, than the history itself: which resuming the broken thread of the narration, relates, that . . . (Part I, Chapter 28)

Thus begins the next segment of *Don Quixote*.

And indeed, the thread of the action in *Don Quixote* is tattered and broken. The inset stories can be divided into several categories based on the way in which they have been inserted into the novel.

But I will insert this classification after describing the stories.

If we separate the stories based on their depiction of "everyday life," we will, first of all, find a series of pastoral stories. The series begins with the episode about the shepherdess Marcela (Part I, Chapters 12-14). Or rather, it begins with Don Quixote's speech on the Golden Age (which I have already discussed), and proceeds with a rather naively inserted poem: "That your worship, Señor knight-errant, may the more truly say, that we entertain you with a ready goodwill, we will give you some diversion and amusement, by making one of our comrades sing, who will soon be here" (Part I, Chapter 11). After which comes the poem. As you can see, the insertion of the poem is motivated in almost the same way as couplets introduced into a vaudeville act, or verses in *The Arabian Nights*, which the heroes recite to not only the beautiful women, but also the devils.

The episode with Marcela begins soon thereafter. The story is inserted as follows:

> While this passed, there came another of those young lads, who brought them their provisions from the village, and said:
>   "Comrades, do you know what passes in the village?"
>   "How should we know?" answered one of them.
>   "Know then," continued the youth, "that this morning died that famous shepherd and scholar, Chrysostom; and it is whispered that he died for love of that devilish untoward lass Marcela, daughter of William the Rich; she, who rambles about these woods and fields in the dress of a shepherdess."
> (Part I, Chapter 11)

As we see, for the introduction of the story, Cervantes uses "the courier" as a storyteller who presumably resembles "the messenger" of ancient tragedy. The messenger communicated events that were necessary for understanding the main plot development of the tragedy. In *Don Quixote*, however, the courier is used as a motivation for inserting a story into the main plot.

The courier's story begins. Meanwhile, all the goatherds have gone to the place where the death had occurred. In order to interweave and connect the inset story with the main plot of the novel, Cervantes brings in Don Quixote, who makes stylistic corrections to the story: "'Friend,' quoth Don Quixote, 'the obscuration of those two greater luminaries is called an eclipse, and not a clipse.'" But Pedro, not dwelling on such petty details, goes on with his story:

> "He also foretold when the year would be plentiful, or estril."
>
> "Sterile, you would say, friend," quoth Don Quixote.
>
> "Sterile or estril," answered Pedro, "comes all to the same thing. And as I was saying, his father and friends who gave credit to his words, became very rich thereby; for they followed his advice in everything. This year, he would say, sow barley, and now wheat; in this you sow vetches, and not barley: the next year there will be plenty of oil: the three following there will not be a drop."
>
> "This science they call astrology," said Don Quixote.
>
> "I know not how it is called," replied Pedro; "but I know that he knew all this, and more too. . . . For perhaps, and even without perhaps, you may never have heard the like in all the days of your life, though you were as old as the itch."
>
> "Say, 'as old as Sarah'," replied Don Quixote, not being able to endure the goatherd's mistaking words.
>
> "The itch is old enough," answered Pedro; "and Sir, if you must at every turn be correcting my words, we shall not have done this twelvemonth." (Part I, Chapter 12)

As the story progresses, the interruptions become less frequent. This is a rather widespread technique of interweaving an inset story with the main plot through constant reminders of the main characters of the plot.

In Sterne's *Tristram Shandy*, Trim's protracted sermon about the Inquisition is repeatedly interrupted by the listeners and Trim's own emotional outbursts (Vol. II, Chapters 15-17). In other places the author himself interrupts the narrative, reminding the reader about other motifs (knots and loops, or Jenny) or the main story by repeating the last phrase, which had been interrupted by another story. But I will discuss this in my analysis of Sterne.

Cervantes interweaves the inset stories in the following ways:

1) *The hero of the main story interrupts the actions of the secondary story.* In addition to the example with Pedro, which I discussed above, Don Quixote interrupts the tangled web of stories with his speech comparing the fates of the scholar and the warrior. Besides verbal interruptions, it is more characteristic of Don Quixote to interrupt with actions. Thus, for example, Don Quixote's battle with the wineskins interrupts the endlessly drawn-out "Novel of the Curious Impertinent" (interpolated into the novel with the help of the "found manuscript" device):

> There remained but little more of the novel to be read, when from the room, where Don Quixote lay, Sancho Panza came running out all in a fright, crying aloud: "Run, sirs, quickly, and succor my master, who is over head and ears in the toughest and closest battle my eyes have ever beheld. As God shall save me, he has given the giant, that enemy of the princess Micomicona, such a stroke, that he has cut off his head close to his shoulders, as if it had been a turnip." (Part I, Chapter 35)

2) *The characters of the inset story take part in the action of the main story.* The most complicated form of this kind is the story of Dorothea (the heroine of the most prominent inset story), who takes part in the hoax played upon Don Quixote. She is introduced to him as the Princess Micomicona:

> [Sancho Panza] then recounted to Cardenio and Dorothea what they had contrived for Don Quixote's cure, or at least for decoying him to his own house. Upon which Dorothea said, she would undertake to act the distressed damsel better

than the barber, especially since she had a woman's apparel, with which she could do it to the life; and they might leave it to her to perform what was necessary for carrying on their design, she having read many books of chivalry, and being well acquainted with the style the distressed damsels were wont to use, when they begged their boons of the knights-errant. (Part I, Chapter 29)

We can see a less complicated application of this method in two episodes, where Don Quixote quarrels with the characters of the inset stories:

"I cannot get it out of my mind, nor can any one persuade me to the contrary, and he must be a blockhead who understands or believes otherwise, but that that great villain master Elisabat lay with Queen Madásima." "It is false, I swear," answered Don Quixote, in great wrath; "it is extreme malice, or rather villainy, and it is not to be presumed, that so high a princess should lie with a quack; and whoever pretends she did, lies like a very great rascal; and I will make him know it on foot or on horseback, armed or unarmed, by night or by day, or how he pleases." (Part I, Chapter 24)

Similarly, the connection between the main novel and one of the pastoral episodes is renewed when a goatherd tells the story of a soldier who won the heart of the proud Leandra with his soldier's suits. The comments that follow the story are quite interesting:

The goatherd's tale gave a general pleasure to all that heard it, especially to the canon, who, with an unusual curiosity, took notice of his manner of telling it, in which he discovered more of the polite courtier, than of the rude goatherd; and therefore he said, that the priest was very much in the right in affirming that the mountains produced men of letters. (Part I, Chapter 52)

Here the author is directly alluding to the "bookishness" of his story.

Cervantes has a curious short novel; it was written, if I am not mistaken, around 1613, in the interval between the publication of the first and second parts of *Don Quixote*. It is called *The Dialogue of the Dogs*.

The structure of this short novel is as banal as a newspaper article, but the main characters—the two dogs—are very unusual; or rather one dog, Berganza, is unusual, while the other dog, Cipión, merely listens to the former tell the story of his life. As is typical in works that employ the stringing device, this short novel is stitched together from a series of episodes, some of which are simply brief outlines, which evolve around the dog's search for a place (employment) as he goes from one master to the next. *The Dialogue* is the canine version of *Lazarillo de Tormes* or *Gil Blas*. It is interesting to note that the search for a place as a motivation for linking episodes is still used in literature today. This is how Octave Mirbeau's *Diary of a Chambermaid* (1900) and Maxim Gorky's *On His Own* (1916) are constructed. Over the course of his life, the dog works in a slaughterhouse, then as a shepherd's dog, then he works for the police, soldiers, gypsies, a *morisco*, a poet, a theater company, and finally a hospital. Each of these new employments has its own story, but sometimes they serve only as a motivation for the inclusion of a short depiction of mores.

Let us look at what Berganza observed among the shepherds. Most of all, the dog was struck by the fact that the life of the shepherds bore no resemblance to the stories in the books he had heard his first master's lady read aloud. The shepherds did not play flutes and shawms, but only sometimes sang "to the sound of crooks being knocked together or a few tiles clicking between their fingers."[67] They spent most of the day removing fleas or mending their sandals, and certainly not daydreaming about shepherdesses.

---

[67] Miguel de Cervantes, *The Dialogue of the Dogs* in *The Complete Exemplary Novels*, ed. Barry Ife and Jonathan Thacker, trans. John Jones and John Macklin (Oxford: Oxbow Books, 2013). All subsequent quotations from *The Dialogue of the Dogs* are taken from this translation.

They didn't call each other Lisardo, Lauso, Jacinto, or Riselo, but Anton, Domingo, Pablo, or Llorente. It would be interesting to compare this protest against unrealistic depictions of a shepherd's life to how Cervantes described the shepherds before and after writing *The Dialogue*. For the purpose of comparison, let me just quote the conclusion of the story about Leandra from *Don Quixote*.

> "There is no hollow of a rock, nor brink of a rivulet, nor shade of a tree, that is not occupied by some shepherd, who is recounting his misfortunes to the air: the echo, wherever it can be formed, repeats the name of Leandra: the mountains resound 'Leandra'; the brooks murmur 'Leandra': in short, Leandra holds us all in suspense and enchanted, hoping without hope, and fearing without knowing what we fear. Among these extravagant madmen, he who shows the least and the most sense is my rival Anselmo, who, having so many other causes of complaint, complains only of absence, and to the sound of a rebeck, which he touches to admiration, pours forth his complaints in verses, which discover an excellent genius. I follow an easier, and, in my opinion, a better way, which is to inveigh the levity of women, their inconstancy, and double-dealing, their lifeless promises, and broken faith; and, in short, the little discretion they show in placing their affections, or making their choice.
>
> "This, gentlemen, was the occasion of the expressions and language I used to this goat when I came hither; for, being a female, I despise her, though she be the best of all my flock. This is the story I promised to tell you: if I have been tedious in the relation I will endeavor to make you amends by my service: my cottage is hard by, where I have new milk, and very savory cheesy, with variety of fruits of the season, not less agreeable to the sight than to the taste." (Part I, Chapter 51)

The story of Leandra was interpolated in a rather unsophisticated way: Don Quixote and his company, who had contrived a plan to take him back home, are approached by a goatherd who tells them his story. However, let us look more closely at the manner in which the story is interwoven with the rest of the material. This is achieved by means of a quarrel, in the same manner as the episode with Cardenio. Don Quixote takes offense at the goatherd, who has taken him for a madman:

> And, so saying, and muttering on, he snatched up a loaf that was near him, and with it struck the goatherd full in the face, with so much fury, that he laid his nose flat. The goatherd, who did not understand raillery, perceiving how much in earnest he was treated, without any respect to the carpet or tablecloth, or to the company that sat about it, leaped upon Don Quixote, and, gripping him by the throat with both hands, would doubtless have strangled him, had not Sancho Panza come up in that instant, and, taking him by the shoulders, thrown him back on the table, breaking the dishes and platters, and spilling and overturning all that was upon it. Don Quixote, finding himself loose, ran at the goatherd, who, being kicked and trampled upon by Sancho, and his face all over blood, was feeling about, upon all fours, for some knife or other, to take a bloody revenge withal: but the canon and the priest prevented him; and the barber contrived it so, that the goatherd got Don Quixote under him, on whom he poured such a shower of buffets, that there rained as much blood from the visage of the poor knight as there did from his own. (Part I, Chapter 52)

This is the second approach to interweaving the inset stories with the main story. Let me say two more words about this. After freeing himself from the goatherd's grip, Don Quixote throws himself into a new adventure without even taking the time to wipe the blood off his face. I am talking about the episode with the disciplinants. He is assaulted and beaten once again. I am not surprised at the barbarities of the novel—these fights belong to the realm of the circus and the fairy tale. Even the tears shed for the novel's hero are merely a game of tears.

Now let us discuss a more fundamental question—the method of interpolating an inset story. As we saw previously, the episode with Marcela was introduced by way of narration. The first part of the Cardenio-Lucinda-Dorothea-Don Fernando story is introduced in the same way. At first, it is narrated to Don Quixote by Cardenio with an interruption occasioned by the quarrel, then Cardenio continues to narrate the story to the barber and the priest, after which they listen to Dorothea's account. Both Cardenio and Dorothea attract everyone's attention by singing:

> While they reposed themselves in the shade, a voice reached their ears, which, though unaccompanied by any instrument, sounded sweetly and delightfully: at which they were not a little surprised, that being no place where they might expect to find a person who could sing so well; for, though it is usually said, there are in the woods and fields shepherds with excellent voices, it is rather an exaggeration of the poets, than what is really true; and especially when they observed, that the verses they heard sung, were not like the compositions of rustic shepherds, but like those of witty and courtly persons. And the verses, which confirmed them in their opinion, were these following . . . (Part I, Chapter 27)

The verses are then followed by this discourse:

> The hour, the season, the solitude, the voice, and the skill of the person who sung, raised both wonder and delight in the two hearers, who lay still, expecting if perchance they might hear something more: but, perceiving the silence continued a good while, they resolved to issue forth in search of the musician, who had sung so agreeably. And, just as they were about to do so, the same voice hindered them from stirring, and again reached their ears with this sonnet. . . .
> The song ended with a deep sigh, and they again listened very attentively in hopes of more; but finding that the music

was changed into groans and laments, they agreed to go and find out the unhappy person whose voice was as excellent as his complaints were mournful. (Part I, Chapter 27)

The second leading character of this story, Dorothea, is introduced in a similar way.

[A]s the priest was preparing himself to comfort Cardenio, he was hindered by a voice, which, with mournful accents, spoke in this manner:

"O heavens! is it possible I have at last found a place that can afford a secret grave for the irksome burden of this body, which I bear about so much against my will? yes, it is, if the solitude, which these rocks promise, do not deceive me. Ah, woe is me! how much more agreeable society shall I find in these crags and brakes, which will at least afford me leisure to communicate my miseries to heaven by complaints, than in the conversation of men, since there is no one living from whom I can expect counsel in doubts, ease in complaints, or remedy in misfortunes." (Part I, Chapter 28)

Here I am compelled to relate in a few words the story, which Cervantes interpolated into his novel and which I, in turn, have inserted into my own work.

A man of noble birth, Cardenio, introduces his friend Don Fernando, who is the second son of a Spanish Duke, to his beloved Lucinda. Don Fernando promptly falls in love with her, sends Cardenio away on some false pretense, and pursues Lucinda's hand in marriage. The latter notifies her beloved, who rushes to her defense, but arrives too late, when the wedding is already in progress. Cardenio mistakenly hears Lucinda say "I will" to Fernando at the altar, after which he loses his mind and flees to the mountains. Meanwhile, Don Fernando was bound to marry Dorothea, a rich and beautiful country girl, whom he leaves for Lucinda. In grief, Dorothea also flees to the mountains and turns up in Cervantes's novel. Eventually, both Cardenio and Dorthea come to the same inn where Sancho was once tossed in a blanket.

This is indeed a remarkable inn. It was created by Cervantes and patented with strictly literary purposes in mind. The inn is a place where many characters and stories interconnect with each other. It is a geometrical plane where the separate storylines of the novel intersect. Don Fernando and Lucinda also end up in this "compositional" inn. Here we see a new method of introducing stories by means of a meeting. This is where Dorothea meets Don Fernando, and Cardenio meets Lucinda. It turns out that Don Fernando had found a letter in Lucinda's bosom when she fainted during the wedding ceremony. The letter revealed Lucinda's love for Cardenio—she declared that she was his wife. Lucinda takes refuge in a convent from which Don Fernando abducts her, but soon after she meets Cardenio in the inn. In a speech addressed to Don Fernando, Dorothea proves point by point why he is obliged to love her. The speech resembles a *suasoria*, examples of which we can find in Ovid.

"I am that humble country girl, whom you, through goodness or love, did deign to raise to the honor of calling herself yours. I am she, who, confined within the bounds of modesty, lived a contented life, until, to the voice of your importunities, and seemingly sincere and real passion, she opened the gates of her reserve, and delivered up to you the keys of her liberty: a gift by you so ill requited, as appears by my being driven into the circumstances in which you find me, and forced to see you in the posture you are in now. Notwithstanding all this, I would not have you imagine that I am brought hither by any dishonest motives, but only by those of grief and concern, to see myself neglected and forsaken by you. You would have me be yours, and would have it in such a manner, that though now you would not have it be so, it is not possible you should cease to be mine. Consider, my lord, that the matchless affection I have for you may balance the beauty and nobility of her, for whom I am abandoned. You cannot be the fair Lucinda's, because you are mine; nor can she be yours, because she is Cardenio's. And it is easier, if you take it right, to reduce your inclination to love her, who adores you, than to bring her to love, who abhors you. You importuned my indifference; you solicited my integrity; you were not ignorant of my condition; you know very well in what manner I gave myself up entirely to your will; you have no room to pretend any deceit; and if this be so, as it really is, and if you are as much a Christian as a gentleman, why do you, by so many evasions delay making me as happy at last, as you did at first? And if you will not acknowledge me for what I am, your true and lawful wife, at least admit me for your slave; for, so I be under your power, I shall account myself happy and very fortunate. . . ."

These and other reasons did the afflicted Dorothea urge so feelingly, and with so many tears, that all who accompanied Don Fernando, and all who were present besides, sympathized with her. . . . [A]fter he had attentively beheld Dorothea for a good while, opened his arms, and, leaving Lucinda free, said:

"You have conquered, fair Dorothea, you have conquered; for there is no withstanding so many united truths." (Part I, Chapter 36)

There is yet another inset story titled "The Novel of the Curious Impertinent" within this long and drawn-out story, which, according to Cervantes himself, is "about eight sheets in manuscript" (Part I, Chapter 32). It is interpolated into the story using the "found manuscript" device. I would like to emphasize here the priest's remark, as he is also a critic of the novel (see the episode of Don Quixote's library, the conversation with the innkeeper, etc.):

"I like this novel very well," said the priest; "but I cannot persuade myself it is a true story: and if it be a fiction, the author has erred against probability: for it cannot be imagined, there can be any husband so senseless, as to desire to make so dangerous an experiment, as Anselmo did: had this case been supposed between a gallant and his mistress, it might pass; but, between husband and wife, there is something impossible in it: however, I am not displeased with the manner of telling it." (Part I, Chapter 35)

The remark is similar to the verdict that the priest pronounced in connection with another inset story, which I have already discussed above. It seems to me that this is a means to evoke "the manner of expression," which is so typical of art. The writer examines the parts of his novel, first, as individual phenomena (the manner of telling in *this* particular story), and second, as literary phenomena (the literary merit of the pastoral style).[68]

Later, the method of introducing inset stories through the "found manuscript" device became very popular. It was extensively used by Sterne: Yorick's speeches in *Tristram Shandy* are interpolated into the text as found papers, and there is an episode in *A Sentimental Journey* that is inserted in a similar fashion. The same device was employed by Dickens in *The Pickwick Papers*—a book written as a frame novel ("The Madman's Manuscript") and combined with elements of stringing, which produced (before our very eyes) the Pickwick type. It is also very likely that the character of Sam Weller is derived from Cervantes: he too, like Sancho Panza, is used for stringing together proverbs, although Sancho's sayings are slightly different from those of Pickwick's servant. Sam's proverbs are consciously *estranged*. Their humor lies in the inappropriateness—the out-of-placeness—of their application and their non-coincidence with the meaning of the situation at hand. It is even possible that Dickens here reveals one of the essential modes of how to employ proverbs: the most important thing is that they be used with a sense of irony. Allow me here to quote a couple of Wellerisms to show what I mean: "There's nothin' so refreshin' as sleep, sir, as the servant-girl said afore she drank the egg-cupful

---

[68] See the beginning of Part I, Chapter 52: "The goatherd's tale gave a general pleasure to all that heard it, especially to the canon, who, with an unusual curiosity, took notice of his manner of telling it, in which he discovered more of the polite courtier, than of the rude goatherd; and therefore he said, that the priest was very much in the right in affirming that the mountains produced men of letters."

of laudanum" (Chapter 16), or "'If you walley my precious life don't upset me, as the gen'l'm'n said to the driver when they was a-carryin' him to Tyburn" (Chapter 19).[69]

But I am beginning to feel the influence of *Don Quixote*—I am inserting episode after episode, while forgetting about the main flow of the chapter. What did Cervantes do in such cases? He usually interrupted the action by reminding the reader of the novel's main character through one of his typical acts of madness. And so, "The Novel of the Curious Impertinent," along with the story about Cardenio, is interrupted by Don Quixote's famous battle with the wineskins. As I have mentioned before, this episode is most likely taken from *The Golden Ass*, which in turn borrowed from the Milesian fables.

The inn where Cardenio meets Don Fernando and Lucinda later becomes the hovel in *King Lear*. This is where all the characters meet; their actions are connected merely by the fact that they all turn up in the same place at the same time. But while in Shakespeare the characters belong to the same complex of events, in Cervantes they are connected only by their common meeting place and the author's whim of bringing them into his novel. Perhaps the only relation between them is that they are either surprised or enthralled by each other. In this, they remind us of the linkages that occur in *The Arabian Nights*, the only difference being that in Cervantes they coexist, whereas in *The Arabian Nights* they are only co-narrated. The difference is not radical, as in Cervantes the element of storytelling is present, though barely noticeable, by the mere fact that the novel is loosely framed as the manuscript "written by Cid Hamet Ben Engeli, Arabian historiographer" (Part I, Chapter 9).

And so to this inn, which I will call "the inn of literary device," comes a man who looks to be about forty or more, followed by a beautiful Muslim woman. After dinner, or, rather, after Don Quixote's introductory speech, this former captive relates the

---

[69] Charles Dickens, *The Pickwick Papers* (London, Amalgamated Press, 1905).

story of his life and adventures, including the standard (or what would later become the standard) story of escape with the help of a beautiful native woman. The story includes a strategic analysis of the battle of the Goleta fortress. One of the captive's comrades turns out to be the brother of Don Fernando—a slight hint of the intersection of the stories. Then Don Fernando recites the sonnets written by his brother. After reciting the sonnets, the captive finishes his detailed story. All in all, it goes on for about five chapters.

As is typical to Cervantes, the literary merits of the story are assessed at the end. Here, again, the inset story is immediately appraised and commented on by one of its listeners:

> Here the captive ended his story; to whom Don Fernando said:
> "Truly, captain, the manner of your relating this strange adventure has been such, as equals the surprising novelty of the event itself. The whole is extraordinary, uncommon, and full of accidents, which astonish and surprise those who hear them. And so great is the pleasure we have received in listening to it, that though the story should have held until tomorrow, we should have wished it were to begin again." (Part I, Chapter 2)

The literary inn, however, continues to fill up. Cervantes introduces more characters, who in turn introduce new stories using the same device. This time, the new guest is a judge, traveling with his beautiful sixteen-year-old daughter. In addition to the device of interweaving a story by means of luring a character into the same place, Cervantes uses yet another device—the judge turns out to be the brother of the captive-narrator (one of the three brothers, which is a conventional fairy-tale device, like in the motif of a father dividing up his property between his three sons, who choose different professions: scholarship, arms, and commerce). The following chapter introduces yet another new episode by the old way of a meeting. It is the "agreeable history of the young muleteer, with other strange accidents that happened in the inn" (Part I, Chapter 43).

A young man dressed as a muleteer comes to the inn. His name is Don Louis and he is in love with the judge's daughter Doña Clara, for whom he sings love songs. Here, again, Cervantes inserts Don Quixote. This is the episode in which the servants of the inn mock the knight errant by tying his hand to the staple of the hayloft door. This is followed by the conclusion of the episode with Don Louis, and finally the action returns to the main story.

Incidentally, the barber from whom Don Quixote had once stolen the brass basin, mistaking it for Mambrino's helmet, and from whom Sancho Panza had stolen the harness and bridle for his mule, arrives at the inn, the magnetic powers of which we have already discussed. The barber recognizes his basin.

This leads to a bizarre argument at the inn, during which all the guests take the side of Don Quixote, asserting that the basin is indeed a helmet. This is one of the many hoaxes that make up the novel. At first, at the beginning of the novel, the hoaxes are explained through Don Quixote's delusions, who takes a prostitute for a princess, a countryman beating his servant, the young Andres, for a knight, and his stick for a lance. But toward the end of the first part, the motivation for the hoaxes changes. Don Quixote is no longer deluded so much as he is a victim of hoaxes. The whole episode in the duke's palace with the magical wooden horse, with the help of which Don Quixote is supposed to disenchant Dulcinea, is an example of such a grandiose hoax (Part II, Chapters 38-41).

The series of hoaxes begins with the argument about the helmet and the fake enchantment whereby Don Quixote is brought home in a cage—that is, if we don't count the comic episode in which the innkeeper dubs Don Quixote a knight (the innkeeper is not the author of the hoax, but merely supports Don Quixote's delusions). Along the way, Don Quixote is let out of the cage on his word of honor, and he gets into an argument with the Canon of Toledo regarding books of chivalry. The conversation begun by the canon and the priest earlier is a genuine critical survey of chivalric literature, the introduction of which was motivated so well by the scrutiny of Don Quixote's library before it was burned at the beginning of the novel, as well as the following conversation on the same subject between the priest and the innkeeper:

"We want here our friend's housekeeper and niece."

"Not at all," answered the barber; "for I myself can carry them to the yard, or to the chimney, where there is a very good fire."

"What, sir, would you burn my books?" said the innkeeper.

"Only these two," said the priest, "that of Don Cirongilio, and that of Felixmarte."

"What, then, are my books heretical, or phlegmatical, that you have a mind to burn them?"

"Schismatical, you would say, friend," said the barber, "and not phlegmatical."

"It is true," replied the innkeeper; "but if you intend to burn any, let it be this of the Grant Captain, and this of Diego de Garcia; for I will sooner let you burn one of my children, than either of the others."

"Dear brother," said the priest, "these two books are great liars, and full of extravagant and foolish conceits; and this of the Grant Captain is a true history, and contains the exploits of Gonçalo Hernandez of Córdova, who, for his many and brave actions, deserved to be called by all the world the Grand Captain; a name renowned and illustrious, and merited by him alone. As for Diego Garcia de Paredes, he was a gentleman of note, born in the town of Truxillo in Estremadura, a very brave soldier, and of such great natural strength, that he could stop a millwheel, in its greatest rapidity, with a single finger; and, being once posted with a two-handed sword at the entrance upon a bridge, he repelled a prodigious army, and prevented their passage over it. And he performed other such things, that if, instead of being related by himself, with the modesty of a cavalier who is his own historian, they had been written by some other dispassionate and unprejudiced author, they would have eclipsed the actions of the Hectors, Achilleses, and Orlandos." (Part I, Chapter 32)

We find the same thing in the conversation with the canon:

> The priest listened to him with great attention, and took him to be a man of good understanding, and in the right in all he said; and therefore he told him, that, being of the same opinion, and bearing an old grudge to books of chivalry, he had burnt all those belonging to Don Quixote, which were not a few. Then he gave him an account of the scrutiny he had made, telling him which of them he had condemned to the fire, and which he had reprieved. (Part I, Chapter 47)

These reminders are like internal staples that join together episodes of a similar type within the novel.

The canon too finds the chivalric romance to be distasteful and begins talking about art in general and drama in particular. This is followed by Don Quixote's speech, on which I have already touched briefly in my analysis of his speeches.

The first part of the novel ends with the inset episode involving the lost she-goat and Don Quixote's attack on the religious procession.

I do not intend to analyze the second part of *Don Quixote* with the same rigor with which I have tried to follow the course of the first part. I wish only to emphasize what is new in the construction of the second part of the book.

I have already mentioned that the second parts of novels, or rather their sequels, often alter their structure. The main story is broken off, as it were, and exists only conventionally; the action in the sequel follows a different principle. Thus, at the end of Rabelais's novel we see a transition to the picaresque form, where the individual islands/allegories are connected through the wanderings of the heroes. The structure of this final part of *Gargantua* and *Pantagruel* laid the ground for the construction of *Gulliver's*

Travels. Swift went even further in his ending—the satirical material supplants the adventure material (this was noted by one of my students, Lev Lunts).

The most distinctive feature of the second part of *Don Quixote* is the abundance of minor anecdotes interpolated into the novel from other sources. Another distinctive feature is that here we see Don Quixote being tricked and deceived in every possible way. The members of the duke's family and their servants amuse themselves at the expense of the poor knight, and Sancho's short stint as a governor is nothing but a great hoax. The bachelor Sampson Carrasco lets Don Quixote out of the house to resume his knight-errantry as a hoax. Don Quixote's battle with the Knight of the Looking-Glasses and later the battle with the Knight of the White Moon are both hoaxes. In Barcelona, they play a hoax on Don Quixote by pinning a sign on his back that says: "This is Don Quixote de la Mancha" (Part II, Chapter 62).

Similarly, in restoring Falstaff to the stage by the order of the queen (as they say), Shakespeare had to make him the object of a hoax in *The Merry Wives of Windsor.*

Very interesting, indeed, is the fact that in the second part, Don Quixote is aware that the first part of the novel has been written, and polemicizes against the "simulated" second part. It is rather a curious situation. The main character of the novel thinks of himself as a real person, and not as someone imitating the sensation of being alive. This is motivated in Cervantes by the fact that Don Quixote considers his illegitimate double to be crude and trivial, and he takes offense not as the fictional Don Quixote, but as the real, living Don Quixote:

> "Then, I presume, your worship is that Don Alvaro Tarfe, mentioned in the second part of the history of Don Quixote de la Mancha, lately printed and published by a certain modern author."
>
> "The very same," answered the gentleman, "and that Don

Quixote, the hero of the said history, was a very great friend of mine; and I was the person, who drew him from his native place; at least I prevailed upon him to be present at certain jousts and tournaments held at Saragossa, whither I was going myself; and in truth, I did him a great many kindnesses, and saved his back from being well stroked by the hangman for being too bold."

"Pray, tell me, Señor Don Alvaro," quoth Don Quixote, "am I anything like that Don Quixote you speak of?"

"No, in truth," answered the guest, "not in the least."

"And this Don Quixote," said ours, "had he a squire with him called Sancho Panza?"

"Yes, he had," answered Don Alvaro; "and though he had the reputation of being very pleasant, I never heard him say any one thing that had any pleasantry in it." (Part II, Chapter 72)

Then Don Quixote asks the gentleman to make a written declaration before the magistrate of the town, stating that he has met the real Don Quixote.

It seems to me that what we have here is a something of an exposure of the footlights—a device that gives away and accentuates the artifice of art. To this type belongs King Lear's speech, when his daughters inform him that fifty knights are more than adequate for his needs; he turns to an elegantly dressed lady in the audience and says:

> Why, nature needs not what thou gorgeous wear'st,
> Which scarcely keeps thee warm. (2.4.263-6)[70]

Similarly, in Gogol's *The Government Inspector*, the governor breaks the conventional fourth wall, which supposedly makes the audience invisible to the characters on the stage, and addresses

---

[70] William Shakespeare, *King Lear*, ed. George Ian Duthie and John Dover Wilson (Cambridge University Press, 1960).

the audience with these famous words: "What are you laughing at? You're laughing at yourselves, that's what!" (Act V, Scene 8). Ostrovsky does the same in *A Family Affair*, when Rispolozhensky rushes to the footlights, showing the worn-out soles of his shoes to the audience. In Tieck and Hoffmann, the main characters are sometimes aware of the fact that they are characters in a novella or capriccio ("a story in which we all appear and act").[71] This is also a typical vaudeville device, with couplets addressed to the audience.

When it comes to theater, the illusion, in all likelihood, ought to flicker—i.e. appear and then completely disappear. The viewer must experience within himself a back-and-forth movement in his perception of the action onstage, switching from something "deliberate" to something "natural" or "real." Leoncavallo's *Pagliacci* and Schnitzler's *The Green Cockatoo* are based on the perception of a flickering illusion. In these works, the action on stage is perceived sometimes as performance, sometimes as life. However, it is time for us to return to Don Quixote.

In his conversation with the bachelor Sampson Carrasco, Sancho Panza tells how his mule was stolen. This detail had been omitted in the first part of the book:

> "That very night, when, flying from the Holy Brotherhood, we entered into the Sierra Morena, after the unlucky adventure of the galley-slaves and of the dead body being carried to Segovia, my master and I got into a thicket, where, he leaning upon his lance, and I sitting upon Dapple, being both of us mauled and fatigued by our late skirmishes, we fell asleep as soundly as if we had had four featherbeds under us; especially I for my part slept so fast, that the thief, whoever he was, had leisure enough to suspend me on four stakes, which he planted under the four corners of the pannel, and in this manner leaving me mounted thereon, got Dapple from under me, without my feeling it."
>
> "That is an easy matter, and no new accident," said Don

E. T. A. Hoffmann, "Princess Brambilla" in *The Golden Pot and Other Tales*, trans. Ritchie Robertson (Oxford University Press, 2000).

Quixote: "for the like happened to Sacripante at the siege of Albracca, where that famous robber Brunello, by this self-same invention, stole his horse from between his legs." (Part II, Chapter 4)

Cervantes has incorporated a vagrant plot here. It is a common occurrence in more recent literature. For instance, different "historical" statements and actions are anonymously ascribed to the hero of the novel. This device was widely used by Alexandre Dumas, for example. We encounter the same thing, albeit tinged with parody, in Tolstoy (the conversation between Bolkonsky's valet Petrushka and Napoleon in *War and Peace*). We see the same thing in Gogol's *Dead Souls*. Referring to a scam by contrabandists who made use of a flock of sheep in double fleece to smuggle Flemish lace, Gogol first says: "The reader doubtless has heard of the oft-repeated story of . . ." and then, after retelling the anecdote, adds: "If he himself had not been in the know, no Jews in the wide world would have succeeded in carrying through such a scheme" (Part I, Chapter 11).[72]

In the fifth chapter of the second part, Sancho utters such complex sentences that the author himself calls them apocryphal, "because in it Sancho talks in another style than could be expected from his shallow understanding, and says such subtle things, that [the translator of this history] reckons impossible that he should know them."

After his speech on fame, Don Quixote sets out for El Toboso, where Sancho tricks him into believing that a passing country girl is Dulcinea. Then comes the episode where Don Quixote meets a traveling troupe of actors and later battles the Knight of the Wood, which again is motivated by a hoax. The next episode of the main story is the knight's famous battle with the lions. The episode interrupts the long discourse between Don Quixote and a certain gentleman from La Mancha. Starting from Chapter 19, we find

---

[72] Nikolai Gogol, *Dead Souls*, trans. George Reavey, ed. George Gibian (New York: Norton, 1985).

ourselves again in an inset pastoral to do with cunning, in which a shepherd steals the bride of a rich farmer. The pastoral includes a description of an allegorical play performed at the wedding. The play most certainly carries the sense of being inserted from elsewhere and, typically for Cervantes, it is immediately evaluated by the spectators:

> Don Quixote asked one of the nymphs, who it was that had contrived and ordered the show. She answered, a beneficed clergyman of that village, who had a notable headpiece for such kind of inventions.
>
> "I will lay a wager," quoth Don Quixote, "that this bachelor or clergyman is more a friend to Camacho than to Basilius, and understands satire better than vespers: for he has ingeniously interwoven in the dance the abilities of Basilius with the riches of Camacho." (Part II, Chapter 20)

But let's not follow every step of Don Quixote, and instead move on to the inset episodes. In Chapter 24, Cervantes inserts an anecdote about a youth walking down the road without trousers on, lest he wear them out, while in Chapters 25–27 he inserts another anecdote about two villages at loggerheads because one has mocked the other by braying like a donkey. This little story is connected to the novel only by the fact that its characters, the villagers, beat up Don Quixote. Later on, the novel narrates a *féerie-ballet* given at the duke's castle. Then we come across an inset episode, similar to the anecdote about the brayers, involving two young men discussing whether it is necessary to know the art of fencing (Part II, Chapter 19), and an argument about how to compensate for the different weights of a lean man and a fat man who are to compete in a running race (Part II, Chapter 66).

Sancho Panza's governorship is also a long and complexly fragmented inset episode. Its origin is quite clear. It is common in frame novels to select material based on a certain systematizing sign, sometimes even by external features. For instance, the stories in *The Arabian Nights* are often selected according to an identical injury caused by their denouements. The story of the three royal mendicants (each blind in one eye, but for a different reason) is of this type. At other times, these stories are selected based on the identical nature of their resolutions—for example, the magical transformation of the enemy in the sheikhs' tales at the beginning of *The Arabian Nights*, which are told with the aim of reclaiming the merchant's blood. This type didn't really survive for long, but it persistently reemerged: we see it in the eighteenth-century Georgian text called *The Book of Wisdom and Lies*. This is also how some of Boccaccio's tales are arranged in *The Decameron*. And it is the same device that Voltaire employs in Candide, where six deposed monarchs *accidentally* assemble at the same inn:

> The servants having vanished, the six strangers, together with Candide and Martin, sat on in deep silence. It was broken at last by Candide. "Gentlemen," he said, "this is presumably some kind of joke. How can you all be kings? I can assure you that neither Martin nor I are anything of the kind."
>
> Cacambo's master then spoke up and said gravely in Italian: "I am no joker, and my name is Achmed III; for several years I was Grand Sultan; I deposed my brother; my nephew deposed me; my viziers had their throats cut; I live out my days in the old seraglio; my nephew the Grand Sultan Mahmud sometimes lets me travel for my health, and I have come to spend Carnival in Venice."
>
> A young man who was next to Achmed spoke next, and said: "My name is Ivan; I was Emperor of all the Russias; I was deposed in my cradle; my father and mother were locked away; I was brought up in prison; occasionally I have permission to travel, accompanied by my guards, and I have come to spend Carnival in Venice."
>
> The third said: "I am Charles Edward, King of England. My father renounced his claims to the throne in my favor; I have fought long and hard to uphold them; eight hundred of my

followers had their hearts ripped out and their cheeks slapped with them; I have been put in prison; I am now on my way to Rome to visit the King my father, deposed like myself and my grandfather, and I have come to spend Carnival in Venice."

The fourth then spoke up and said: "I am King of Poland; the fortunes of war have deprived me of my hereditary states; my father suffered the same reverses; I entrust myself to the will of Providence, just like Sultan Achmed, Emperor Ivan and King Charles Edward, whom God preserve; and I have come to spend Carnival in Venice."

The fifth said: "I too am King of Poland; I have lost my kingdom twice, but Providence has given me another state, in which I have done more good than all the Sarmatian kings combined have managed to do on the banks of the Vistula. I too entrust myself to Providence, and have come to spend Carnival in Venice."

It remained for the sixth monarch to speak. "Gentlemen," he said, "I am not as great a ruler as any of you; but for all that I have been a king just like everyone else; I am Théodore; I was elected King of Corsica; they called me 'Your Majesty,' who now barely call me 'Sir'; I once minted my own coin, and now do not own a farthing; I once had two secretaries of state, and now have scarcely a valet; I once sat on a throne, but then for a long time slept on straw in a London prison; I am much afraid I shall be treated in the same fashion here, although I have come like Your Majesties to spend Carnival in Venice."

The other five kings listened to this speech with regal compassion. Each of them gave King Théodore twenty sequins to buy clothes and shirts, and Candide made him a present of a diamond worth two thousand sequins. "Who can this be?" said the five kings. "A mere commoner who is in a position to give a hundred times as much as each of us, and who moreover gives it?"

Just as they were getting up from the table, there arrived in the same hostelry four Serene Highnesses, who had likewise lost their states through the fortunes of war, and who had come to spend what remained of the Carnival in Venice. But Candide did not even notice these newcomers. All he could now think about was getting to Constantinople and finding his dear Cunégonde.

Chapter 27
Candide's voyage to Constantinople

The faithful Cacambo had already obtained permission, from the Turkish captain who was to escort Sultan Achmed back to Constantinople, for Candide and Martin to join them on board. They made their way to the ship, after duly prostrating themselves before His doleful Highness. On the way, Candide said to Martin: "Six deposed kings, if you please! All of whom supped with us, and one of whom had to accept alms from me. Perhaps there are any number of other princes who are even more unfortunate. As for me, all I have lost is a hundred sheep and here I am flying to the arms of Cunégonde. My dear Martin once again I see that Pangloss was right: all is well." – "I hope so," said Martin. – "Nonetheless," said Candide, "was this not a fairly singular adventure we have just had in Venice? Who ever saw or heard of six deposed kings having supper together in a tavern." (Chapters 26-27)[73]

If this is not a motivation for the device, then it is an attempt to conceptualize it or, at the very least, draw attention to it. It would be interesting to look at a passage from Conan Doyle as an analogous attempt to motivate another "device convention"—the convention of the adventure novel with its "favorable confluence" of circumstances:

"But this is pure coincidence, Holmes! Fate is favorably disposed toward you!"

"My dear Watson, I see it a bit differently than you. Anyone

---

[73] Voltaire, *Candide, or Optimism*, trans. Theo Cuffe (Penguin Books, 2005).

who stubbornly pursues something, whose thoughts are constantly preoccupied with one and the same thing, who is guided by an insistent desire to bring something to a close, unwittingly contributes everything to this cause. You may call it hypnosis, inflexible willpower, but it is so! Pulling toward itself all the iron and steel from everywhere like a magnet, this drive forces all the details, all the petty circumstances to arrange themselves into the steps of a staircase that will lead us to the exposure of the crime."[74]

This principle of selecting material based on some external sign has been widely used in novels. Sometimes, especially in the organic novel, the inset parts are made to interact with each other—for example, they are constructed as parallels. Sancho Panza's governorship represents a summary of folkloric episodes involving wise judgments. It even includes the echoes of Solomon's judgments and Talmudic passages (for example, the story about the stick of gold coins). Sancho himself admits that his wisdom is derivative:

All were struck with admiration, and took their new governor for a second Solomon. They asked him, whence he had collected, that the ten crowns were in the cane. He answered, that, upon seeing the old man give it his adversary, while he was taking the oath, and swearing that he had really and truly restored them into his own hands, and, when he had done, ask for it again, it came into his imagination, that the money in dispute must be in the hollow of the cane. Whence it may be gathered, that God Almighty often directs the judgments of those who govern, though otherwise mere blockheads: besides, he had heard the priest of his parish tell a like case; and, were it not that he was so unlucky as to forget all he had a mind

---

[74] From *Nozh Tantsovshchitsy* [The Dancer's Knife], a pseudotranslation that appeared in a collection of stories supposedly by Arthur Conan Doyle titled *Poslednie priklyucheniya Sherloka Kholmsa* [The Last Adventures of Sherlock Holmes], "translated from the original manuscript" into Russian by a certain G. S. and published in 1908 by Gerold Press. [—Trans.]

to remember, his memory was so good, there would not have been a better in the whole island. (Part II, Chapter 45)

The other episodes, such as the one featuring the woman who falsely accuses a swineherd of raping her, have many parallels that emerge according to the laws of plot construction.

Some of the episodes from Sancho's governorship include picaresque proverbs and fables. Apart from such inset episodes and various folkloric "problems," Cervantes introduced his own administrative considerations into the depiction of Sancho's governorship in the same way as he had done earlier with Don Quixote's speeches. Sometimes these ideas, conveyed through the mouth of Sancho, radically differ from the type of discourse that we are accustomed to hearing from Don Quixote's squire. In such cases, Cervantes himself reveals the incongruity, exposing the device:

"I now plainly perceive, that judges and governors must or ought to be made of brass, if they would be insensible of importunities of your men of business, who, being intent upon their own affairs alone, come what will of it, at all hours, and at all times, will needs be heard and dispatched; and if the poor judge does not hear and dispatch them, either because he cannot, or because it is not the proper time for giving them audience, presently they murmur and traduce him, gnawing his very bones, and calumniating him and his family. Foolish man of business, impertinent man of business, be not in such haste; wait for the proper season and conjuncture for negotiation: come not at dinner-time, nor at bed-time; for judges are made of flesh and blood, and must give to their nature what their nature requires; except only poor I, who do not so by mine, thanks to Señor Pedro Recio Tirteafuera here present, who would have me die of hunger, and affirms that this kind of dying is in order to live: God grant the same life to him and all those of his tribe; I mean, bad physicians; for good ones deserve palms and laurels."

All who knew Sancho Panza were in admiration to hear him talk so elegantly, and could not tell what to ascribe it to, unless that offices and weighty employments quicken and enliven some understandings, as they confound and stupefy others. (Part II, Chapter 49)

In the account of Sancho's governorship, Cervantes has also inserted a brief, underdeveloped story about a young woman who runs away from her father's house dressed in men's clothing.

All of these episodes are tightly conjoined in a single motley kaleidoscope. However, Sancho's speech of abdication from his governorship is not a simple conglomeration of statements. The reconceptualization of the old material is obvious here. This is already a step into a new novel. The writer has realized the possibility of presenting his hero not just as the butt of jokes who undergoes various ordeals, but also as someone who survives them.

Humanism is inserted into the novel as new material for constructions, for example, through Cervantes's remark condemning the duke and the duchess for mocking Don Quixote.

The effect here consists of the alternation of the two masks and the re-experiencing of the old material in the new.

Returning from the island of Barataria, Sancho Panza meets his friend and neighbor Ricote the Morisco who, under the guise of a pilgrim, is trying to get back to his native village in Spain, where he had once buried a treasure (Part II, Chapter 54). After a short conversation, the friends part. This episode has no independent significance, but it is introduced into the novel to tie in even more tightly the story about the fair Morisca in Chapter 63. In short, the chapter narrates the capture of a "Moorish" galley, the captain of which turns out to be a Christian woman, the daughter of Ricote the Morisco, dressed as a man. As chance would have it, Ricote happens to be on that galley as well.

The fact that we are already familiar with Ricote from his earlier meeting with Sancho draws the inset story closer to the main plot.

Another story, or rather a story within a story, is the account of Don Quixote's meeting with Roque and his bandits. The painterly description of the noble outlaw is interrupted by a story about an unreasonably jealous woman, Claudia Jerónima, who shot her lover, wrongly accusing him of infidelity. These stories are linked to the main plot only because Don Quixote is present when they unfold. This is a near perfect type of stringing. For the purpose of introducing episodes in this manner it has always been especially convenient to concoct a journey, which would motivate the contact between the hero and the inset stories.

The hero unifies these episodes in the same way as the viewer unifies paintings in an art gallery.

This is similar to the device used in Le Sage's *The Devil upon Two Sticks*, where Don Cleophas and Asmodeus inspect the interiors of people's dwellings by the magical removal of the roofs. Asmodeus's remarks accompanying their tour have the same function as the hero's emotional reaction to the episodes strung onto his journey, or the princes' astonishment at the inset tales they hear in *The Arabian Nights*.

Sometimes frame stories may include not only anecdotes, but also collections of scientific data. So, for example, we come across arithmetical problems interpolated into the Georgian *Book of Wisdom and Lies*, or we see encyclopedic entries on scientific topics and lists of geographical discoveries in the novels of Jules Verne. The Old Russian poem of *The Book of the Dove* is wholly based on the exposition of knowledge considered scientific at the time, framed as a story about a holy book. Aeschylus interpolated a description of an optical telegraph into his tragedy on the same principle. I have noted on multiple occasions the inclusion of such material in Cervantes. One of the most vivid examples of this is when Don Quixote, immediately after his speech on liberty, encounters a dozen men carrying statues of saints (Part II, Chapter 58).

In another instance, Cervantes inserts a description of a talking brass head, with all the details of its mechanism. This is Chapter 62, which "treats of the adventure of the enchanted head, with other trifles that must not be omitted."

Elsewhere, during a conversation about the baselessness of omens, with parallels from ancient history, an explication of the Spanish battle cry, and so on, Don Quixote suddenly finds himself entangled in some nets of silk thread. It turns out that several young men and women had decided to recreate a new pastoral Arcadia close by. This game, in which they dress as shepherds and shepherdesses, is in fact the source of all the novel's pastoral scenes. Cervantes himself wrote pastoral novels in that same conventional spirit. There are numerous pastoral scenes in *Don Quixote* and at times we are led to think that the entire novel will set off on a new trajectory, turning into a pastoral. And indeed, Don Quixote returns home intent on becoming a shepherd after his defeat by the Knight of the White Moon.

But the approach of death removes from Don Quixote the mask of madness, in order to give him a new mask—the mask of the meek Christian Alonso the Good.

THE MYSTERY STORY

1) It is possible to narrate a story in such a way that the reader will be able to see how its events unfold and how they progress, one after the other. Such a narration usually progresses in chronological order and without any significant omissions.

As an example we may take Tolstoy's *War and Peace*.

2) It is also possible to narrate in such a way that the reader will not be able to understand what is happening. The story is riddled with "mysteries" that are resolved only later.

To this kind belong Turgenev's "Knock, Knock, Knock," Dickens's novels, and detective stories, which I will discuss below.

The second type of narration usually employs temporal transposition—i.e. the omission of the description of a particular event and its occurrence after the revelation of the consequences of that event. A single temporal transposition is often sufficient to create a mystery. A good illustration of this is the mysterious appearance of Svidrigailov at the bedside of the ailing Raskolnikov in *Crime and Punishment*; although it is earlier hinted that a certain man had overheard the address, the mystery is renewed by Raskolnikov's dream.

The mystery of this second meeting is achieved through simple omission of the fact that Svidrigailov has discovered the address.

In an adventure novel that has several parallel threads, the surprise effect is achieved by having one plot thread progress either at the same pace as or faster than another, parallel thread, so that when we switch from one thread to another, the rhythm of the first thread is preserved—i.e. we find ourselves in the midst of consequences whose causes are unknown to us.

This is how Don Quixote finds Sancho in the pit among the ruins of the old buildings.

This device seems perfectly natural, but it is a modern achievement. The Greek epic was unfamiliar with it. As Zieliński has shown, there is no simultaneity of action in *The Odyssey*: although there are parallel storylines (Odysseus and Telemachus), the events unfold alternately in each storyline.

Temporal transposition can serve to create a "mystery," but we must not think that the mystery resides in transposition alone.

For example, Chichikov's childhood, related after he had already been introduced by the author, would ordinarily have been found in the opening of a classic adventure novel; but the transposition of this description does not make the hero mysterious.

Tolstoy's later work employs this device to achieve a *reverse* effect. In other words, temporal transposition is done in such a way that it diffuses the interest toward the denouement. Here is an example from *The Kreutzer Sonata*:

> "Yes, undoubtedly there are critical episodes in married life," said the lawyer, wishing to end this disturbingly heated conversation.
>
> "I see you have found out who I am!" said the gray-haired man softly, and with apparent calm.
>
> "No, I have not that pleasure."
>
> "It is no great pleasure. I am that Pozdnyshev in whose life that critical episode occurred to which you alluded; the episode when he killed his wife," he said, rapidly glancing at each of us.

In *Hadji Murad*, a Cossack shows Butler the decapitated head of Hadji Murad; the drunken officers examine it and kiss it.

And then we come to the scene of Hadji Murad's last battle.

But besides this, the fate of Hadji Murad, his entire story is conveyed through the image of the broken thistle, which nevertheless yearns for life.

The Death of Ivan Ilych opens as follows:

> During an interval in the Melvinsky trial in the large building of the Law Courts the members and public prosecutor met in Ivan Egorovich Shebek's private room, where the conversation turned on the celebrated Krasovsky case. . . . Peter Ivanovich, not having entered into the discussion at the start, took no part in it but looked through the *Gazette* which had just been handed in.
>
> "Gentlemen," he said, "Ivan Ilych has died!"[75]

In these three examples, there seems to be a conflict with the *fabula* (storyline), rather than an attempt to impede it. Tolstoy evidently wanted to deflect interest away from the plot and shift the emphasis onto the analysis, the "details," as he used to say.

We know the date of Ivan Ilych's death and we know the fate of Pozdnishev's wife, including the result of Pozdnishev's trial. We know the fate of Hadji Murad and what people will say when they see his decapitated head.

The interest in this aspect of the work is removed.

The artist required a new way of conceptualizing things, an alteration of the habitual chain of thought, so he rejected the plot, giving it a merely perfunctory role.

In this excursus I have been trying to show the difference between temporal transposition, which can be used in particular cases to create "mysteries," and the use of mystery itself as a plot device.

I think that even the most careless reader of adventure novels will be able to notice the number of mysteries that figure therein.

The word "mystery" often appears in titles of works, for

---

[75] Lev Tolstoy, *The Death of Ivan Ilych* in *Collected Short Fiction, Volume II*, trans. Louise and Aylmer Maude and Nigel J. Cooper (New York: Alfred A. Knopf, 2001).

example, *Mysteries of the Madrid Court, The Mysterious Island, The Mystery of Edwin Drood*, etc.

Mysteries are usually inserted into an adventure novel or story with the aim of enhancing interest in the action and creating the possibility of more than one interpretation.

Detective novels, which represent a special type of "crime fiction," have gained an advantage over novels about outlaws probably due to the convenience of providing motivation for a mystery. At first the crime is presented as a riddle, then the detective is introduced as a professional riddle solver.

Crime and Punishment similarly makes broad use of the device of preparation (when Raskolnikov designs the noose for the axe, or when he changes his hat, etc.—these details are exposed before the crime, and we know their purpose). The motives for the crime in this novel are given after the crime, which is their consequence.

In novels of the *Arsène Lupin* type, the main character is not a detective, but a "gentleman thief." The detective is present as someone who discovers the mystery and functions as a motif of delay. But Lupin also often works as a detective.

Let us take one of Conan Doyle's stories about the adventures of Sherlock Holmes in order to get a better sense of what I mean by a story constructed on a mystery.

I am going to discuss "The Speckled Band" and will draw a few parallels from the same collection of stories, so that it is easier for the reader to follow me if he should choose to do so with the collection of stories in his hands.[76]

Conan Doyle's stories open in a rather uniform way: they often begin with a listing of Holmes's adventures recounted by his friend, Dr. Watson—it is as if he is selecting what to narrate and what to omit. He drops hints about certain affairs along the way and presents the details.

The most common opening is the arrival of a client, which,

---

[76] Arthur Conan Doyle, *The Adventures of Sherlock Holmes*, ed. Richard Lancelyn Green (Oxford University Press, 1993). All subsequent quotations from *The Adventures of Sherlock Holmes* are taken from this edition.

again, is constructed in a rather uniform way. Let's take, for example, "A Case of Identity":

> He had risen from his chair, and was standing between the parted blinds, gazing down into the dull, neutral-tinted London street. Looking over his shoulder, I saw that on the pavement opposite there stood a large woman with a heavy fur boa round her neck, and a large curling red feather in a broad-brimmed hat which was tilted in a coquettish Duchess-of-Devonshire fashion over her ear. From under this great panoply she peeped up in a nervous, hesitating fashion at our windows, while her body oscillated backwards and forwards, and her fingers fidgeted with her glove buttons. Suddenly, with a plunge, as of the swimmer who leaves the bank, she hurried across the road, and we heard the sharp clang of the bell.
>
> "I have seen those symptoms before," said Holmes, throwing his cigarette into the fire. "Oscillation upon the pavement always means an *affaire de cœur*. She would like advice, but is not sure that the matter is not too delicate for communication. And yet even here we may discriminate. When a woman has been seriously wronged by a man she no longer oscillates, and the usual symptom is a broken bell wire. Here we may take it that there is a love matter, but that the maiden is not so much angry as perplexed, or grieved. But here she comes in person to resolve our doubts."

Let's take another example, from "The Adventure of the Beryl Coronet":

> "Holmes," said I as I stood one morning in our bow-window looking down the street, "here is a madman coming along. It seems rather sad that his relatives should allow him to come out alone." . . .
>
> He was a man of about fifty, tall, portly, and imposing, with a massive, strongly marked face and a commanding figure. He was dressed in a sombre yet rich style, in black frock-coat,

shining hat, neat brown gaiters, and well-cut pearl-grey trousers. Yet his actions were in absurd contrast to the dignity of his dress and features, for he was running hard, with occasional little springs, such as a weary man gives who is little accustomed to set any tax upon his legs. As he ran he jerked his hands up and down, waggled his head, and writhed his face into the most extraordinary contortions.

"What on earth can be the matter with him?" I asked. "He is looking up at the numbers of the houses."

"I believe that he is coming here," said Holmes, rubbing his hands.

As one can see, there isn't much variety in these openings. Remember that both of these passages come from the same collection of stories.

But before we move on to further critiques of Conan Doyle, let us first clarify why he needs Dr. Watson.

Watson has a two-fold role. First, as a narrator, he tells us about Holmes and conveys to us his anticipation of Holmes's solutions, while he himself does not take part in the latter's process of thought. Holmes indulges Watson in some of his half-solutions only occasionally.

Watson, therefore, slows down the action and simultaneously regulates the flow of events. He might simply have been replaced by a particular way of dividing the story into chapters.

Second, Watson is necessary as a "constant fool" (the term is crude, and I don't insist on introducing it into the theory of prose). In this regard, he shares the fate of Inspector Lestrade, whom I will discuss later in the chapter.

Watson misconstrues the meaning of the clues, therefore making it possible for Sherlock Holmes to correct him.

Watson motivates the false solution.

In addition to this, Watson's role is to carry on a dialogue and give cues—in other words, he plays the role of a pitcher, tossing the ball to Sherlock Holmes for him to bat.

Coming to Sherlock Holmes, the client usually relates all the known circumstances of the case in great detail.

If there is no such person (i.e. when Holmes is summoned to a crime scene), then it is Holmes who relates the details of the case to Watson.

Holmes likes to baffle his visitors (and Watson too) with his omniscience.

His methods of analysis are monotonous: in three out of twelve stories in the collection, Holmes first focuses on a person's sleeve:

"There is no mystery, my dear madam," said he, smiling. "The left arm of your jacket is spattered with mud in no less than seven places. The marks are perfectly fresh. There is no vehicle save a dog-cart which throws up mud in that way, and then only when you sit on the left-hand side of the driver." ("The Speckled Band")

Elsewhere Holmes says:

"My first glance is always at a woman's sleeve. In a man it is perhaps better first to take the knee of the trouser. As you observe, this woman had plush upon her sleeves, which is a most useful material for showing traces. The double line a little above the wrist, where the typewritist presses against the table, was beautifully defined. The sewing-machine, of the hand type, leaves a similar mark, but only on the left arm, and on the side of it farthest from the thumb, instead of being right across the broadest part, as this was. I then glanced at her face, and observing the dint of a pince-nez at either side of her nose, I ventured a remark upon short sight and typewriting, which seemed to surprise her."

"It surprised me." ("A Case of Identity")

In "The Red-Headed League," Holmes baffles again his client by pointing out that the latter had done a considerable amount of writing lately.

"Ah, of course, I forgot that. But the writing?"

"What else can be indicated by that right cuff so very shiny for five inches, and the left one with the smooth patch near the elbow where you rest it upon the desk?"

This monotony of method might be explained by the fact that the stories were written one after another, and the writer may have forgotten that he had already used it in the previous stories. And yet, it should be said, that self-repetition is far more frequent in literature than is commonly thought.

The mystery device is sometimes incorporated into the body of the novel, into the main characters' mode of expression and the author's comments on them. I will show this with respect to Dickens in the next chapter.

Conan Doyle's Sherlock Holmes expresses himself in rather mysterious ways, which is often achieved through circumlocution.

The inspector tells Holmes that he has hired a cab and asks whether he wants to see the crime scene:

"It was very nice and complimentary of you," Holmes answered. "It is entirely a question of barometric pressure."

Lestrade looked startled. "I do not quite follow," he said.

"How is the glass? Twenty-nine, I see. No wind, and not a cloud in the sky. I have a caseful of cigarettes here which need smoking, and the sofa is very much superior to the usual country hotel abomination. I do not think that it is probable that I shall use the carriage to-night."

Sherlock Holmes stays in the hotel (where he has absolutely nothing to do). Not long thereafter we are given a clue as to his mysterious remark:

"The glass still keeps very high," he remarked as he sat down. "It is of importance that it should not rain before we are able to go over the ground. On the other hand, a man should be at his very best and keenest for such nice work as that, and I did not wish to do it when fagged by a long journey." ("The Boscombe Valley Mystery")

A shorter and less ambiguous version of this circumlocution would be: If it doesn't rain.

The passage must have been important enough for Conan Doyle to have included it here, although it bears no significance to the unfolding plot.

But in order to include it there, Holmes had to be left behind in the hotel and, as I already said, he is redundant there and has even more reason than before to feel angry: "Oh, how simple it would all have been had I been here before they came like a herd of buffalo and wallowed all over it."

Apart from giving Holmes an opportunity to show off his wit and express his foresight, the author uses the awkward delay at the hotel to introduce analytical conversations.

In the case of "The Speckled Band," the story is broken down into two parts: the first part summarizes the cause of the crime, while the second narrates the crime in as detailed a manner as possible.

I will now quote a few excerpts from the young woman's story about the death of her sister. This is in the first part of the story. Since I myself am not writing a mystery story here, I will provide a preface to the evidence that I am about to produce.

The excerpts below provide certain clues, some of which are intended to mislead. Others are given indirectly (or in passing: in subordinate clauses on which the narrator does not dwell, but which are nonetheless of major importance). And so, here is a warning: (1) is a false lead; (2) is an incomplete clue regarding the method of committing the crime; (3) illustrates the communication of an important clue in a subordinate clause; (4) and (5) offer details about the murder; (6) shows how the dead woman's words are construed in such a way as to lead to a false solution (i.e. that the woman was killed by the gypsies).

According to the information provided at the beginning of the story, we are led to think that the stepfather had a motive for the murder. And now, here are the excerpts:

(1)

"He had no friends at all save the wandering gypsies, and he would give these vagabonds leave to encamp upon the few acres of bramble-covered land which represent the family estate, and would accept in return the hospitality of their tents, wandering away with them sometimes for weeks on end."

(2)

"He has a passion also for Indian animals, which are sent over to him by a correspondent, and he has at this moment a cheetah and a baboon, which wander freely over his grounds and are feared by the villagers almost as much as their master."

(3–4)

"The windows of the three rooms open out upon the lawn. That fatal night Dr. Roylott had gone to his room early, though we knew that he had not retired to rest, for my sister was troubled by the smell of the strong Indian cigars which it was his custom to smoke. She left her room, therefore, and came into mine, where she sat for some time, chatting about her approaching wedding. At eleven o'clock she rose to leave me, but she paused at the door and looked back.

"'Tell me, Helen,' said she, 'have you ever heard anyone whistle in the dead of the night?'

"'Never,' said I.

"'I suppose that you could not possibly whistle, yourself, in your sleep?'

"'Certainly not. But why?'

"'Because during the last few nights I have always, about three in the morning, heard a low, clear whistle. I am a light sleeper, and it has awakened me. I cannot tell where it came from—perhaps from the next room, perhaps from the lawn. I thought that I would just ask you whether you had heard it.'

"'No, I have not. It must be those wretched gypsies in the plantation.'"

(5)

"As I opened my door I seemed to hear a low whistle, such as my sister described, and a few moments later a clanging sound, as if a mass of metal had fallen."

(6)

"At first I thought that she had not recognised me, but as I bent over her she suddenly shrieked out in a voice which I shall never forget, 'Oh, my God! Helen! It was the band! The speckled band!' . . . It is certain, therefore, that my sister was quite alone when she met her end. Besides, there were no marks of any violence upon her."

The catch here is that in English the word "band" is a homonym, i.e. it has two meanings: a ribbon and a gang. The significance of the existence of two possible interpretations is evident from the following dialogue:

"Ah, and what did you gather from this allusion to a band—a speckled band?"

"Sometimes I have thought that it was merely the wild talk of delirium, sometimes that it may have referred to some band of people, perhaps to these very gypsies in the plantation. I do not know whether the spotted handkerchiefs which so many of them wear over their heads might have suggested the strange adjective which she used."

Holmes shook his head like a man who is far from being satisfied.

The use of homonyms is quite frequent in Conan Doyle. We find similar wordplay in the following passage from "The Boscombe Valley Mystery":

"The Coroner: Did your father make any statement to you before he died?

"Witness: He mumbled a few words, but I could only catch some allusion to a rat."

Holmes interprets this word quite differently:

"What of the rat, then?"

Sherlock Holmes took a folded paper from his pocket and flattened it out on the table. "This is a map of the Colony of Victoria," he said. "I wired to Bristol for it last night." He put his hand over part of the map. "What do you read?"

"ARAT," I read.

"And now?" He raised his hand.

"BALLARAT."

"Quite so. That was the word the man uttered, and of which his son only caught the last two syllables. He was trying to utter the name of his murderer. So-and-so of Ballarat."

There are many such examples in Conan Doyle's stories. It is a popular literary device. For example, Jules Verne makes use of the different meanings of a word in two languages in *Children of Captain Grant*, where a mysterious document, partially illegible due to water damage, can be read in several different ways, depending on the language in which the traveler had written the message in the bottle. The search is complicated by the fact that the writer of the message uses a geographic synonym (Isle Tabor) when referring to the place of his shipwreck.

Those interested in this device may easily find other parallels.

As you can see, the main question is whether it is possible to trace two perpendiculars to the same straight line from only one point. The writer searches for the coincidence of two non-coincident things based on a single shared feature. Of course, in detective stories the coinciding feature isn't always a word. In "The Queer Feet" (*The Innocence of Father Brown*), to create an analogous construction, Chesterton makes use of the plain fact that a gentleman's evening dress is the same as a waiter's uniform.

But let us not digress.

Mystery fiction abounds in hints alluding to the solution and making it more veridical when one arrives at it.

Conan Doyle's "The Man with the Twisted Lip" is based on the story of a gentleman who dresses like a beggar in order to collect alms. A series of primitively built coincidences leads to the arrest of St. Clair the beggar, who is accused of murdering St. Clair the gentleman.

Sherlock Holmes investigates the case and reaches a false conclusion. The problem is that St. Clair is nowhere to be found; however, the police have found a dress coat with pockets full of coins not far from the site of the alleged murder. Sherlock Holmes constructs a new hypothesis:

> "No, sir, but the facts might be met speciously enough. Suppose that this man Boone had thrust Neville St. Clair through the window, there is no human eye which could have seen the deed. What would he do then? It would of course instantly strike him that he must get rid of the tell-tale garments. He would seize the coat then, and be in the act of throwing it out, when it would occur to him that it would swim and not sink. He has little time, for he has heard the scuffle downstairs when the wife tried to force her way up, and perhaps he has already heard from his Lascar confederate that the police are hurrying up the street. There is not an instant to be lost. He rushes to some secret hoard, where he has accumulated the fruits of his beggary, and he stuffs all the coins upon which he can lay his hands into the pockets to make sure of the coat's sinking. He throws it out, and would have done the same with the other garments had not he heard the rush of steps below, and only just had time to close the window when the police appeared."

This is a false solution.

Meanwhile, we already have a hint suggesting that St. Clair is the same person as Boone. During their search of Boone's apartment the police find traces of blood on the windowsill and on the wooden floor. Mrs. St. Clair faints at the sight of the blood and the police send her home in a cab, as her presence is of no help to them in their investigation. Inspector Barton, who is in charge of the case, makes a very careful examination of the premises, but finds nothing. One mistake is not to have arrested Boone instantly, giving him an opportunity to communicate with his friend the Lascar. But this fault is soon remedied; Boone is seized and searched, without anything being found that might incriminate him. There are, it is true, some bloodstains on his right shirtsleeve, but he shows them his ring finger, which has a cut near the nail, and explains that the bleeding came from there, adding that he was at the window not long before, and that the stains observable there doubtlessly came from the same source.

As we see, the cut on Boone's finger is presented indirectly and the main focus is on the blood on the windowsill.

Meanwhile, Mrs. St. Clair says the following about her presentiment in connection with her husband: "There is so keen a sympathy between us that I should know if evil came upon him. On the very day that I saw him last he cut himself in the bedroom, and yet I in the dining-room rushed upstairs instantly with the utmost certainty that something had happened."

The emphasis in this passage is placed on Mrs. St. Clair's feeling that her husband had injured himself and not on the injury itself. And yet, this is the clue that establishes the fact that St. Clair and Boone are the same person (based on the injury).

The purpose of the passage is not to reveal the recognition, but to make it apparent in retrospect. According to Chekhov's principle, if a story tells us there is a rifle hanging on the wall, then later it must go off.

At its most intense, this motive is transformed into what Ibsen called "doom." This principle in its usual form does indeed correspond to the general rule governing artistic means, but in the mystery novel, it is not the rifle on the wall that goes off. It is another that does.

It is very interesting to follow how the artist gradually prepares the material for such a denouement. Let's take a distant example. In *Crime and Punishment*, Svidrigailov overhears Raskolnikov's confession, but does not give him away. Svidrigailov poses a different kind of threat.

But I shouldn't write about Dostoevsky in a chapter on Conan Doyle.

Before this digression I observed that the word "band," with its ambiguity and allusion to the gypsies, prepares us for a false denouement. Holmes says:

> "When you combine the ideas of whistles at night, the presence of a band of gypsies who are on intimate terms with this old doctor, the fact that we have every reason to believe that the doctor has an interest in preventing his stepdaughter's marriage, the dying allusion to a band, and, finally, the fact that Miss Helen Stoner heard a metallic clang, which might have been caused by one of those metal bars which secured the shutters falling back into their place, I think that there is good ground to think that the mystery may be cleared along those lines."

As one can see, the originator of the "false lead" in this case is Holmes himself. This is due to the fact that there is not the official inspector in "The Speckled Band" who would normally come up with a false solution (like Watson, who always misinterprets the details). Subsequently, as there is no inspector in the story, Holmes himself has to err.

The same happens in "The Man with the Twisted Lip."

One critic has explained the perpetual failure of the state inspector and the constant victory of the private detective in Conan Doyle as reflecting the opposition between the state and private capital.

I don't know if Conan Doyle had any basis for juxtaposing the English state, which is essentially bourgeois, against the English bourgeoisie, but I do think that if these stories were written by someone from a proletarian state, they would still include an inspector who fails. In this latter case, the state detective would probably be the successful one, while the private detective would be constantly erring. So, hypothetically speaking, Sherlock Holmes would be working for the state, while Lestrade would be the free-lancer; but even so, the structure of the story (and particularly, the issue at hand) would be unaltered.

Let us now return to "The Speckled Band."

Sherlock Holmes and his friend travel to the scene of the alleged crime and inspect the house.

They inspect the room of the deceased, to which her sister has now been moved; she fears a similar fate might await her.

> "Where does that bell communicate with?" he asked at last, pointing to a thick bell-rope which hung down beside the bed, the tassel actually lying upon the pillow.
>
> "It goes to the housekeeper's room."
>
> "It looks newer than the other things?"
>
> "Yes, it was only put there a couple of years ago."
>
> "Your sister asked for it, I suppose?"
>
> "No, I never heard of her using it. We used always to get what we wanted for ourselves."
>
> "Indeed, it seemed unnecessary to put so nice a bell-pull there. You will excuse me for a few minutes while I satisfy myself as to this floor." He threw himself down upon his face with his lens in his hand, and crawled swiftly backward and forward, examining minutely the cracks between the boards. Then he did the same with the woodwork with which the chamber was paneled. Finally he walked over to the bed and spent some time in staring at it and in running his eye up and down the wall. Finally he took the bell-rope in his hand and gave it a brisk tug.

"Why, it's a dummy," said he.

"Won't it ring?"

"No, it is not even attached to a wire. This is very interesting. You can see now that it is fastened to a hook just above where the little opening for the ventilator is."

"How very absurd! I never noticed that before."

"Very strange!" muttered Holmes, pulling at the rope. "There are one or two very singular points about this room. For example, what a fool a builder must be to open a ventilator into another room, when, with the same trouble, he might have communicated with the outside air!"

"That is also quite modern," said the lady.

"Done about the same time as the bell-rope?" remarked Holmes.

"Yes, there were several little changes carried out about that time."

"They seem to have been of a most interesting character—dummy bell-ropes, and ventilators which do not ventilate."

We have three clues: the bell, the floor, and the ventilator. Pay attention to how Sherlock Holmes talks only about the first and the second clues, whereas the third is presented in the form of a hint. See point (3), which I made earlier, regarding the divulgation of an important clue intentionally given in a subordinate clause.

After examining his client's room, Holmes proceeds to the adjacent room belonging to her stepfather, Dr. Grimesby Roylott. Holmes examines everything in the room and stops by the safe:

"There isn't a cat in it, for example?"

"No. What a strange idea!"

"Well, look at this!" He took up a small saucer of milk which stood on the top of it.

"No; we don't keep a cat. But there is a cheetah and a baboon."

"Ah, yes, of course! Well, a cheetah is just a big cat, and yet a saucer of milk does not go very far in satisfying its wants, I

daresay. There is one point which I should wish to determine."
He squatted down in front of the wooden chair, and examined
the seat of it with the greatest attention.

"Thank you. That is quite settled," said he, rising and putting his lens in his pocket.

Suddenly Holmes notices a small coiled lash, tied so as to make a
loop of whipcord. He says:

"What do you make of that, Watson?"

"It's a common enough lash. But I don't know why it
should be tied."

"That is not quite so common, is it? Ah, me! it's a wicked
world, and when a clever man turns his brains to crime it is the
worst of all. I think that I have seen enough now, Miss Stoner,
and with your permission we shall walk out upon the lawn."

As you can see, Holmes's findings are not communicated immediately. Our attention is drawn to certain objects, but the result
of his examination is revealed later. Finally, Holmes stresses the
previously unstressed detail about the ventilator and divulges the
fact that the bed is clamped to the floor—something he failed to
do earlier:

"I saw nothing remarkable save the bell-rope, and what purpose that could answer I confess is more than I can imagine."

"You saw the ventilator, too?"

"Yes, but I do not think that it is such a very unusual thing
to have a small opening between two rooms. It was so small
that a rat could hardly pass through."

"I knew that we should find a ventilator before ever we
came to Stoke Moran."

"My dear Holmes!"

"Oh, yes, I did. You remember in her statement she said
that her sister could smell Dr. Roylott's cigar. Now, of course
that suggested at once that there must be a communication

between the two rooms. It could only be a small one, or it would have been remarked upon at the Coroner's inquiry. I deduced a ventilator."

"But what harm can there be in that?"

"Well, there is at least a curious coincidence of dates. A ventilator is made, a cord is hung, and a lady who sleeps in the bed dies. Does not that strike you?"

"I cannot as yet see any connection."

"Did you observe anything very peculiar about that bed?"

"No."

"It was clamped to the floor. Did you ever see a bed fastened like that before?"

"I cannot say that I have."

"The lady could not move her bed. It must always be in the same relative position to the ventilator and to the rope—for so we may call it, since it was clearly never meant for a bell-pull."

In this way, the new detail first appears as a hint and is only then connected with the other details of the story. We are presented with a series of clues: ventilator, bell-pull, clamped bed. What remains undisclosed is what Holmes saw on the seat of the wooden chair, and the significance of the lash.

Watson is still unable to put the clues together. Holmes does not tell him, or, subsequently, us—we are separated from him by the narrator.

Generally speaking, Sherlock Holmes never bothers to explain, and always brings the case to an effective close. But the effective close is preceded by anticipation.

The detective and his friend are sitting in the room and waiting for the crime to be committed. They wait for a while.

How shall I ever forget that dreadful vigil? I could not hear a sound, not even the drawing of a breath, and yet I knew that my companion sat open-eyed, within a few feet of me, in the same state of nervous tension in which I was myself.

The shutters cut off the least ray of light, and we waited in absolute darkness. From outside came the occasional cry of a night-bird, and once at our very window a long drawn cat-like whine, which told us that the cheetah was indeed at liberty. Far away we could hear the deep tones of the parish clock, which boomed out every quarter of an hour. How long they seemed, those quarters! Twelve struck, and one, and two, and three, and still we sat waiting silently for whatever might befall.

Suddenly there was the momentary gleam of a light up in the direction of the ventilator . . .

I am not criticizing Conan Doyle, but I must point out the repetitiousness of not only his plot schemes but also the elements of their execution.

Let me cite a parallel from "The Red-Headed League":

What a time it seemed! From comparing notes afterwards it was but an hour and a quarter, yet it appeared to me that the night must have almost gone, and the dawn be breaking above us. My limbs were weary and stiff, for I feared to change my position, yet my nerves were worked up to the highest pitch of tension, and my hearing was so acute that I could not only hear the gentle breathing of my companions, but I could distinguish the deeper, heavier in-breath of the bulky Jones from the thin, sighing note of the bank director. From my position I could look over the case in the direction of the floor. Suddenly my eyes caught the glint of a light.

In both cases, the suspense (obviously employed for deceleration) ends with an attempt to commit a crime.

In "The Speckled Band," the criminal releases a snake through the ventilator, which crawls down the rope. Sherlock Holmes strikes it, and shortly afterwards a scream is heard. Holmes and his assistant run into the adjacent room:

It was a singular sight which met our eyes. On the table stood a dark lantern with the shutter half open, throwing a brilliant beam of light upon the iron safe, the door of which was ajar. Beside this table, on the wooden chair, sat Dr. Grimesby Roylott clad in a long grey dressing-gown, his bare ankles protruding beneath, and his feet thrust into red heelless Turkish slippers. Across his lap lay the short stock with the long lash which we had noticed during the day. His chin was cocked upward and his eyes were fixed in a dreadful, rigid stare at the corner of the ceiling. Round his brow he had a peculiar yellow band, with brownish speckles, which seemed to be bound tightly round his head. As we entered he made neither sound nor motion.

"The band! the speckled band!" whispered Holmes.

I took a step forward: in an instant his strange headgear began to move, and there reared itself from among his hair the squat diamond-shaped head and puffed neck of a loathsome serpent.

As you can see, all of the information is summed up in this short passage. Everything is clear about the band and the looped whipcord. Here is Holmes's analysis:

"I had," said he, "come to an entirely erroneous conclusion, which shows, my dear Watson, how dangerous it always is to reason from insufficient data. The presence of the gypsies, and the use of the word 'band,' which was used by the poor girl, no doubt, to explain the appearance which she had caught a hurried glimpse of by the light of her match, were sufficient to put me upon an entirely wrong scent. I can only claim the merit that I instantly reconsidered my position when, however, it became clear to me that whatever danger threatened an occupant of the room could not come either from the window or the door. My attention was speedily drawn, as I have already remarked to you, to this ventilator, and to the bell-rope which hung down to the bed. The discovery that this was a dummy, and that the bed was clamped to the floor, instantly gave rise to the suspicion that the rope was there as a bridge for something passing through the hole, and coming to the bed. The idea of a snake instantly occurred to me, and when I coupled it with my knowledge that the Doctor was furnished with a supply of creatures from India, I felt that I was probably on the right track. The idea of using a form of poison which could not possibly be discovered by any chemical test was just such a one as would occur to a clever and ruthless man who had had an Eastern training. The rapidity with which such a poison would take effect would also, from his point of view, be an advantage. It would be a sharp-eyed coroner, indeed, who could distinguish the two little dark punctures which would show where the poison fangs had done their work. Then I thought of the whistle. Of course, he must recall the snake before the morning light revealed it to the victim. He had trained it, probably by the use of the milk which we saw, to return to him when summoned. He would put it through this ventilator at the hour that he thought best, with the certainty that it would crawl down the rope and land on the bed. It might or might not bite the occupant, perhaps she might escape every night for a week, but sooner or later she must fall a victim.

"I had come to these conclusions before ever I had entered his room. An inspection of his chair showed me that he had been in the habit of standing on it, which, of course, would be necessary in order that he should reach the ventilator. The sight of the safe, the saucer of milk, and the loop of whipcord were enough to finally dispel any doubts which may have remained. The metallic clang heard by Miss Stoner was obviously caused by her stepfather hastily closing the door of his safe upon its terrible occupant."

Of course, all of these devices are more or less masked—it is true that every novel assures us of its reality. It is common for every writer to draw a distinction between his story and "literature." Lyudmila (in Pushkin's *Ruslan and Lyudmila*) isn't just eating fruits in Chernomor's garden, but she is violating the literary tradition with this act: "The princess thought, and—started eating."[77]

This is even more applicable to detective novels that try to mask themselves as real documents or reports. Watson says in "The Boscombe Valley Mystery":

> I walked down to the station with them, and then wandered through the streets of the little town, finally returning to the hotel, where I lay upon the sofa and tried to interest myself in a yellow-backed novel. The puny plot of the story was so thin, however, when compared to the deep mystery through which we were groping, and I found my attention wander so continually from the action to the fact, that I at last flung it across the room and gave myself up entirely to a consideration of the events of the day.

Other such masking devices include referencing other cases (yet to be turned into stories) and indicating that the publication of the given story was made possible due to the death of such and such a lady, etc.

But the diversity of types in Conan Doyle is very limited, and if we are to judge based on the author's success in the world, then it becomes obvious that there is no need for a wider diversity. From the standpoint of technique, the devices employed by Conan Doyle in his stories are, of course, simpler than the devices used in the English mystery novel; however, they are much more concentrated.

The mystery story entails nothing but a crime and its investigation, whereas in Radcliffe or Dickens we always find descriptions of nature, psychological analysis, etc. A landscape is very rare in

---

[77] Aleksandr Pushkin, *Ruslan and Lyudmila*, trans. Walter Arndt (Ann Arbor: Ardis, 1974). In this passage, the princess mourns her captivity and contemplates suicide in a poetic vein (Ah, jailer, whose pernicious lust / Would now indulge me, now torment me / Your evil might cannot prevent me / From choosing death: I can! I must . . . / I want no meals, no tunes, no meeting, / I'll die amidst your opulence!" / The princess thought, and—started eating.). The final line, however, stands in direct contradiction to both the form and the content of the preceding lines. [—Trans.]

Conan Doyle, and, if there is one, it usually serves to remind and underscore that nature is good, while man is evil.

The general scheme of Conan Doyle's stories is as follows:

1. Anticipation; conversation about previous cases; analysis.
2. The appearance of a client (the business part of the story).
3. The introduction of clues (the secondary facts are the most important clues arranged in such a way that the reader pays little or no attention to them); the introduction of material for creating a false lead.
4. Watson misinterprets the clues.
5. A visit to the crime scene (often the crime has not been committed yet, and this is how the action begins in the narrative, allowing the crime story to infiltrate the detective story); the gathering of evidence.
6. The state inspector comes up with a false solution; if the story does not have an inspector, the false solution is presented either by the newspaper, the victim, or Sherlock Holmes himself.
7. The interval is filled with Watson's speculations (who doesn't have a clue about anything); Holmes smokes, or plays the violin (sometimes he connects and groups the facts without offering a final conclusion).
8. The denouement, ideally, is unexpected (it often includes an attempted crime).
9. Sherlock Holmes analyzes the facts.

Conan Doyle did not invent this scheme, nor did he steal it. It is dictated by the genre. Let's compare it with "The Gold-Bug" by Edgar Allan Poe (I presume everyone knows this work, but if there is someone who doesn't, then I congratulate him on the prospect of reading such a good story). I will outline the story in such a way that it will not ruin the pleasure of reading it for the first time.

1. Exposition: a description of a friend.
2. Accidental discovery of a document; the friend calls

attention to the reverse side of the document (a device used by Holmes).

3. The friend's bizarre actions, recounted by the negro servant (Watson).

4. A treasure hunt; failure due to an error made by the negro servant (a deferment device, comparable with the false solution).

5. The discovery of treasure.

6. The friend's account with an analysis of facts.

Anyone who aims to create such plots in Russian literature must pay attention to Conan Doyle's use of hints and how those hints propel the narrative toward a denouement.

THE MYSTERY NOVEL

Anyone who has studied riddles will surely have noticed that a riddle usually allows not one, but several solutions.

A riddle is not merely a parallelism with an omitted part, but a game with the possibility of establishing several parallels.

This is particularly noticeable in erotic riddles.

Erotic riddles constitute a play on words in which indecent images are replaced with decent ones. The indecent images are not eliminated, but simply repressed.

Dmitri Sadovnikov makes the following note to the riddle no. 102 in his collection of Russian riddles:

Almost all of the riddles about the lock and the key have a double meaning, and some of them could not be included in this collection. The percentage of such riddles is quite high, and it can be stated with certainty that they are widespread. Children tell these riddles without inhibition; young men tell them as jokes, old women and girls whisper them into each other's ears. However, the latter case is rare, except for when it is preceded by a warning about the indecency of the riddle (everything is called by its true name and words are not omitted, as it is usually done in songs). Many of these riddles are evidently based on mythical beliefs and parallels, which have now lost their significance and meaning.[78]

I completely disagree with the last argument, as the samples in Sadovnikov's book do not substantiate this hypothesis.

There are riddles, however, that have only a single answer, such as Samson's riddle: "Out of the eater came something to eat. Out of the strong came something sweet" (Judges 14:14).

Such riddles are about one specific object known only to the riddle-teller. In fairy tales such a riddle is usually posed as the third in a series (as the most difficult one), or it serves as a response riddle. At times the answer is not spoken, but shown. For example, in Andersen's "The Traveling Companion," the princess asks: "What am I thinking of?" In response, her suitor shows the severed head of a troll.[79]

Sometimes the series of riddles begin with a riddle of the following type, here posed by Ivan the Fool (no. 78 in *Tales and Songs of the Belozersk Region*):

The riddle: "I rode my father, sat on my mother, restrained my brother, and whipped my sister." The answer: "My father gave me the horse on which I was riding, my mother gave me money for the saddle, my brother—the bridle, my sister—the horsewhip."

A similar type of riddle with only a single answer is that posed by Solomon's wife: "I'm sitting on the tsar, but looking at the king."

In the well-known vagrant folk song "The King and the Bishop," the king poses three questions, the last of which is: "What am I thinking?" and the answerer (a teacher, laborer, or acolyte) says: "You are thinking that I am so-and-so, but in fact I

---

[78] *Zagadki russkovo naroda*, a collection of over 2,500 Russian riddles, first published in 1876. *Riddles of the Russian People: A Collection of Riddles, Parables and Puzzles*. Compiled by Dmitri Sadovnikov, trans. Ann C. Bigelow (Ann Arbor: Ardis, 1986).

[79] Hans Christian Andersen, "The Travelling-Companion" in *Hans Andersen's Fairy Tales: A Selection*, trans. L. W. Kingsland (Oxford University Press, 1998).

am such-and-such." So, the last question, the third, has a single answer (substitution).

In essence, this type of riddle cannot be guessed or solved. It does not have a "false" answer. And yet it is perceived as a regular riddle.

Let us take a look at another riddle similar to that cited above (regarding the horse bought with the father's money):

> After passing the night at home, Ivan resolved to return to her and pose another riddle. Ivan, the son of a peasant, washed himself with the sweat of his horse, dried himself with the horse's mane, and went off to meet her. She asked: "Why did you come here, to tell a riddle, or to solve it?" "To tell a riddle," said Ivan. "I sat on the horse, washed myself, but not with dew or with water, and then I dried myself, but not with silk or with cloth." Tsarevna Marfa could not solve the riddle.
>
> On his third trip, Ivan took a gun with him. He saw a flock of geese in the air and shot down a goose. He dug two holes in the ground, one shallow, the other deep. He roasted the goose in the shallow hole, made a fire in the deep one, then climbed a tree and ate the goose on the treetop. When he arrived at Tsarevna Marfa's, she asked: "Are you here to tell a riddle?" "Yes," said Ivan. "I was riding on my horse, saw a flock of geese in the air, and shot down a goose. I cooked it but not on the ground or on water, and I ate it above the forest." She looked in her book of riddles and couldn't find the answer.

The second part of the tale offers riddles of an entirely different kind.[80]

Note how the above excerpt stresses the fact that these are unique riddles—they cannot be found in ordinary books. Such riddles remind us of the contemporary oral tradition of "Armenian riddles," which also cannot be solved. These riddles are perceived against the background of the traditional (solvable) riddle.

---

[80] They are erotic. [—Trans.]

Story Built on a Mistake

As I have already written, the simplest form of plot is the stepped construction, where each succeeding step varies either quantitatively or qualitatively from the previous one. The stepped construction usually extends into a circular construction.

In Jules Verne's *Around the World in Eighty Days*, for example, the steps are the adventures, while the circular story is the mistake in the date (the travelers gain a day by traveling eastward).

In adventure novels the circular story is very often built on a recognition.

In *Gil Blas*, for example, one of the stories is used as a denouement. Structurally speaking, it does not differ from the other stories. Rather, the sense of closure is achieved in this novel by a change in the author's relation to his hero. At the end of the novel we see Gil Blas (very much like his precursor Lazarillo in the picaresque novel *Lazarillo de Tormes*) married, settled, and apparently deceived. The author introduces a note of irony in his relation to the hero.

It is more common to see a frame story built on a mistake, such as the one in the abovementioned Jules Verne novel.

For the sake of simplicity, let's first examine how the mistake functions in the story, and then in the novel.

There are many stories built on a mistake.

Let us take Chekhov's story "At the Bathhouse." It is a given that both clergymen and socialists have long hair. The task it to mix them up. The motivation for this mix-up is the bathhouse.

In Maupassant, real diamonds are mixed up with imitation diamonds. There are two possibilities:

1) *Fake diamonds are mistaken for real ones*. This is the case of "The Necklace." A young woman borrows a diamond necklace from her friend, then loses it. She buys a similar necklace on credit and returns it to her friend. She spends her whole youth paying off the debt, only to find out in

the end that the original necklace was just costume jewelry and not worth anything.

2) *Real jewels are mistaken for fake ones.* This is the case of "The Jewels." A man lives happily with his wife. She has only one flaw: a love of imitation jewelry. The wife dies. Needing money, the husband decides to sell her imitation jewelry expecting to get very little in return. They turn out to be real jewels. They were gifts from her lovers.

In folklore, in the legend of St. Julian the Hospitaller, we see the son killing his sleeping mother and father, whom he mistakes for his wife and her lover.

In Chekhov, a man ends up in someone else's room and mistakes the sleeping couple for his wife and her lover.

Elsewhere, brothers, sons, and husbands are mistaken for lovers.

In love, one pursues and the other resists—the same relationship holds true for the battle. From here we have the frequent image of love as a battle.

> Poor ropes, you are beguiled,
> Both you and I, for Romeo is exiled.
> He made you for a highway to my bed,
> But I, a maid, die maiden-widowèd.
> Come, cords; come, nurse: I'll to my wedding-bed,
> And death, not Romeo, take my maidenhead! (Act III, Scene 2)[81]

The same motif appears in Lucretius, *On the Nature of Things*, and Apuleius, *The Golden Ass.*

Folk poetry makes use of the reverse metaphor, comparing a battle to a love scene or a wedding (see *The Song of Igor's Campaign*, for example).

---

[81] William Shakespeare, *Romeo and Juliet* (Wordsworth Classics, 1992). In the Russian translation used by Shklovsky, Juliet addresses the rope ladder in lines 5-6: "Дай мне совет, как выиграть мне битву, / В которой потерять должна я непорочность" [Give me counsel, how am I to win this battle / In which I must lose my maidenhead]. This version erroneously constructs a pursuit/resistance continuum between Romeo and Juliet—Juliet has to lose to Romeo—whereas the conflict in the original resides elsewhere. [—Trans.]

People wrestle—whether loving or killing each other. This gives rise to another parallel. Maupassant has a story called "Father Boniface's Crime," in which an old mailman overhears the groans and sighs of a couple in bed and mistakes them for sounds of a crime.[82]

A woman might also find herself in bed with her own children. Coming home to his wife, the husband sees her asleep with a young man, who turns out to be her son. Here is an example of such a misrecognition: "He arrived at his dwelling and looked in through the small window, just above the ground; he saw a woman sleeping with two young lads on each side. He took out his sword, wanting to cut off their heads, but remembered the words of the old man: 'Raise your sword, but do not strike.' He then entered the dwelling and woke up his wife. She didn't recognize him. He asked her: 'Who are these men, dear?' She replied: 'These are my sons.'" (See also "Ivan the Unfortunate" in Onchukov's collection).

In conclusion, stories built on a mistake are similar to stories built on a pun. The pun gives the standard meaning of a word, then a new meaning of that word and a substantiation for the mix-up.

The mix-up is motivated by the commonality of the verbal sign, which is used to mean two different things.

In the story built on a mistake, the mix-up of two concepts is motivated by an external similarity of situations that allows for a dual interpretation.

And yet, the mystery story, which is the same as the story built on a mistake, differs from the story built on a parallelism.

The latter mode is common, as I have already mentioned, in Maupassant.

Story Built on a Parallelism

The story built on a parallelism deals with a comparison of two objects.

---

[82] The title of the story is also translated as "A Mistake." [—Trans.]

For example, the fate of a woman is compared with the fate of a dog, or with the fate of a hunted doe, etc. The comparison is usually made up of two parts—two independent stories, as it were, often only connected by the same narrator or setting.

I won't cite any examples, as almost all of Maupassant's stories can serve as examples of parallelism.

In the mystery story as well as the mystery novel, however, we are dealing not so much with a comparison as with a displacement of one object by another.

When a story unfolds into a novel, the solution of the mystery loses its meaning. The parallelism prevails over the intersection of storylines.

The possibility of delaying the denouement with the help of a mystery has led to the fact that stories built on puns are rarely used as frame stories, whereas mystery stories are often chosen specifically for that purpose.

The history of the mystery novel shows that the "denouement" has lost its significance; it has become awkward, imperceptible, useless.

The novel of pure parallelism, which doesn't intersect storylines, battles against the technique of the mystery novel.

The technique of the mystery novel was often employed by Dostoevsky, while Tolstoy preferred pure parallelism.

Tolstoy even preferred to employ parallelism in order to frame a story, playing with the paradoxical relationship between the length of one part of the parallel and that of the other.

This can be easily seen in *Hadji Murad*. The short novel begins with a description of fields. The narrator is gathering flowers for a bouquet. The pace of the story is intentionally slow and unhurried:

> I gathered myself a large nosegay and was going home when I
> noticed in a ditch, in full bloom, a beautiful thistle plant of the
> crimson variety, which in our neighborhood they call "Tatar"
> and carefully avoid when mowing—or, if they do happen to

cut it down, throw out from among the grass for fear of prick-ing their hands. Thinking to pick this thistle and put it in the center of my nosegay, I climbed down into the ditch, and after driving away a velvety bumble-bee that had penetrated deep into one of the flowers and had there fallen sweetly asleep, I set to work to pluck the flower. But this proved a very diffi-cult task. Not only did the stalk prick on every side—even through the handkerchief I wrapped round my hand—but it was so tough that I had to struggle with it for nearly five minutes, breaking the fibers one by one; and when I had at last plucked it, the stalk was all frayed and the flower itself no longer seemed so fresh and beautiful. Moreover, owing to a coarseness and stiffness, it did not seem in place among the delicate blossoms of my nosegay. I threw it away feeling sorry to have vainly destroyed a flower that looked beautiful in its proper place.

"But what energy and tenacity! With what determination it defended itself, and how dearly it sold its life!" thought I, remembering the effort it had cost me to pluck the flower.

Continuing along his path, the narrator sees another thistle:

In front of me to the right of the road I saw some kind of little clump, and drawing nearer I found it was the same kind of thistle as that which I had vainly plucked and thrown away. This "Tatar" plant had three branches. One was broken and stuck out like the stump of a mutilated arm. Each of the other two bore a flower, once red but now blackened. One stalk was broken, and half of it hung down with a soiled flower at its tip. The other, though also soiled with black mud, still stood erect. Evidently a cartwheel had passed over the plant but it had risen again, and that was why, though erect, it stood twisted to one side, as if a piece of its body had been torn from it, its bowels drawn out, an arm torn off, and one of its eyes plucked out. Yet it stood firm and did not surrender to man who had destroyed all its brothers around it. . . .

"What vitality!" I thought. "Man has conquered everything and destroyed millions of plants, yet this one won't submit." And I remembered a Caucasian episode of years ago, which I had partly seen myself, partly heard of from eye-witnesses, and in part imagined.

The episode, as it has taken shape in my memory and imagination, was as follows.

Then follows the long story of Hadji Murad, which concludes with the frame story, thus returning to the image of the thistle: "It was of this death that I was reminded by the crushed thistle in the midst of the ploughed field."

The relationship between the two parts of this parallelism is most extraordinary.

The parallelism, however, is felt most forcefully due to the opening description of the thistle plant—the pun of *tatarin* (thistle/Tatar)—whereas the ending of the parallelism is deliberately simple. This last sentence, nevertheless, contains the most important moment of the parallel: a thistle plant in the midst of a cultivated field, the last of the Circassians who doesn't want to submit amidst those who submitted. The insistence on the desire for life is not repeated, but it is certainly felt.

The Mystery Novel

In *The Mysteries of Udolpho* by Ann Radcliffe, one of the founders of the mystery novel, the mysteries are montaged in the following way: the heroine enters a haunted castle, where she finds a half-decomposing corpse behind a curtain, someone's voice interrupts a conversation of drunken bandits, and so on. Everything is resolved at the end of the novel: the corpse, as it turns out, was made of wax and was placed there by one of the ancestors of the Udolpho family, who had been condemned by the Pope to contemplate the "human corpse" as a form of penance. The mysterious voice belongs to a prisoner, who had been wandering in the castle through secret passageways. As you can see, and as one of Radcliffe's contemporaries remarked, these explanations are only partially satisfactory.

In the second part of the novel, the story begins all over again. A new castle, new mysterious voices. Later it turns out that the voices belonged to some contrabandists. The protagonists hear mysterious music near the castle, and later find out that it had been played by a nun.

I am not listing all of Radcliffe's mysteries, as I don't have the book in front of me.

It is interesting to note, that at first these mysteries initially lead to false solutions (as in Dickens). We often suspect something far more awful than is actually the case. For example, in the second part of the novel, the author alludes to incest. The novel uses the same device as the one employed in those indecent songs, such as the well-known but rarely quoted song "In Knopp's Shop," with the solution: "nothing vulgar . . . just yellow gloves!"[83]

I should remind the reader that this is a typical device in Russian folk riddles of the type: "It hangs and swings, it's within everyone's reach," to which the answer is: "A towel."

There is often a pause that suggests the "false" (usually obscene) solution of the riddle. Let me illustrate how such a riddle is developed into a plot.

Boris and Yuri Sokolov recorded the following "anecdote" told by an old woman (no. 131 in *Tales and Songs of the Belozersk Region*, 1915). Pay attention to how the anecdote accentuates the moment of the "false" solution. It is a game of riddles: "A young tailor once visited me and posed the following riddle: 'What happens to a crow after two years?' And I said to him: 'He'll enter his third year.' The tailor started laughing because I had solved the riddle. Then it was my turn: 'If not for my father's skill, my

[83] The Russian song plays with the rhyme *Knoppa/zhopa* [Knopp's/ass], however the singer merely insinuates the word "ass" by only pronouncing half of the word (zho--), which in the next line is completed as another word, *zholtye* [yellow]: "*V magazine Knoppa vystavlena zho . . . Ne podumayte durnovo, zholtye perchatki!*" [—Trans.]

mother would be overgrown.' The young tailor went in the wrong direction, he thought of you know what, but couldn't guess the right answer. So I told him: 'Weeds grow fast on a strip of land— our Mother Earth.'"

As we can see, the false solution is a key element in the mystery story or novel. Here is the technique of constructing a mystery: false solution—correct solution; the transitional moment from one solution to the other is the moment of the denouement. The relationship between parts is the same as the relationship in plots based on puns.

The mystery plot is closely associated with the device of inversion, i.e. transposition.

The most common type of mystery in a novel is a narration that follows a reverse chronology, starting with the present and moving backward. Good examples of this are the mysteries of the watch and the double in *Little Dorrit*.

The mysteries of the house, Amy Dorrit's love for Arthur Clennam, and Clennam's love for Minnie Meagles are constructed without the use of inversion.

Here the mystery is achieved by means of exposition. The metaphoric axis forms a parallel with the factual axis. In cases of a mystery based on the transposition of cause and effect, the parallel is formed by the false solution.

The construction of mystery is quite intriguing in Dickens's final novel, *Our Mutual Friend*.

The first mystery is that involving John Rokesmith. The author pretends to conceal from us the fact that John Rokesmith is none other than John Harmon. Dickens himself says that he never intended to conceal Rokesmith's real name from the reader. The second mystery involves Boffin. We see how wealth spoils the "Golden Dustman," and we don't know that Boffin is, in fact, tricking us.

The mystery of John Harmon is a false lead; it does not give us an opportunity to solve or even notice the mystery of Boffin. The technique at work in this novel is extremely sophisticated.

The direct heir of the mystery novel is the detective novel, in which the detective is nothing other than a professional mystery solver.

At first, we are presented with a mystery: a crime, which is usually followed by a false solution—a failed police investigation, for example—after which the full picture of the crime is exposed. Inversion is necessary in a work of this type, and it is sometimes used in its most complex form: the omission of certain elements.

This is how the mystery of *The Brothers Karamazov* is constructed (but without a detective). I have chosen Dickens's *Little Dorrit* for a more detailed analysis of the mystery technique.

Little Dorrit

The novel is built around several simultaneous actions. The connection between the parallels is achieved by: a) involving the characters of one storyline in the actions of another storyline, b) connecting the characters by place. So, for example, the protagonists live in close proximity to each other. Clennam moves to Bleeding Heart Yard, which is where Patriarch and John Baptist live.

The storylines of the novel are as follows: 1) the love story between Amy Dorrit and Arthur Clennam, 2) the coming into wealth and subsequent ruin of the Dorrit family, and 3) the blackmail attempt by Rigaud, who threatens to expose Mrs. Clennam.

The novel can be summarized in this way only after one has read it to the end. When we are in the middle of it, however, we have before us a whole series of mysteries, including the relationships between the characters. These mysteries are woven into one another. We can discern the following mysteries when we read the book for the first time:

1) The mystery of the watch. ⎱ Main mysteries: they frame the plot, but
2) The mystery of the dreams. ⎰ are essentially left unresolved.
3) The mystery of Pancks (the discovery of the inheritance). This is a partial mystery, as it does not run throughout the

entire novel. It introduces an imbalance between Arthur
Clennam and Amy Dorrit, and it is based on an inversion.

4) The mystery of Mr. Merdle (again, a subsidiary mystery).

5) The mystery of the strange noises in the house. It prepares
the denouement of the first two mysteries.

6) The mystery of the love story (Dorrit and Clennam). It
belongs to the central plot but represents the technique of
an extended negative parallelism.

1. The Mystery of the Watch

Arthur Clennam has just arrived at his mother's house. On her
little table lie two or three books, her handkerchief, a pair of steel
spectacles, and an old-fashioned gold watch in a heavy double
case. They are both staring at this last object.

"I see that you received the packet I sent you on my father's
death, safely, mother."

"You see."

"I never knew my father to show so much anxiety on any
subject, as that his watch should be sent straight to you."

"I keep it here as a remembrance of your father."

"It was not until the last, that he expressed the wish. When
he could only put his hand upon it, and very indistinctly say to
me 'your mother.' A moment before, I thought him wandering
in his mind, as he had been for many hours—I think he had
no consciousness of pain in his short illness—when I saw him
turn himself in his bed and try to open it."

"Was your father, then, not wandering in his mind when
he tried to open it?"

"No. He was quite sensible at that time."

Mrs. Clennam shook her head; whether in dismissal of
the deceased or opposing herself to her son's opinion, was not
clearly expressed.

"After my father's death I opened it myself, thinking there
might be, for anything I knew, some memorandum there.

However, as I need not tell you, mother, there was nothing but the old silk watch-paper worked in beads, which you found (no doubt) in its place between the cases, where I found and left it." (Chapter 3)[84]

The conversation between mother and son continues in Chapter 5:

"I want to ask you, mother, whether it ever occurred to you to suspect—"

At the word Suspect, she turned her eyes momentarily upon her son, with a dark frown. She then suffered them to seek the fire, as before; but with the frown fixed above them, as if the sculptor of old Egypt had indented it in the hard granite face, to frown for ages.

"—that he had any secret remembrance which caused him trouble of mind—remorse? Whether you ever observed anything in his conduct suggesting that; or ever spoke to him upon it, or ever heard him hint at such a thing?"

"I do not understand what kind of secret remembrance you mean to infer that your father was a prey to," she returned, after a silence. "You speak so mysteriously."

". . . Time and change (I have tried both before breaking silence) do nothing to wear it out. Remember, I was with my father. Remember, I saw his face when he gave the watch into my keeping, and struggled to express that he sent it as a token you would understand, to you. . . . For Heaven's sake, let us examine sacredly whether there is any wrong entrusted to us to set right."

There is a hint toward the end of the chapter that this mystery may have something to do with the young seamstress nicknamed "Little Dorrit." The riddle of the watch continues to be intertwined with that of Amy Dorrit. In the following passage she is telling Mrs. Clennam about her life:

---

[84] Charles Dickens, *Little Dorrit* (London: Oxford University Press, 1967). All subsequent quotations from *Little Dorrit* are taken from this edition.

"I have been here many a time when, but for you and the work you gave me, we should have wanted everything."

"We," repeated Mrs. Clennam, looking towards the watch, once her dead husband's, which always lay upon her table. (Chapter 29)

Then, in Chapter 30, Rigaud comes to the house, obviously with the intention of blackmailing the family; he doesn't say anything directly, but he takes the watch in his hands and says: "A fine old-fashioned watch." He makes other similar remarks.

Earlier, in Chapter 8, Clennam imagines his mother saying to him: "He withers away in his prison; I wither away in mine; inexorable justice is done; what do I owe on this score!"

In Chapter 15, Mrs. Clennam says in Mrs. Flintwinch's dream: "Then say no more. Say no more. Let Little Dorrit keep her secret from me, and do you keep it from me also. Let her come and go, unobserved and unquestioned. Let me suffer, and let me have what alleviation belongs to my condition. Is it so much, that you torment me like an evil spirit?"

Left alone, Arthur Clennam feels that all his old doubts and suspicions are returning to him. The riddles, of course, are interspersed throughout the novel, separated by chapters describing "everyday life," whereas the mysteries are used for the purpose of binding the parts together.

So, for example, there are descriptions of the Dorrit family in Chapters 6 and 7, but they do not include or reveal any new mysteries. The compositional function of these chapters is to impede the progress of the unfolding events. If, however, we consider them to be central to the novel, then we must note that, clamped between riddles, they bear the pressure of the plot. The descriptive chapters in Dickens usually conclude with condensed images, such as the image of "the shadows of the yard" (Chapter 6).

The Circumlocution Office and the Barnacle family are described in a similar way. Tolstoy would have called this part of the novel "details."

Let us now turn to the next mystery.

2. The Mystery of the Dreams

Having got her mistress into bed, lighted her lamp, and given her good night, Mrs. Flintwinch went to roost as usual, saving that her lord had not yet appeared. It was her lord himself who became—unlike the last theme in the mind, according to the observation of most philosophers—the subject of Mrs. Flintwinch's dream.

It seemed to her that she awoke, after sleeping some hours, and found Jeremiah not yet abed. That she looked at the candle she had left burning, and, measuring the time like king Alfred the Great, was confirmed by its wasted state in her belief that she had been asleep for some considerable period. . . .

The staircase was as wooden and solid as need be, and Affery went straight down it without any of those deviations peculiar to dreams. . . .

She expected to see Jeremiah fast asleep or in a fit, but he was calmly seated in a chair, awake, and in his usual health. But what—hey?—Lord forgive us!—Mrs. Flintwinch muttered some ejaculation to this effect, and turned giddy.

For, Mr. Flintwinch awake, was watching Mr. Flintwinch asleep. He sat on one side of the small table, looking keenly at himself on the other side with his chin sunk on his breast, snoring. The waking Flintwinch had his full front face presented to his wife; the sleeping Flintwinch was in profile. The waking Flintwinch was the old original; the sleeping Flintwinch was the double. (Chapter 4)

The double asks for wine, drinks to "her health" and leaves, taking away an iron box.

The chapter thus introduces two mysteries: the mystery of the double and the mystery of the box.

The end of this scene is rather unusual: Mrs. Flintwinch remains standing on the staircase, frightened to such an extent that she cannot bring herself to enter the room:

Consequently when he came up the staircase to bed, candle in hand, he came full upon her. He looked astonished, but said not a word. He kept his eyes upon her, and kept advancing; and she, completely under his influence, kept retiring before him. Thus, she walking backward and he walking forward, they came into their own room. They were no sooner shut in there, than Mr. Flintwinch took her by the throat, and shook her until she was black in the face.

"Why, Affery, woman—Affery!" said Mr. Flintwinch. "What have you been dreaming of? Wake up, wake up! What's the matter?"

Flintwinch then tries to convince his wife that she has been dreaming.

In terms of composition, Dickens presents some of the mysterious scenes with a special motivation—eavesdropping at night. Because the dream seems to be a reality, it is therefore possible to have a twofold construction: not a reality, but a dream.

Thus, the real situation is given in negative form. I could explain this much better by excerpting some twenty pages from the novel, but the expensiveness of paper holds me back. This construction that employs dream as a motivation is quite common in literature. In folklore, for example, it takes the following form: A maiden wanders into the house of bandits and witnesses a murder. She carries away the severed hand of the victim. The leader of the bandits asks for her hand in marriage, and during the wedding she tells of everything that she has seen. Everyone is convinced that she is talking about a dream. Then finally she shows the severed hand. The parody of this motif can be found in Vasili Zhukovsky's poem "Svetlana," in which the dream really is a dream.[85]

---

[85] Compare with "The Merchant's Daughter and the Bandits" (no. 13 in Onchukov's collection). "The bandits come to the wedding and sit in the chamber, meanwhile the young daughter describes everything that she had seen in a dream about the bandits that night. The bandits listen to her and then refute each one of her words with the following: 'An amazing dream, but that is all, my maiden.' She then identifies them by showing a severed ear." Also compare with "The Priest's Wife and the Bandits" (no. 83 in Onchukov's collection). Here the identification is achieved by showing a severed finger with a ring. "And apparently she has a finger with a ring under her bed.' 'No, no, holy Mother,' said the

Mrs. Flintwinch later confirms the first part of the negative parallel (that the dream was reality). The "severed hand" in this case is the evidence produced by Rigaud.

In Chapter 15, Mrs. Flintwinch has another dream about Mrs. Clennam having a conversation with her servant, Mr. Flintwinch. There is an allusion to some secrets.

In Chapter 30, the riddle of the double is affirmed when Rigaud takes Mr. Flintwinch for someone else.

3. The Mystery of the Inheritance

Every riddle usually has its own motivation. For example, in Poe's "The Gold-Bug," the protagonist is a man who likes to decipher codes. The exposition of the protagonist, in general, does not coincide with the beginning of the action. And this is true for *Little Dorrit*: as soon as Pancks appears we learn that he has an interest in locating the heirs to escheated properties.

> "Mr. Clennam," he then began, "I am in want of information, sir."
>
> "Connected with this firm?" asked Clennam.
>
> "No," said Pancks.
>
> "With what then, Mr. Pancks? That is to say, assuming that you want it of me."
>
> "Yes, sir; yes, I want it of you," said Pancks, "if I can persuade you to furnish it. A, B, C, D. DA, DE, DI, DO. Dictionary order. Dorrit. That's the name, sir?" (Chapter 23)

Pancks asks Clennam a few questions without revealing the purpose of his inquiry. He then pays a visit to Mrs. Clennam's house and speaks with Little Dorrit. He tells her fortune by reading her palm. He tells her about her past, about her father and uncle. He says that he sees himself in her fate, calls himself "Pancks the gipsy" and "a fortune-teller."

---

bandit. She then took out the finger with the ring from her pocket and showed it to everyone. At this point the bandit tried to run away, but was seized by the people."

Such predictions and premonitions tighten the novel.

Compare them with the premonitions in Stendhal and in *David Copperfield*. The mystery of the inheritance evolves rather consistently and continuously, in contrast to the mystery of the frame story (the secret of Arthur's mother). The next chapter is about the gathering at the house of General Agent Mr. Rugg:

> "There's a Church in London; I may as well take that. And a Family Bible; I may as well take that, too. That's two to me. Two to me," repeated Pancks, breathing hard over his cards. "Here's a Clerk at Durham for you, John, and an old seafaring gentleman at Dunstable for you, Mr. Rugg."

Pancks makes a brief appearance in Chapter 29, uttering just a few words: "Pancks the gipsy, fortune-telling." The mystery surrounding the inheritance is resolved at the end of Chapter 32:

> "You are to understand"—snorted Pancks, feverishly unfolding papers, and speaking in short high-pressure blasts of sentences, "Where's the Pedigree? Where's Schedule number four, Mr. Rugg? Oh! all right! Here we are.—You are to understand that we are this very day virtually complete. We shan't be legally for a day or two. Call it at the outside a week. We've been at it, night and day, for I don't know how long. Mr. Rugg, you know how long? Never mind. Don't say. You'll only confuse me. You shall tell her, Mr. Clennam. Not till we give you leave. Where's that rough total, Mr. Rugg? Oh! Here we are! There sir! That's what you'll have to break to her. That man's your Father of the Marshalsea!"

Just before this passage we see a wildly rejoicing Pancks, but the source of his joy is still unknown to us.

The function of this mystery, as I mentioned earlier, is to create an imbalance between Clennam and Little Dorrit: Dorrit is rich now, while Clennam is, relatively speaking, poor. More specifically, the function of the "details" of this mystery is to tie together the descriptions of Marshalsea Prison.

4. The Mystery of Mr. Merdle

Mr. Merdle is the richest of all. His shadow hovers over the novel. He thrills Dorrit, who has recently come into a fortune, and the poor inhabitants of Bleeding Heart Yard. But we find Mr. Merdle suffering from some mysterious illness. At first it seems to be a rather common illness, but gradually the signs and symptoms of a mystery emerge.

> "Do I ever say I care about anything?" asked Mr. Merdle.
>
> "Say? No! Nobody would attend to you if you did. But you show it."
>
> "Show what? What do I show?" demanded Mr. Merdle hurriedly. (Chapter 33)

In the second part of the novel, Mr. Merdle, "evasively rolling his eyes round the Chief Butler's shoes without raising them to the index of that stupendous creature's thoughts, had signified to him his intention . . ." (Part II, Chapter 12)

In Chapter 16, Mr. Merdle offers his advice and assistance to Mr. Dorrit: "'You know we may almost say we are related, sir,' said Mr. Merdle, curiously interested in the pattern of the carpet, 'and, therefore, you may consider me at your service.'"

We hear again Mr. Merdle's mysterious phrases in Chapter 24. Fanny asks him whether her governess will receive anything from her father's will:

> "*She* won't get anything," said Mr. Merdle.
>
> Fanny was delighted to hear him express the opinion. Mr. Merdle, after taking another gaze into the depths of his hat as if he thought he saw something at the bottom, rubbed his hair and slowly appended to his last remark the confirmatory words, "Oh dear no. No. Not she. Not likely."

He asks Fanny to lend him a penknife:

> "Edmund," said Mrs. Sparkler, "open (now, very carefully, I beg and beseech, for you are so very awkward) the mother-of-pearl box on my little table there, and give Mr. Merdle the mother-of-pearl penknife."
>
> "Thank you," said Mr. Merdle; "but if you have got one with a darker handle, I think I should prefer one with a darker handle."
>
> "Tortoise-shell?"
>
> "Thank you," said Mr. Merdle; "yes. I think I should prefer tortoise-shell."
>
> Edmund accordingly received instructions to open the tortoise-shell box, and give Mr. Merdle the tortoise-shell knife. On his doing so, his wife said to the master-spirit graciously:
>
> "I will forgive you, if you ink it."
>
> "I'll undertake not to ink it," said Mr. Merdle.

The following chapter describes Mr. Merdle's suicide. His secret is revealed—he was a speculator and a bankrupt who had brought thousands of people to ruin.

> The room was still hot, and the marble of the bath still warm; but the face and figure were clammy to the touch. The white marble at the bottom of the bath was veined with a dreadful red. On the ledge at the side, were an empty laudanum-bottle and a tortoise-shell handled penknife—soiled, but not with ink. (Part II, Chapter 25)

So, the little mystery of the knife and its negative parallelism (soiled not with ink, but with blood) resolves the mystery of Mr. Merdle.

The purpose of this mystery is to level the circumstances of the heroes. Dorrit is just as poor as Clennam. In addition, the "details" of the mystery "pull" the descriptions together.

5. The Mystery of the Noises in the House

In the dwindling light of a winter afternoon, Mrs. Flintwinch has the following dream:

> She thought she was in the kitchen getting the kettle ready for tea, and was warming herself with her feet upon the fender and the skirt of her gown tucked up, before the collapsed fire in the middle of the grate, bordered on either hand by a deep cold black ravine. She thought that as she sat thus, musing upon the question whether life was not for some people a rather dull invention, she was frightened by a sudden noise behind her. She thought that she had been similarly frightened once last week, and that the noise was of a mysterious kind—a sound of rustling, and of three or four quick beats like a rapid step; while a shock or tremble was communicated to her heart, as if the step had shaken the floor, or even as if she had been touched by some awful hand. She thought that this revived within her certain old fears of hers that the house was haunted; and that she flew up the kitchen stairs without knowing how she got up, to be nearer company. (Part I, Chapter 15)

Mrs. Flintwinch never says anything to attract the attention of Mr. Flintwinch or Mrs. Clennam, except on certain occasions:

> "There, Jeremiah! Now! What's that noise?"
> Then the noise, if there were any, would have ceased, and Mr. Flintwinch would snarl, turning upon her as if she had cut him down that moment against his will, "Affery, old woman, you shall have a dose, old woman, such a dose! You have been dreaming again!"

Rigaud makes his first appearance in Mrs. Clennam's house in Part I, Chapter 29:

> "Now, my dear madam," he said, as he took back his cloak and threw it on, "if you have the goodness to——what the Devil's that!"

The strangest of sounds. Evidently close at hand from the peculiar shock it communicated to the air, yet subdued as if it were far off. A tremble, a rumble, and a fall of some light dry matter.

The noises are mentioned again in the second part of the novel:

> At that moment, Mistress Affery (of course, the woman with the apron) dropped the candlestick she held, and cried out, "There! O good Lord! there it is again. Hark, Jeremiah! Now!"
> If there were any sound at all, it was so slight that she must have fallen into a confirmed habit of listening for sounds; but Mr. Dorrit believed he did hear a something, like the falling of dry leaves. (Part II, Chapter 17)

In the following passage Mrs. Flintwinch refers to Rigaud as her witness:

> "I'll tell you then," said Affery, after listening, "that the first time he ever come he heard the noises his own self." (Part II, Chapter 23)

On the following page there is a hint, although imperceptible to the reader, that the outer door cannot be opened, as if someone were holding it.

Like many mysteries, the mystery of the house has a false solution at first. The mystery of the watch finally begins to unravel. It turns out that Mrs. Clennam is not Arthur's mother. Arthur is the illegitimate son of his father's lover, who has been locked up in a mental asylum by Mrs. Clennam and her husband's uncle. The watch serves as a reminder of the need to rectify the wrong. Affery thinks that Arthur's biological mother is hidden in the house. She says:

> "Only promise me, that, if it's the poor thing that's kept here

secretly, you'll let me take charge of her and be her nurse. Only promise me that, and never be afraid of me."

Mrs. Clennam stood still for an instant, at the height of her rapid haste, saying in stern amazement:

"Kept here? She has been dead a score of years or more. Ask Flintwinch—ask *him*. They can both tell you that she died when Arthur went abroad."

"So much the worse," said Affery, with a shiver, "for she haunts the house, then. Who else rustles about it, making signals by dropping dust so softly? Who else comes and goes, and marks the walls with long crooked touches when we are all a-bed? Who else holds the door sometimes?" (Part II, Chapter 30)

As you can see, the thread with the noises is already being determined. We are now close to the true answer: the house is subsiding and threatens to collapse. But the reader doesn't know this yet.

6. Denouements

The main mystery of the novel—the mystery of the watch—has already been revealed. The secret of Arthur's birth has also been uncovered. One after another, the secondary mysteries are resolved. First, the mystery of the house is revealed. In one stroke, the novelist also eliminates Rigaud, who in essence plays the role of someone who knows the secret. So when the secret is revealed, Rigaud is discarded, because he is no longer needed.

Mrs. Clennam runs back home with Little Dorrit:

They were in the gateway. Little Dorrit, with a piercing cry, held her back.

In one swift instant the old house was before them, with the man lying smoking in the window; another thundering sound, and it heaved, surged outward, opened asunder in fifty places, collapsed, and fell. Deafened by the noise, stifled, choked, and blinded by the dust, they hid their faces and stood rooted to the spot. The dust storm, driving between them and the placid sky, parted for a moment and showed them the stars. As they looked up, wildly crying for help, the great pile of chimneys, which was then alone left standing like a tower in a whirlwind, rocked, broke, and hailed itself down upon the heap of ruin, as if every tumbling fragment were intent on burying the crushed wretch deeper. . . .

The mystery of the noises was out now; Affery, like greater people, had always been right in her facts, and always wrong in the theories she deduced from them. (Part II, Chapter 31)

It is important to note that Dickens is very consistent in his use of the mystery device in all parts of *Little Dorrit*. Even events that begin to unfold right in front of our eyes are given as mysteries. The device is thus extended.

Dorrit's love for Clennam and Clennam's love for Minnie are also presented as "mysteries" and not as simple descriptions.

It is as if the writer negates this love, while confirming it at the same time.

In Part I, Chapter 16, Clennam is glad that he has resolved not to fall in love when, in fact, he is in love.

Chapter 17 employs the same device and concludes in the following way:

The rain fell heavily on the roof, and pattered on the ground, and dripped among the evergreens and the leafless branches of the trees. The rain fell heavily, drearily. It was a night of tears.

If Clennam had not decided against falling in love with Pet; if he had had the weakness to do it; if he had, little by little, persuaded himself to set all the earnestness of his nature, all the might of his hope, and all the wealth of his matured character, on that cast; if he had done this and found that all was lost; he would have been, that night, unutterably miserable. As it was——

As it was, the rain fell heavily, drearily.

The technique of affirmation through negation is employed here in the following way: the passage presents a false interpretation of Clennam's action—he is not in love, while his actual mood is given through the metaphor of the rain.

Amy Dorrit's love for Arthur Clennam is also presented in the form of a riddle. Little Dorrit tells Maggy a fairy tale about a "tiny woman" who loved the shadow and who died without ever revealing the secret.

Dickens connects the riddle of Dorrit's love with the riddle of Pancks through the title of the chapter ("Fortune-Telling"):

> "Who's he, Little Mother?" said Maggy. She had joined her at the window and was leaning on her shoulder. "I see him come in and out often."
>
> "I have heard him called a fortune-teller," said Little Dorrit. "But I doubt if he could tell many people even their past or present fortunes."
>
> "Couldn't have told the Princess hers?" said Maggy.
>
> Little Dorrit, looking musingly down into the dark valley of the prison, shook her head.
>
> "Nor the tiny woman hers?" said Maggy.
>
> "No," said Little Dorrit, with the sunset very bright upon her. "But let us come away from the window." (Part I, Chapter 24)

The device is the same as the one in the previous excerpt: "with the sunset very bright upon her" can be read as "blushing from the excitement of hope," while "let us come away from the window" leads in a false direction: the brightness of the sunlight (blushing) depends on the change in light from the window.

Maggy recalls the secret of the Princess in Clennam's presence, during his conversation with Little Dorrit:

> "So you said that day upon the bridge. I thought of it much afterwards. Have you no secret you could entrust to me, with

hope and comfort, if you would!"

"Secret? No, I have no secret," said Little Dorrit in some trouble.

They had been speaking in low voices; more because it was natural to what they said to adopt that tone, than with any care to reserve it from Maggy at her work. All of a sudden Maggy stared again, and this time spoke:

"I say! Little Mother!"

"Yes, Maggy."

"If you an't got no secret of your own to tell him, tell him that about the Princess. *She* had a secret, you know." (Part I, Chapter 32)

Clennam understands nothing and torments Little Dorrit by telling her that someday she will fall in love. Maggy explains further:

"It was the little woman as had the secret, and she was always a spinning at her wheel. And so she says to her, why do you keep it there? And so the t'other one says to her, no I don't; and so the t'other one says to her, yes you do; and then they both goes to the cupboard, and there it is. And she wouldn't go into the Hospital, and so she died. You know, Little Mother; tell him that. For it was a reg'lar good secret, that was!" cried Maggy, hugging herself.

Clennam is still clueless. What we have here is a game that mimics the game of the peripeteia in classical tragedy: the mystery has been solved, but the heroes don't know it yet.

For the purpose of comparison, let us look at how Dickens uses the device of recognition in *The Cricket on the Hearth*. The first hint that the mysterious elderly stranger is in disguise is given in the incoherent words of the nanny:

"Did its mothers make it up a Beds then!" cried Miss Slowboy to the Baby; "and did its hair grow brown and curly, when its caps was lifted off, and frighten it, a precious Pets, a-sitting by the fires!"

With that unaccountable attraction of the mind to trifles, which is often incidental to a state of doubt and confusion, the Carrier, as he walked slowly to and fro, found himself mentally repeating even these absurd words, many times. So many times that he got them by heart, and was still conning them over and over, like a lesson, when Tilly, after administering as much friction to the little bald head with her hand as she thought wholesome (according to the practice of nurses), had once more tied the Baby's cap on.

"And frighten it, a precious Pets, a-sitting by the fires. What frightened Dot, I wonder!" mused the Carrier, pacing to and fro. ("Chirp the First")[86]

Here the clue (of the disguise) has been provided, but it has not been recognized. The non-recognition is motivated by the incoherence of the form (plural, etc.).

On the stage and in the novel, the mystery or recognition is nearly always given first as a hint. For example, the presence of the Boffin couple at the wedding of John Harmon and Bella Wilfer in *Our Mutual Friend* is hinted at via "a mysterious rustling and a stealthy movement somewhere in the remote neighborhood of the organ" (Book IV, Chapter 4: "A Runaway Match").[87]

In plays, the character in disguise usually reveals himself to the audience first and only then does he begin his act on the stage.

Chaplin's reversal of this device is quite interesting.

He was expected to perform at a well-known venue, but his name was not announced in the program.

One of the performers in the show was a young man in a tailcoat who read a banal poem. He had impeccable poise. But when he turned his back to the audience and walked off the stage, or

---

[86] Charles Dickens, "The Cricket on the Hearth" in *A Christmas Carol and Other Christmas Books*, ed. Robert Douglas-Fairhurst (London: Oxford University Press, 2006).

[87] Charles Dickens, *Our Mutual Friend* (London: Oxford University Press, 1967).

rather shuffled, with his feet turned outwards, in Chaplin's inimitable style, the audience finally recognized Chaplin.

This is analogous to the device of the false solution.

The solution is given in a conversation between John, who is in love with Amy Dorrit, and Clennam who has landed in the debtors' prison.

> "Mr. Clennam, do you mean to say that you don't know?"
>
> "What, John?"
>
> "Lord," said Young John, appealing with a gasp to the spikes on the wall. "He says, What!"
>
> Clennam looked at the spikes, and looked at John; and looked at the spikes, and looked at John.
>
> "He says What! And what is more," exclaimed Young John, surveying him in a doleful maze, "he appears to mean it! Do you see this window, sir?"
>
> "Of course I see this window."
>
> "See this room?"
>
> "Why, of course I see this room."
>
> "That wall opposite, and that yard down below? They have all been witnesses of it, from day to day, from night to night, from week to week, from month to month. For how often have I seen Miss Dorrit here when she has not seen me!"
>
> "Witnesses of what?" said Clennam.
>
> "Of Miss Dorrit's love."
>
> "For whom?"
>
> "You," said John. (Part II, Chapter 27)

But this semantic solution does not yet solve the verbal riddle.

The equation (Dorrit and Clennam – tiny woman = shadow) remains unsolved. The theme of the shadow reappears via Maggy.

Love is one step away, but Clennam rejects it. There is an imbalance in their relationship (like the one between Eugene Onegin and Tatyana Larina).

Maggy, who had fallen into very low spirits, here cried, "Oh get him into a hospital; do get him into a hospital, Mother! He'll never look like hisself again, if he an't got into a hospital. And then the little woman as was always a spinning at her wheel, she can go to the cupboard with the Princess, and say, what do you keep the Chicking there for?" (Part II, Chapter 29)

Here the theme has been complicated by Maggy's delirious outbursts (she had been treated in a hospital, and the hospital and chickens are her paradise). It's the same device as the one used in *The Cricket on the Hearth*.

The closure of the plot, which may be called "The Love between Arthur and Dorrit, and the Obstacle to their Marriage," is presented in rather a banal way via Mr. Merdle's mystery. Old Dorrit entrusted his entire fortune to Mr. Merdle, and now Little Dorrit is ruined. The situation has balanced out. The resolution follows suit. What still remains unsolved is the framing mystery of the watch.

In Turgenev's *Home of the Gentry*, the imbalance is constructed in the following way: Lavretsky cannot love Liza, as he is already married. He then finds himself free due to a newspaper report about his wife's death. His wife's return (the rumor of her death was false) restores the difficulty of the situation. A false ending is necessary because the composition is left unresolved. Let me remind the reader of what I mean by a false ending: it is when the author ends the work with a new motif, creating a parallel with the old one. Here is the false ending of *Home of the Gentry*:

Lavretsky went out of the house into the garden, and sat down on the bench that was so familiar to him—and in that dear place, face to face with the house where for the last time he had vainly stretched out his hands to promised cup in which there bubbles and sparkles the golden wine of pleasure— he, a lonely, homeless, wanderer, his ears filled with the gay shouts of a younger generation that had already taken his place, looked back upon his life. He grew sad at heart, but not oppressed and not ashamed: there were things to regret, nothing to be ashamed of. "Play on, enjoy yourselves, grow up, forces of youth," he thought, and there was no bitterness in his thoughts.[88]

In Knut Hamsun, failed love is presented entirely as a psychological motivation. In *Pan*, Lieutenant Glahn and Edvarda love each other, but when one says "yes," the other says "no." I don't mean to say, of course, that Hamsun's motivation or composition is better or more artistic than that of Ariosto or Pushkin. It is simply different. Maybe Hamsun's device will seem preposterous in the future, just as, for instance, the tendency of some nineteenth-century artists to conceal their technique seems strange to us today.

Connection Between Parallels as a Mystery

The device of several simultaneous actions, the connection of which the author does not immediately make apparent, can be understood as an impediment, and as a distinctive continuation of the mystery technique.

That is how *Little Dorrit* begins. The novel has two simultaneous plot threads—the Rigaud thread and the Clennam thread. The beginning of each thread is developed into a full chapter.

We encounter Rigaud and John Baptist in Chapter 1, which is titled "Sun and Shadow." They are in prison—Rigaud for murder and John Baptist for contraband trade. Rigaud is led to trial. The crowd gathered outside the prison is raging and wants to tear him to pieces. However, neither Rigaud nor his fellow inmate are the main characters of the novel.

This manner of beginning a novel with a minor character rather

---

[88] Ivan Turgenev, *Home of the Gentry*, (trans. Richard Freeborn. Penguin, 1974).

than the main hero is common to Dickens. He does the same in *Nicholas Nickleby, Oliver Twist, Our Mutual Friend,* and *Martin Chuzzlewit.* This device is quite possibly connected with the riddle technique.

The second group of characters is presented in the second chapter, titled "Fellow Travelers." This chapter is connected with the first through the statement, "'No more of yesterday's howling, over yonder, to-day, Sir; is there?'"

Little Dorrit is a multilayered novel. In order to connect the various levels of the work, it was necessary to connect the characters in some artificial way at the beginning of the novel. Hence, Dickens came up with the quarantine quarters. The quarantine quarters are analogous to the inn or abbey in a collection of stories (such as *The Heptameron* of Marguerite of Navarre or *The Canterbury Tales*). Mr. and Mrs. Meagles, their daughter Minnie (Pet), the maid whom everyone calls Tattycoram, Mr. Clennam, and Miss Wade are all placed in the quarantine quarters before they can depart to different destinations.

A similar device is used in *Our Mutual Friend.* In the first chapter, titled "On the Look Out," we are introduced to Gaffer and his daughter Lizzie; they are towing a corpse attached to their boat. The chapter makes use of the mystery device: we do not know precisely what these people on the boat are searching for, and the description of the corpse is given negatively:

> Lizzie's father, composing himself into the easy attitude of one who had asserted the high moralities and taken an unassailable position, slowly lighted a pipe, and smoked, and took a survey of what he had in tow. What he had in tow, lunged itself at him sometimes in an awful manner when the boat was checked, and sometimes seemed to try to wrench itself away, though for the most part it followed submissively. A neophyte might have fancied that the ripples passing over it were dreadfully like faint changes of expression on a sightless face; but Gaffer was no neophyte and had no fancies.

Compare this with the "fishing" scene in *A Tale of Two Cities* where one of the protagonists digs up corpses to sell them to scientists.

The second chapter of *Our Mutual Friend*, titled "The Man from Somewhere," describes the home of the Veneerings. It introduces the lawyer Mortimer and fellow members of an inner circle of high society, who later in the novel serve as a "chorus," similar to Anna Pavlovna's salon in *War and Peace*.

The second chapter is connected back to the first chapter toward its end, where we learn that a certain man who was due to come into a very large fortune has drowned. We immediately link his fate to the corpse towed by the boat.

In the third chapter, titled "Another Man," Dickens introduces a new character, Julius Handford. In the fifth chapter he introduces the Boffin family, in the sixth chapter the Wilfer family, and so on.

These plot threads hold out until the end of the novel and don't intersect so much as occasionally touch each other.

The plot threads in *A Tale of Two Cities* intersect even less. We perceive the transition from one plot thread to another, without obvious links between them, as some kind of a riddle. The identification of characters from different plot threads has been pushed back from the beginning of the novel to the middle.

It seems that today we are on the eve of a revival of the mystery novel. There is great interest in complex and intricate constructs. The technique of mystery is refracted rather remarkably in Andrei Bely.

Let us take a brief look at Bely's revival of the mystery technique in *Kotik Letaev*.

There are two planes in this work: *roi* (swarm) and *stroi* (form). "Swarm" represents life *before* the moment of becoming, whereas "form" is life that has already come into being.

"Swarm" consists of either a series of metaphors or puns. We are first introduced to "swarm" and then to "form"—i.e. an inversion. The pun is presented as a riddle. Sometimes we also get the mystery technique in its purest form:

The Lion

Among the strangest deceptions mistily glinting at me, a very strange one appears before me: before me looms a maned lion's snout; the time to shout had come; everything is kind of sandy yellow; from there the ragged fur calmly looks at me; and—the snout: there is a shout:

—"Lion's coming . . ."

. . . .

In this strange event all the sullenly flowing images conglomerated for the first time; and were sliced open by the deceptive light of looming darkness; rays had illuminated the labyrinths; in the midst of the yellow, sunny dry spots I recognized myself: here it is—a circle; along its edges are little benches; on them sit the dark images of women, like—images of night; they are nannies, and nearby in the light—children are pressed to their dark skirts; multinosed curiosity is in the air; and in the midst of it all is a *Lion*—

—(Later I used to see a yellow sand circle—between the Arbat and Dog Square, and to this day when passing by from Dog Square, you will see a place encircled with greenery; there the silent nannies sit; and—the children run around) . . . (Part I, "The Lion")[89]

This is the first clue to the riddle.

The lion's image reappears in the same chapter: " . . . from under the circle the big-headed animal, the *lion*, began to crawl out onto the circle toward us: and again everything—disappeared."

And then the mystery is solved. Twenty years later, the author is talking to a friend at the university:

I sketch my childhood life in bright colors: the old woman and the reptiles; I talk about the circle and the *lion*: and his yellow snout . . .

A fellow student laughs:

---

[89] Andrei Bely, *Kotik Letaev*, trans. Gerald J. Janecek (Northwestern University Press, 1999). All subsequent quotations from *Kotik Letaev* are taken from this translation.

—"Come now . . . Your *lion snout* is a fantasy."

—"Well, yes: a dream . . ."

—"Not a dream, but a fantasy: a fabrication . . ."

—"I assure you: I did see it in a dream."

—"The point is that you didn't see it in a dream . . ."

—"?"

—"You simply saw a Saint Bernard . . ."

—"A lion . . ."

—"Well, yes, 'Lion' . . ."

—"?"

—"That is, 'Lion,' the Saint Bernard . . ."

—"What do you mean?"

—"I remember this 'Lion' . . ."

—"?"

—"I remember the yellow snout . . . not a lion's but—a dog's . . ."

—"??"

—"Your lion snout is a fantasy: it belongs to a Saint Bernard by the name of 'Lion.'"

—"And how do you know?"

—"When I was a child, I lived near Dog Square for a while too . . . They took me out for walks—on the circle; I saw 'Lion' there too . . . He was a good-natured dog; sometimes he would run out on the circle; he carried a whip in his teeth; we were afraid of him: we would run off screaming . . ."

—"Do you remember someone screaming 'Lion's —coming'?"

—"Of course I remember . . ." (Part I, "After Twenty Years—after Thirty-two Years")

This is followed by a reconfirmation of "Lion" as something mystical.

But this is not an exceptional device either.

It is fairly conventional to confirm a metaphoric or fantastical axis after the exposition of the factual axis.

This is occasionally followed by a second and final solution.

Let me give two examples from Turgenev.

The solutions to the mysteries in *Klara Milich* (*After Death*) are constructed according to the first type—the lock of hair in the hand is an irreducible remainder, as it were. The denouement refutes itself.

Of the second type is the story "Knock, Knock, Knock": the first riddle of the knock has been clarified, but the riddle of the "name" remains unsolved (one of the characters hears a mysterious voice calling his name). The mystery is revealed at the end: the voice belonged to the girlfriend of the village peddler who had the same name as the main protagonist (the officer who is now dead).

In Bely, however, we are dealing with the mystery technique in its purest form (take *Petersburg*, for example).

The successors and imitators of Bely, particularly Boris Pilnyak, have further developed the device of parallelism—the kind of parallelism in which the connection between the axes is pushed aside and concealed. These works tend to give the impression of having a complex structure—in reality, however, they are quite elementary. The connection between the parts is given either through the simplest device of "kinship bonds" or the episodic appearance of a character from one axis in another axis (see, for example, "The Tale of St. Petersburg," "Ryazan-Apple," and "The Snowstorm"). It would be worthwhile to trace Pilnyak's accretion of stories into a novel.

I am going to write a separate book on contemporary Russian prose, and at this point I wish only to assert, rather indiscriminately, that the mystery technique is likely to play a decisive role in the future novel, as it has already made its way into works constructed on the principle of parallelism.

There is a growing interest in plot. The time of the Tolstoyan device seems to be over, where a story (such as *The Death of Ivan Ilych*) might start with a death and not bother with "what happens next."

Tolstoy himself liked the works of Alexandre Dumas very much and certainly had a sense of plot, but his focus was on something else.

Both the solution and the riddle are important in a mystery novel.

The riddle makes it possible to accentuate the exposition, to estrange it, to strain the reader's attention—the main goal is not to let the reader recognize the object. A recognized object is not so terrible any more. For this reason, in Charles Maturin's novel *Melmoth the Wanderer*, we are unable to uncover the "mystery" of Melmoth's proposal, which he makes to people living in terrible conditions—for example, to prisoners of the Inquisition, people dying of starvation and selling their own blood, inmates of an insane asylum, people lost in underground passages, and so on. The manuscript breaks off each time the action arrives at the moment of the actual proposal (the novel consists of separate parts, connected with each other in intricate ways).

For many novelists the task of solving a mystery is a burdensome tradition, and yet they do not resort to fantastic solutions. If they do introduce fantasy, then it is only at the end, during the denouement. The fantastic element is presented as the cause of action, but rarely features during the action itself. And even when it does, it is presented in a special way, as a prediction, for example, helping the novel develop against the backdrop of a certain inevitability.

Matthew Lewis's *The Monk* includes fantastic elements and characters such as Lucifer and his Attendant Spirit and the ghost of the Bleeding Nun. Lucifer carries the monk away at the end of the novel and recounts to him the whole intrigue.

This revelation of the intrigue is by no means accidental in the novel. Dickens, with his complex plot structures that do not unfold through action, is often compelled to resort to such devices.

This is how the mystery of the watch is resolved in *Little Dorrit*; it is typical that in order to elucidate it Dickens gathers together everyone in one room. The device is used by many novelists and has been parodied by Veniamin Kaverin in his story "Chronicle of the City of Leipzig in the Year 18—."

The protagonists in *Little Dorrit* are quite literally dragged into the room by their collars. Rigaud is escorted like this to Mrs. Clennam's house by Pancks and John Baptist.

> "And now," said Mr. Pancks, whose eye had often stealthily wandered to the window-seat and the stocking that was being mended there, "I've only one other word to say before I go. If Mr. Clennam was here . . . he would say, 'Affery, tell your dreams!'" (Part II, Chapter 30)

The denouement is constructed in the following way: Affery describes her dreams. The dreams represent a new ironic motivation, estranging the old device of eavesdropping. In Dickens, the eavesdroppers are usually the clerks (*Nicholas Nickleby*) and occasionally the main characters.

In Dostoevsky's *The Adolescent*, eavesdropping is presented as something that happens by accident. This is an innovation of the device.

The main artificiality of the denouement in *Little Dorrit* is that it takes place without any outside witnesses, and the characters tell each other what they already know all too well. Affery, in this case, cannot be considered to be an eavesdropper.

The denouement in *Our Mutual Friend* is organized more successfully. There, too, everyone is brought together and the secret of the bottle is revealed to Wegg, who is then thrown out of the house; the whole story, from the very beginning, is then recounted to John Harmon's wife.

The denouement of *Martin Chuzzlewit* is organized in a similar way.

The leading characters are all gathered in one place. Old Martin (the trickster and director of the whole novel) explains all the riddles that he himself had constructed.

Let me now cite the denouement of *Little Dorrit*:

> The determined voice of Mrs. Clennam echoed "Stop!"
> Jeremiah had stopped already.
>   "It is closing in, Flintwinch. Let her alone. Affery, do you
> turn against me after these many years?" (Part II, Chapter 30)

This is followed by an unravelling of the riddles. We first find out
what Rigaud needs from the Clennam household and why he
disappeared when he did, making people search for him.

It turns out that he knew a secret, wanted money for keeping
the secret, and when he wasn't given anything, he left with the
intention to blackmail.

Rigaud takes Mrs. Clennam's wrist to check her pulse as he
proceeds to relate "a secret history of a house."

Rigaud's story and Mrs. Clennam's revelation of the secrets of
the house take up approximately twenty-four pages of printed text
and unfortunately cannot be quoted in their entirety here.

Mrs. Clennam's revelation is motivated by the fact that she does
not wish to hear her story from the mouth of a scoundrel.

I now turn to the analysis of the denouement.

First to be solved is the mystery of Affery's dreams.

Rigaud commences "a history of a strange marriage, and a
strange mother."

Jeremiah Flintwinch tries to interrupt, but Affery cries out:

> "Jeremiah, keep off from me! I've heerd, in my dreams, of
> Arthur's father and his uncle. He's a talking of them. It was
> before my time here; but I've heerd in my dreams that Arthur's
> father was a poor, irresolute, frightened chap, who had had
> everything but his orphan life scared out of him when he was
> young, and that he had no voice in the choice of his wife even,
> but his uncle chose her. There she sits! I heerd it in my dreams,
> and you said it to her own self." (Part II, Chapter 30)

Rigaud continues: The auspicious nuptials take place; the newly married come home to their charming mansion. Soon the young wife makes a singular and terrible discovery:

> "Thereupon, full of anger, full of jealousy, full of vengeance, she forms—see you, madame!—a scheme of retribution, the weight of which she ingeniously forces her crushed husband to bear himself, as well as execute upon her enemy. What superior intelligence!"
>
> "Keep off, Jeremiah!" cried the palpitating Affery, taking her apron from her mouth again. "But it was one of my dreams that you told her, when you quarreled with her one winter evening at dusk—there she sits and you looking at her—that she oughtn't to have let Arthur when he come home, suspect his father only."

You are already familiar with the technique of interruption. Several secrets are woven into one and exposed.

Mrs. Clennam then breaks her silence and begins to talk. It turns out that Arthur is not her son, but the son of her husband's lover. The mystery of the watch is revealed.

> She turned the watch upon the table, and opened it, and, with an unsoftening face, looked at the worked letters within.
>
> "They did *not* forget."

It appears that the watch was sent to Mrs. Clennam as a reminder.

Little Dorrit's secret is revealed here too.

Arthur's father's uncle, Mr. Gilbert Clennam, repented on his deathbed and left, according to Rigaud, "'One thousand guineas to the little beauty you slowly hunted to death. One thousand guineas to the youngest daughter her patron might have at fifty, or (if he had none) brother's youngest daughter, on her coming of age.'"

This patron was Frederick Dorrit, Amy's uncle.

I should probably not repeat the whole story here and limit myself only to revealing the mystery of the double, who turns out to be Mr. Flintwinch's brother.

We can now make the following remark. As you can see, the connection between Little Dorrit and Arthur's secret is very weak. She is the niece of Arthur's mother's patron. Indeed, her role in this mystery is purely formal and not very effective. The will of Gilbert Clennam is awfully contrived.

The secret, in essence, is not part of the novel's plot; it has been appended to the plot. Arthur's question about his biological mother is very important to him, yet he never finds out who she was.

Mrs. Clennam gives the documents containing information about this secret to Amy Dorrit, and the latter has them burned by her husband, Arthur Clennam:

> "I want you to burn something for me."
>
> "What?"
>
> "Only this folded paper. If you will put it in the fire with your own hand, just as it is, my fancy will be gratified."
>
> "Superstitious, darling Little Dorrit? Is it a charm?"
>
> "It is anything you like best, my own," she answered, laughing with glistening eyes and standing on tiptoe to kiss him, "if you will only humor me when the fire burns up." . . .
>
> "You can say (if you don't mind) 'I love you!'" answered Little Dorrit. So he said it, and the paper burned away. (Part II, Chapter 34)

The secret is threaded throughout the entire novel, although it does not serve as a basis for the novel's action. It is left unrevealed to the only person who would supposedly be interested in it—Arthur Clennam.

The author didn't really need a mystery, in effect, but wanted to accentuate the mysteriousness of the action.

Rigaud's mystery is interwoven with the main mystery of the birth. Rigaud is the one who knows the secret. According to the author's design, he frames all the actions. However, this seems to have remained an intention that was not fully realized.

Rigaud surfaces in the most incongruous situations. It is perhaps interesting to see how Dickens underscores his connection to all the main characters of the novel:

> Throwing back his head in emptying his glass, he cast his eyes upon the travelers' book, which lay on the piano, open, with pens and ink beside it, as if the night's names had been registered when he was absent. Taking it in his hand, he read these entries.

> William Dorrit, Esquire
> Frederick Dorrit, Esquire
> Edward Dorrit, Esquire
> Miss Dorrit
> Miss Amy Dorrit
> Mrs. General
> } And suite. From France to Italy.
> Mr. and Mrs. Henry Gowan. From France to Italy.

> To which he added, in a small complicated hand, ending with a long lean flourish, not unlike a lasso thrown at all the rest of the names:
> Blandois. Paris. From France to Italy.
> And then, with his nose coming down over his moustache, and his moustache going up and under his nose, repaired to his allotted cell. (Part II, Chapter 1)

This grimace is none other than the writer's "inscription."

Rigaud has just adopted a new name here. Each time the author brings him onto the stage, while continuing to employ the technique of mystery in all the details of the novel, he puts new makeup on him, as it were. But we recognize Rigaud, either

by the song he had picked up in prison ("Who passes by this road
so late?") or by his smile. This is how the song is introduced into
the novel—it is sung by the jailer's young daughter as part of her
game:

> "Who passes by this road so late?
>   Compagnon de la Majolaine!
> Who passes by this road so late?
>   Always gay!"

John Baptist then joins in (though a little hoarsely):

> "Of all the king's knights 'tis the flower,
>   Compagnon de la Majolaine!
> Of all the king's knights 'tis the flower,
>   Always gay!" (Part I, Chapter 1)

Later this song becomes Rigaud's—we recognize him by it. The
author perhaps chose this song because it is a children's song and,
at the same time, it is "boastful." The boastfulness is characteristic of Rigaud, while the childishness—emphasized by the fact
that it was first sung by a child—is necessary for the creation of
a contrast.

I am afraid that my analysis is becoming overly detail-oriented
and interesting only to specialists; as it is difficult for a non-spe-
cialist to discern the general laws of art in every trifling detail, and
I am not a storyteller, but a demonstrator.

Nevertheless, I will give you one more detail. When Rigaud
appears in his new role, the author first describes him by his "secondary sign," nobody can tell whether he is handsome or ugly,
and only then does he unfold the second sign—we recognize him
after the second indication (Part I, Chapter 11).

Here we have what is commonly known in art as a stepped
construction.

The same is true with the mystery of the noises in the house.

By confusing us with Affery's intentionally misleading story and keeping us from the true solution, Dickens keeps producing new technical details: first, a simple noise, then a more specific sound of a rumble and a fall of some light dry matter, then a sound of rustling, "like the falling of dry leaves" (Part II, Chapter 17). Then the door will not open. On the one hand, we have Affery's false lead (that someone is "kept here secretly"), on the other hand, the evidence that she produces is very technical and precise:

"Who else comes and goes, and marks the walls with long crooked touches when we are all a-bed?" (Part II, Chapter 30)

But let us return to Rigaud, who slipped away from us into the stepped construction.

Rigaud himself is nothing more than a thief of documents; he is the passive carrier of a secret.

He does not have "his own plot," as Svidrigailov does in *Crime and Punishment*, for example.

Miss Wade plays even more of an ancillary role.

How can we explain the success of the mystery novel—from Ann Radcliffe to Charles Dickens?

This is how I see it. The adventure novel had become obsolete. They were trying to revive it with satire. The elements of the adventure novel in Swift (*Gulliver's Travels*) already had a purely ancillary role.

An epoch of crisis followed. Fielding parodied the old novel in *Tom Jones* by introducing an immoral protagonist. Instead of the traditional faithfulness of the lover subjected to various adventures, we have the happy escapades of Tom Jones.

Sterne carried out a much more radical parody. He parodied the very structure of the novel by rethinking all its devices. Simultaneously, a younger genre—the letter—began to rear its head and aspire to canonization. This was achieved by Samuel Richardson.

As legend goes, Richardson wanted to write a new letter-writing manual, but ended up writing an epistolary novel instead.

This period also marked the rise of the horror story, the Pinkertons of that era; Ann Radcliffe and Charles Maturin gave birth to the Gothic novel.

The old novel attempted to extend the longevity of its devices by introducing a parallelism of intrigues.

It was convenient to use the technique of the mystery novel to connect several parallel intrigues.

This led to the creation of complex Dickensian structures.

The mystery novel allowed for the inclusion of long descriptions of everyday life, which, while primarily serving as impediments, relieved the pressure of the plot and were perceived as part of the artistic work. The descriptions of the debtors' prison, the Circumlocution Office, and Bleeding Heart Yard were inserted into *Little Dorrit* with this in mind. And this is why the mystery novel was later incorporated into the "social novel."

Today, as I have already noted, the mystery technique is employed by young Russian writers Boris Pilnyak, Mikhail Slonimsky ("Warsaw"), and Veniamin Kaverin. Kaverin borrows the Dickensian denouement that includes all the main characters—not for the purpose of reminiscence, but as parody.

> "Enough," I said, finally entering the shop. "What is there to be confused about? I don't get it. And it's stupid to get excited over so trivial a thing."
>
> I took the big lamp with the blue lampshade and turned on its bright light to look closely at those present one last time before departing.
>
> "That's enough from you, storyteller!" Frau Bach grumbled. "Why are you bossing people around like it's your own house?!"
>
> "Be quiet, Frau Bach," I said, keeping my cool. "I need to say a few words to all of you, before bidding you farewell."
>
> I stood up on the chair, waved my arms, and said:

"Attention!" and immediately every face turned to me.

"Attention! This is the final chapter, my dear friends, and soon we will have to part. I have come to love each and every one of you, and this separation is going to be very difficult for me. But time moves on, the plot has been exhausted, and nothing could be more boring than to revive the figurine again, turn it around again, and then marry him off to the virtuous . . ."

"If I may be so bold as to suggest," a stranger interrupted, "that it would be very helpful, dear storyteller, if you gave a few explanations first."

"Really?" I said, lifting my eyebrows in surprise. "Is there something that seems unclear to you?"

"May I inquire," the stranger continued with a polite, but cunning smile, "about the charlatan, who . . ."

"Shush!" I stopped him with a cautious whisper. "Do not say a word about the charlatan. If I were you, my dear friend, I would have asked why the professor fell silent."

"You poured some kind of poison into the envelope," said Bor.

"That's nonsense," I replied. "You are an irritating young man, Robert Bor. The professor fell silent, because . . ." But here old Frau Bach turned off the lamp. I carefully climbed down from the chair in the dark, tenderly shook the hands of all present and walked out.[90]

Here Kaverin bares the Dickensian device: the main characters of the work are gathered in a room, but the action is explained by the author himself and not by one of the characters, as it is usually done in Dickens. And the story does not offer a denouement per se, but only points at the device of its resolution. There is no denouement; the motivation is parodistic.

---

[90] Veniamin Kaverin, "Khronika goroda Leiptsiga za 18— god" [Chronicle of the City of Leipzig in the Year 18—], 1922.

THE PARODY NOVEL

Sterne's *Tristram Shandy*

I do not propose to analyze Laurence Sterne's novel in this chapter, but rather to use it to illustrate the general laws of plot. Sterne was an extreme revolutionary of form. His characteristic feature was the baring of the literary device. The artistic form is simply presented as such, without any kind of motivation. The difference between a conventional novel and a novel by Sterne is exactly the same as between a conventional poem, with its phonic instrumentation, and a Futurist poem written in a transrational language (*zaum*). Nothing has yet been written about Sterne, or if there has been, then only a few banalities.

Your first impression upon picking up Sterne's *Tristram Shandy* and starting to read it is one of chaos.

The action is constantly interrupted; the author is constantly going backward or leaping forward; the main storyline, which cannot immediately be found, is constantly intercepted by dozens of pages filled with bizarre reflections about the influence of one's nose or name on one's character, or discussions about fortifications.

The beginning of the book sets the tone of an autobiography, but it strays from its course and becomes a description of the hero's birth. However, the hero can't get born, being pushed aside by peripheral material squeezing into the novel. The book turns into an account of a single day. As Sterne himself explains:

> I will not finish that sentence till I have made an observation upon the strange state of affairs between the reader and myself, just as things stand at present——an observation never applicable before to any one biographical writer since the creation of the world, but to myself——and I believe will never hold good to any other, until its final destruction——and therefore, for the very novelty of it alone, it must be worth your worships attending to.
>
> I am this month one whole year older than I was this time twelve-month; and having got, as you perceive, almost into the middle of my fourth volume——and no farther than to my first day's life——'tis demonstrative that I have three hundred and sixty-four days more life to write just now, than when I first set out; so that instead of advancing, as a common writer, in my work with what I have been doing at it——on the contrary, I am just thrown so many volumes back—— (Volume IV, Chapter 13)[91]

But as you begin to examine the structure of the book, you see first of all that this disorder is intentional—it has its own poetics. It is as logical as a painting by Picasso.

Everything in the book has been displaced and rearranged. The dedication appears on page 15, contrary to the three basic requirements of content, form, and place.

The preface also appears in an unusual place. It takes up nearly eleven pages and is not located at the beginning of the book, but in Volume III, Chapter 20. The placement of the preface is motivated in the following way: "All my heroes are off my hands;—— 'tis the first time I have had a moment to spare,——and I'll make use of it, and write my preface."

---

[91] Laurence Sterne, *The Life and Opinions of Tristram Shandy, Gentleman*, ed. James Aiken Work (New York: Odyssey Press, 1940). All subsequent quotations from *Tristram Shandy* are taken from this edition.

The preface is, of course, written as intricately as possible. But the crowning rearrangement in *Tristram Shandy* is the transposition of chapters. So, for example, Chapters 18 and 19 of Volume IX come after Chapter 25. This is how the transposition of the chapters is motivated: "All I wish is, that it may be a lesson to the world, '*to let people tell their stories their own way.*'"

But this transposition of chapters bares another primary Sternean device—that of decelerating the transposition of the action.

Sterne introduces an anecdote at the beginning of the novel about a sexual act that is interrupted by a question. Here is how the anecdote is inserted. Tristram Shandy's father has relations with his wife on the first Sunday of every month and he also winds the house-clock on that same evening in order to get his domestic duties "out of the way at one time, and be no more plagued and pester'd with them the rest of the month" (Volume I, Chapter 4).

This, however, has caused an inevitable association in his wife's mind: she thinks of something completely different when she hears the clock being wound up, and vice versa. So quite naturally, she interrupts her husband's act with the question: "*Pray my Dear, . . . have you not forgot to wind up the clock?*" (Volume I, Chapter 1).

The anecdote is introduced into the work in the following manner: first, a general remark is made about the inattentiveness of the parents, then the mother asks her question, which seems unrelated to anything at this point. We mistakenly assume that she has interrupted her husband's speech. Sterne plays with our assumption:

> *Good G—!* cried my father, making an exclamation, but taking care to moderate his voice at the same time,——*Did ever woman, since the creation of the world, interrupt a man with such a silly question?* Pray, what was your father saying?—— Nothing. (Volume I, Chapter 1)

This is followed by a discussion of the *homunculus* (fetus), spiced up with anecdotal allusions to its legal rights.

Only in Chapter 4 do we get an explanation of the whole situation and a full description of the father's strange punctuality in his family affairs.

So, from the very beginning of the novel, we see in *Tristram Shandy* a temporal dislocation. The causes are given after the effects; thus, the author himself prepares the ground for false leads. Sterne uses this device constantly. The punning motif of "coitus," connected with that particular day, threads throughout the novel, reappearing here and there to connect the different parts of this masterfully constructed and unusually complicated work.

If we were to visualize this schematically, it would look something like the following. Let's say a cone symbolizes an event, and its apex symbolizes the causative moment. In a conventional novel, such a cone is attached to the main storyline by its apex. In Sterne, however, the cone is attached to the main storyline by its base, so that we immediately fall into a swarm of implications.

Such temporal transpositions appear frequently in the poetics of the novel in general. Consider, for example, the temporal transposition in Turgenev's *Home of the Gentry*, which is motivated by Lavretsky's reminiscence, or in Goncharov's "Oblomov's Dream." The temporal transpositions in Gogol's *Dead Souls* (Chichikov's childhood and Tentetnikov's upbringing) appear to be without motivation. Sterne, however, employs this device throughout the novel.

The exposition, the preparation of a character always occurs after we have paused in puzzlement at a strange word or exclamation uttered by the new character.

It is also an example of the device being bared. Pushkin, in his "Boldino fables" (for example, in the story "The Shot"), makes extensive use of temporal transposition.[92] At first, we see Silvio practicing shooting, then we hear about the unfinished duel, and then we meet the count, Silvio's enemy, and find out

---

[92] *The Tales of Belkin.* Shklovsky is referencing Boris Eikhenbaum's analysis of "The Shot" and "The Snowstorm" in the 1919 article "Boldinskie pobasenki Pushkina" ("The Boldino Fables of Pushkin"). [—Trans.]

the denouement of the story. The parts appear in the following sequence: II—I—III. But this rearrangement has a motivation, while Sterne's transposition is an end in itself: to bare the device.

> What I have to inform you, comes, I own, a little out of its due course;———for it should have been told a hundred and fifty pages ago, but that I foresaw then 'twould come in pat hereafter, and be of more advantage here than elsewhere. (Volume II, Chapter 19)

Sterne even bares the device of stitching together separate stories to make the novel. In general, he accentuates the very structure of the novel; for him, the content of the novel is precisely the awareness of the form through its violation.

I have already outlined several canonical devices for integrating stories into a novel in my chapter on *Don Quixote*.

Sterne employs other methods, or, when using an old one, does not hide its conventionality, but rather thrusts it into the open and plays with it.

In a conventional novel an inset story is interrupted by the main storyline. If there are two or more storylines in the novel, their fragments alternate with one another, as in *Don Quixote*, in which scenes depicting the knight's adventures at the duke's court alternate with scenes depicting the governorship of Sancho Panza. Zieliński observes something entirely different in Homer: he never depicts two simultaneous actions. They are always presented in sequential order, even if the course of events demands simultaneity. The only simultaneous actions permitted are the action of one hero, while the other "rests"—i.e. a state of inaction.

Sterne allowed simultaneous actions, but parodied the unfolding of the story and the intrusion of the new material into it.

In the first part of the novel, Tristram Shandy's birth is used as material for development. The description of the birth spans some two hundred pages, which nevertheless contain almost nothing about the actual birth of Tristram Shandy. Instead, what really unfolds is the conversation between the hero's father and his uncle Toby:

> ——I wonder what's all that noise, and running backwards and forwards for, above stairs, quoth my father, addressing himself, after an hour and a half's silence, to my uncle *Toby*,——who, you must know, was sitting on the opposite side of the fire, smoking his social pipe all the time, in mute contemplation of a new pair of black plush-breeches which he had got on;——What can they be doing, brother? quoth my father,——we can scarce hear ourselves talk.
>
> I think, replied my uncle *Toby*, taking his pipe from his mouth, and striking the head of it two or three times upon the nail of his left thumb, as he began his sentence,——I think, says he:——But to enter rightly into my uncle *Toby*'s sentiments upon this matter, you must be made to enter first a little into his character, the out-lines of which I shall just give you, and then the dialogue between him and my father will go on as well again. (Volume I, Chapter 21)

This is followed by a discourse on inconstancy, which is so whimsical that it would have to be copied out to be conveyed properly. On page 65, Sterne remembers: "But I forget my uncle *Toby*, whom all this while we have left knocking the ashes out of his tobacco-pipe." This leads into a sketch of Uncle Toby, into which the story of Aunt Dinah is inserted. In the next chapter, Sterne remembers again: "I was just going, for example, to have given you the great out-lines of my uncle *Toby*'s most whimsical character;——when my aunt *Dinah* and the coachman came a-cross us, and led us a vagary . . ." Unfortunately, I cannot copy out everything from Sterne, so I continue having omitted a few paragraphs:

> . . . from the beginning of this, you see, I have constructed the main work and the adventitious parts of it with such

intersections, and have so complicated and involved the digressive and progressive movements, one wheel within another,
that the whole machine, in general, has been kept a-going;——and, what's more, it shall be kept a-going these forty
years, if it pleases the fountain of health to bless me so long
with life and good spirits.

Thus ends Chapter 22 of the first volume; Chapter 23 continues: "I have a strong propensity in me to begin this chapter very
nonsensically, and I will not balk my fancy.——Accordingly I set
off thus"—and new digressions follow. The uncle is mentioned
again in Chapter 24: "If I was not morally sure that the reader
must be out of all patience for my uncle *Toby*'s character,——"
and further down the page Sterne begins a description of Uncle
Toby's obsession—his "Hobby-Horse." It turns out that Uncle
Toby, who was wounded in the groin at the siege of Namur, has
a passion for building toy fortresses. Finally, in the next volume,
Uncle Toby is able to complete the action he had begun in Volume
I, Chapter 21:

> —I think, replied my uncle *Toby*,—taking, as I told you, his
> pipe from his mouth, and striking the ashes out of it as he
> began his sentence;——I think, replied he,—it would not be
> amiss, brother, if we rung the bell. (Volume II, Chapter 6)

Sterne continually resorts to this device. As we can see from his
mischievous reminders about Uncle Toby, he is not only aware of
his hyperbolic manner of unfolding the story, but he also actively
plays with it.

This method of development, as I have already observed, is
canonical for Sterne. For example, Uncle Toby's statement—"I
wish . . . you had seen what prodigious armies we had in *Flanders*"
(Volume II, Chapter 18)—is immediately followed by a discourse
about Mr. Shandy's obsession. Tristram's father harbors a list of
obsessions: the injury done by the pressure of the pelvis against

the head in natural births, the influence of a person's name on his character (the motif is developed in great detail), and the influence of the size of one's nose on one's abilities. (The latter motif is developed in an unusually extravagant way, beginning from approximately page 217 and branching off, after a short break, into several curious stories about different types of noses. Especially remarkable is the story of Hafen Slawkenbergius, in Chapter 38, who "has been dead and laid in his grave above fourscore and ten years," and whose book on noses, according to Tristram's father, was highly influential. The discourse on noseology ends on page 272.)

The main storyline picks up from the third volume:

——"I *wish*, Dr. *Slop*," quoth my uncle *Toby*, (repeating his wish for Dr. *Slop* a second time, and with a degree of more zeal and earnestness in his manner of wishing, than he had wished at first)——"I *wish*, Dr. *Slop*," quoth my uncle Toby, "*you had seen what prodigious armies we had in Flanders.*" (Volume III, Chapter 1)

Once again, the main storyline is interrupted with digressions. And then it resumes again in Volume III, Chapter 6: "'——What prodigious armies you had in *Flanders!*'" This conscious exaggeration of the development in Sterne often occurs without any transitions:

The moment my father got up into his chamber, he threw himself prostrate across his bed in the wildest disorder imaginable, but at the same time, in the most lamentable attitude of a man borne down with sorrows, that ever the eye of pity dropp'd a tear for. (Volume III, Chapter 29)

This is followed by a typical Sternean description of the pose:

——The palm of his right hand, as he fell upon the bed,

receiving his forehead, and covering the greatest part of both his eyes, gently sunk down with his head (his elbow giving way backwards) till his nose touch'd the quilt;——his left arm hung insensible over the side of the bed, his knuckles reclining upon the handle of the chamber-pot, which peep'd out beyond the valance,——his right leg (his left being drawn up towards his body) hung half over the side of the bed, the edge of it pressing upon his shin bone.

The cause of Mr. Shandy's despondency is the fact that the midwife's forceps have broken the bridge of his son's nose (which is what motivates the whole epic discourse on the subject of noses mentioned above). In Chapter 2 of Volume IV we return once more to the prostrate father: "My father lay stretched across the bed as still as if the hand of death had pushed him down, for a full hour and a half before he began to play upon the floor with the toe of that foot which hung over the bed-side."

I cannot help but observe a few things about the poses we generally find in Sterne. He was the first to introduce the description of poses into the novel. They are always depicted in a strange way, or, to be more exact, an estranged way.

Here is another example from Volume III, Chapter 2:

Brother *Toby*, replied my father, taking his wig from off his head with his right hand, and with his *left* pulling out a striped *India* handkerchief from his right coat pocket, in order to rub his head, as he argued the point with my uncle *Toby*.——

I skip to the next chapter:

It was not an easy matter in any king's reign, (unless you were as lean a subject as myself) to have forced your hand diagonally, quite across your whole body, so as to gain the bottom of your opposite coat-pocket.—— (Volume III, Chapter 3)

This method of depicting poses, according to Eichenbaum, passed from Sterne to Tolstoy, who used it more moderately and with a psychological motivation.

I now return to the unfolding of the plot, with several examples that clearly establish the Sternean device—i.e. to have the content of the work be the taming of its form.

> What a chapter of chances, said my father, turning himself about upon the first landing, as he and my uncle *Toby* were going down stairs——what a long chapter of chances do the events of this world lay open to us! (Volume IV, Chapter 9)

Then follows a discussion containing an erotic estrangement, which I will discuss later.

> Is it not a shame to make two chapters of what passed in going down one pair of stairs? for we are got no farther yet than to the first landing, and there are fifteen more steps down to the bottom; and for aught I know, as my father and my uncle *Toby* are in a talking humour, there may be as many chapters as steps; . . . (Volume IV, Chapter 10)

Sterne devotes this entire chapter to a discussion of chapters. The following chapter begins: "We shall bring all things to rights, said my father, setting his foot upon the first step from the landing——" And the next chapter: "——And how does your mistress? cried my father, taking the same step over again from the landing . . ." Then the author intervenes again:

> Holla!——you, chairman!——here's sixpence——do step into that bookseller's shop, and call me a *day-tall* critick. I am very willing to give any one of 'em a crown to help me with his tackling, to get my father and my uncle *Toby* off the stairs, and to put them to bed. . . .
>
> I am this month one whole year older than I was this time

twelve-month; and having got, as you perceive, almost into the middle of my fourth volume——and no farther than to my first day's life——'tis demonstrative that I have three hundred and sixty-four days more life to write just now, than when I first set out; so that instead of advancing, as a common writer, in my work with what I have been doing at it——on the contrary, I am just thrown so many volumes back—— (Volume IV, Chapter 13)

This fixation on form—the canonical part of form—is reminiscent of those octaves and sonnets filled with nothing but descriptions of how they were composed. I would like to cite one last example of how the plot unfolds:

My mother was going very gingerly in the dark along the passage which led to the parlour, as my uncle *Toby* pronounced the word *wife*.——'Tis a shrill, penetrating sound of itself, and *Obadiah* had helped it by leaving the door a little a-jar, so that my mother heard enough of it to imagine herself the subject of the conversation: so laying the edge of her finger across her two lips——holding in her breath, and bending her head a little downwards, with a twist of her neck——(not towards the door, but from it, by which means her ear was brought to the chink)——she listened with all her powers:——the listening slave, with the Goddess of Silence at his back, could not have given a finer thought for an intaglio.

In this attitude I am determined to let her stand for five minutes: till I bring up the affairs of the kitchen (as *Rapin* does those of the church) to the same period. (Volume V, Chapter 5)

After an excursus, he returns to his mother again in Chapter 11 of Volume V: "I am a *Turk* if I had not as much forgot my mother, as if Nature had plaistered me up, and set me down naked upon the banks of the river *Nile*, without one."

But here, too, Sterne proceeds by making a digression. The

reminders are necessary only to renew our perception of the "forgotten" subject (here, Tristram Shandy's mother), lest the impression of an unfolding plot be lost. Finally, in Chapter 13, the mother changes her pose: "——Then, cried my mother, opening the door . . ." The plot here unfolds by way of introducing a parallel story. In such cases where there is a reverse movement in the development of plot by means of commentary, time in novels is considered to have stopped or, at least, it is not taken into account. This is how the inset scenes functioned in Shakespeare: inserted into the main action, they diverted attention from the flow of time, and even if the inset dialogue (usually spoken by new characters) continued for only a few minutes, the author thought it possible to carry on the action (presumably without lowering the curtain, which most likely didn't exist in the Shakespearean theater) as though hours or even a whole night had gone by.[93] Sterne, by mentioning and reminding us of the fact that Tristram's mother has been standing with her head bent slightly downwards for the duration of the digression, forces us to notice the unfolding of the plot.

It is generally very interesting to trace the role of time in Sterne's work. "Literary time" is a pure convention; its laws do not coincide with the laws of real time. If we traced, for example, the myriad stories and incidents concentrated in *Don Quixote*, we would see that the succession of day and night plays no compositional role in the sequence of events, and that a day is not even considered as a length of time. We can observe the same in Abbé Prévost's manner of narration in *Manon Lescaut*. The Chevalier des Grieux relates the first part of the novel (a hundred pages) in one breath—without a break—and then, after a slight respite, continues for another hundred pages. Such a narration would last about sixteen hours, and only if read at a tongue-twisting speed.

I have already written about the conventionality of time on the

---

[93] Boris Silversvan, "Teatr i stsena epokhi Shekspira" [The Theater and the Stage of Shakespeare's Time], 1918.

stage. But Sterne conceived of and employed the conventionality of "literary time" as the basis for a game:

> It is about an hour and a half's tolerable good reading since my uncle *Toby* rung the bell, when *Obadiah* was order'd to saddle a horse, and go for Dr. *Slop*, the man-midwife;——so that no one can say, with reason, that I have not allowed *Obadiah* time enough, poetically speaking, and considering the emergency too, both to go and come;——tho', morally and truly speaking, the man perhaps has scarce had time to get on his boots.
>
> If the hypercritick will go upon this; and is resolved after all to take a pendulum, and measure the true distance betwixt the ringing of the bell, and the rap at the door;——and, after finding it to be no more than two minutes, thirteen seconds, and three fifths,——should take upon him to insult over me for such a breach in the unity, or rather probability of time;——I would remind him, that the idea of duration and of its simple modes, is got merely from the train and succession of our ideas,——and is the true scholastic pendulum,——and by which, as a scholar, I will be tried in this matter,——abjuring and detesting the jurisdiction of all other pendulums whatever.
>
> I would, therefore, desire him to consider that it is but poor eight miles from *Shandy-Hall* to Dr. *Slop*, the man-midwife's house;——and that whilst *Obadiah* has been going those said miles and back, I have brought my uncle *Toby* from *Namur*, quite across all *Flanders*, into *England*:——That I have had him ill upon my hands near four years;——and have since travelled him and Corporal *Trim* in a chariot and four, a journey of near two hundred miles down into *Yorkshire*;——all which put together, must have prepared the reader's imagination for the entrance of Dr. *Slop* upon the stage,——as much, at least (I hope) as a dance, a song, or a concerto between the acts.
>
> If my hypercritick is intractable, alledging, that two minutes and thirteen seconds are no more than two minutes and thirteen seconds,——when I have said all I can about

them;——and that this plea, tho' it might save me dramatically, will damn me biographically, rendering my book, from this very moment, a profess'd ROMANCE, which, before, was a book apocryphal:——If I am thus pressed—I then put an end to the whole objection and controversy about it all at once,——by acquainting him, that *Obadiah* had not got above threescore yards from the stable-yard before he met with Dr. *Slop*; . . . (Volume II, Chapter 8)

Sterne employs the old "found manuscript" device almost unchanged from its traditional usage. This is how Yorick's sermon is introduced into the novel. The reading of the found manuscript itself does not deduct time from the main plotline, and it is constantly interrupted, mostly by emotional exclamations. The sermon occupies about fifteen pages, but it is rather protracted due to the usual Sternean insertions.

The reading of the sermon begins with a description of the Corporal's pose, given in Sterne's typical style of markedly awkward portrayal:

He stood before them with his body swayed, and bent forwards just so far, as to make an angle of 85 degrees and a half upon the plain of the horizon;——which sound orators, to whom I address this, know very well to be the true persuasive angle of incidence; . . .

I am skipping a few sentences:

He stood,——for I repeat it, to take the picture of him in at one view, with his body sway'd, and somewhat bent forwards,——his right leg from under him, sustaining seven-eighths of his whole weight,——the foot of his left leg, the defect of which was no disadvantage to his attitude, advanced a little,——not laterally, nor forwards, but in a line betwixt them; . . . (Volume II, Chapter 17)

The description takes up more than one page. The sermon itself is interrupted by a story about Corporal Trim's brother, followed by the theological objections of the Catholic doctor and Uncle Toby's remarks about fortifications.

Thus, the reading of the manuscript in Sterne is far more interwoven into the main plotline than in Cervantes.

The found manuscript became Sterne's favorite device in *A Sentimental Journey*. There he discovers what he thinks is a manuscript by Rabelais; however, as is quite typical of Sterne, he abandons the reading of the manuscript after a brief examination of the lettering. The unfinished story is canonical for Sterne in both its motivated and unmotivated forms. In the case of the manuscript, the interruption is motivated by the loss of its ending. Nothing motivates the conclusion of *Tristram Shandy*, which ends with the narrative simply being cut off:

> L - - d! said my mother, what is all this story about?——
> A COCK and a BULL, said Yorick——And one of the best of its kind, I ever heard.

THE END OF THE NINTH VOLUME

A Sentimental Journey ends similarly:

> So that when I stretch'd out my hand, I caught hold of the *fille de chambre's*—

END OF VOL. II

This, of course, is a specific stylistic device based on differential qualities. Sterne worked against the backdrop of the adventure novel, with its extremely strict forms and its custom of ending with a marriage. The forms of the Sternean novel are constructed by way of displacing and violating the conventional forms. He treated the endings of his novels in the same way. It is as if we plummet into them—there is a slide in the stairwell where we expected to find a landing. Gogol's "Ivan Fyodorovich Shponka and His Aunt" employs the same method of ending a story, but with a motivation: the final pages of the manuscript have been used to wrap pies in (Sterne uses his to wrap currant jam). E. T. A. Hoffmann's *The Life and Opinions of the Tomcat Murr* presents a similar scene with a motivated absence of the ending—however, it is further complicated by temporal transposition (due to a mix-up at the printing house) and parallelism.

Sterne introduces the story of Le Fever in a thoroughly traditional way. At the time of Tristram's birth, during a conversation about the choice of a tutor, Uncle Toby suggests Le Fever's son, and the inset story begins, narrated by the author himself:

> Then, brother *Shandy*, answered my uncle *Toby*, raising himself off the chair, and laying down his pipe to take hold of my father's other hand,——I humbly beg I may recommend poor *Le Fever*'s son to you;——a tear of joy of the first water sparkled in my uncle *Toby*'s eye,——and another, the fellow to it, in the corporal's, as the proposition was made;——you will see why when you read *Le Fever*'s story:——fool that I was! nor can I recollect (nor perhaps you) without turning back to the place, what it was that hindered me from letting the corporal tell it in his own words;——but the occasion is lost,——I must tell it now in my own. (Volume VI, Chapter 5)

The story about Le Fever then begins; it is approximately sixteen pages long.

Tristram's journeys are described in a separate set of stories (in Volume VII), which Sterne later developed, step by step, motif by motif, in his *Sentimental Journey*. Sterne also interpolates the story about the abbess of Andoüillets in Volume VII, Chapters 20-25.

All of this various material, weighed down by long extracts from the works of a variety of pedants, would doubtlessly have

broken the back of the novel, were it not tightly bound together
by its motifs. A motif in Sterne is neither unfolded nor realized—it
is merely mentioned from time to time. Its full materialization is
continually postponed, yet its very presence throughout the novel
unifies the episodes.

There are several such motifs. One of them concerns knots.
Here is how it is introduced: Dr. Slop's bag of obstetrical instruments is tied up in several knots: "'Tis God's mercy, quoth he (to
himself) that Mrs. *Shandy* has had so bad a time of it,——else
she might have been brought to bed seven times told, before one
half of these knots could have got untied" (Volume III, Chapter
9). The motif is continued in the next chapter:

> In the case of *knots*,——by which, in the first place, I would
> not be understood to mean slip-knots,——because in the
> course of my life and opinions,——my opinions concern-
> ing them will come in more properly when . . . (Volume III,
> Chapter 10)

Then begins a discourse about knots, slip-knots, bow-knots, and
so on. In the meantime, Dr. Slop takes a penknife to cut the knots,
but accidentally wounds his hand. Then he begins to swear, whereupon Mr. Shandy, "with the most *Cervantick* gravity," advises the
latter not to curse in vain, but rather to curse in accordance with
the rules of art, and provides, as an example of emulation, "a
form of excommunication of the church of *Rome*." Dr. Slop takes
the form and reads it; the text (in Latin and in English translation) takes up a whole chapter—nine full pages. The curious
thing here is the motivation Sterne uses to unfold the material.
Usually such material has to do with medieval scholarship, which
by Sterne's time was considered amusing (just as dialectal pecu-
liarities are perceived to be amusing when inserted in tales about
foreigners)—and so, Sterne inserts this material as a string of Mr.
Shandy's obsessions. Although the motivation here is slightly more

complex. For example, Sterne doesn't ascribe to Mr. Shandy the material about baptizing a child before his birth, nor the comical argument of the lawyers about whether the mother is akin to her son.

The motif of knots reappears in Chapter VIII of Volume V, but with a new twist: instead of the promised chapter on "*chamber-maids and buttonholes*," Sterne proposes to write another chapter devoted to "*chamber-maids, green-gowns and old hats*." But the question of knots is not yet settled; it resurfaces toward the end of the book in Chapter 14 of Volume IX, where the author again promises to write a special chapter "of *Knots*."

Another motif that runs throughout the novel is the reference to Jenny. This is how Jenny is introduced into the novel:

> ———it is no more than a week from this very day, in which I am now writing this book for the edification of the world;——— which is *March* 9, 1759,———that my dear, dear Jenny, observing I look'd a little grave, as she stood cheapening a silk of five-and-twenty shillings a yard,——— (Volume I, Chapter 18)

A few pages down, Sterne plays with the reader's curiosity concerning who Jenny is in the author's life:

> ———I own the tender appellation of my dear, dear *Jenny*,——— with some other strokes of conjugal knowledge, interspersed here and there, might, naturally enough, have misled the most candid judge in the world into such a determination against me.———All I plead for, in this case, Madam, is strict justice, and that you do so much of it, to me as well as to yourself,——— as not to prejudge or receive such an impression of me, till you have better evidence, than I am positive, at present, can be produced against me.———Not that I can be so vain or unreasonable, Madam, as to desire you should therefore think, that my dear, dear *Jenny* is my kept mistress;———no,———that would be flattering my character in the other extreme, and giving it an

air of freedom, which, perhaps, it has no kind of right to. All I contend for, is the utter impossibility, for some volumes, that you, or the most penetrating spirit upon earth, should know how this matter really stands.———It is not impossible, but that my dear, dear *Jenny!* tender as the appellation is, may be my child.———Consider,———I was born in the year eighteen.——— Nor is there any thing unnatural or extravagant in the supposition, that my dear *Jenny* may be my friend.———Friend!——— My friend.———Surely, Madam, a friendship between the two sexes may subsist, and be supported without———Fy! Mr. *Shandy:*———Without any thing, Madam, but that tender and delicious sentiment which ever mixes in friendship, where there is a difference of sex.

Jenny's motif appears again much later in Chapter 32 of Volume IV:

> ———I shall never get all through in five minutes, that I fear———and the thing I *hope* is, that your worships and reverences are not offended———if you are, depend upon't I'll give you something, my good gentry, next year, to be offended at———that's my dear *Jenny's* way———but who my *Jenny* is——— and which is the right and which the wrong end of a woman, is the thing to be *concealed*———it shall be told you in the next chapter but one, to my chapter of button-holes,———and not one chapter before.

The next mention is in Chapter 13 of Volume VII: "I love the Pythagoreans (much more than ever I dare tell my dear *Jenny*) . . ." There are other references to Jenny in Chapter 11 of Volume VIII and in Chapter 8 of Volume IX. The last of these (I have skipped over a few) has a kind of sentimentality that is quite rare in Sterne:

> I will not argue the matter: Time wastes too fast: every letter I trace tells me with what rapidity Life follows my pen: the days and hours of it, more precious, my dear *Jenny!* than the rubies

about thy neck, are flying over our heads like light clouds of a windy day, never to return more———every thing presses on———whilst thou art twisting that lock,———see! it grows grey; and every time I kiss thy hand to bid adieu, and every absence which follows it, are preludes to that eternal separation which we are shortly to make.———

———Heaven have mercy upon us both!

CHAP. IX.

Now, for what the world thinks of that ejaculation———I would not give a groat.

Chapter 9 ends here.

It would be interesting to say a few words about sentimentality in general. Sentimentality cannot serve as content for art, if only for the reason that art does not have separate content. The narration of things from a "sentimental point of view" is a special method of narration, just like the narration of things from an equine point of view (Tolstoy's "Strider"), or from the point of view of a giant (Swift's *Gulliver's Travels*).

Art, in essence, is unemotional. Remember how in fairy tales people are placed in a barrel studded with nails and thrown into the sea ("The Tale of Tsar Saltan"). In "Little Thumb," an ogre cuts off the heads of his daughters, and the children listening to the fairy tale never let you skip over this detail. It isn't cruel—it is fairy-tale-like.

In his *Ritual Spring Song*, Professor Anichkov cites examples of vernal dance songs.[94] These songs speak of bad, querulous husbands, death, and maggots. This is indeed tragic, but only in the world of song. Blood (*krov'*) in art is not bloody, it rhymes with "love" (*lyubov'*)—it is material for the construction of sounds or images.

For that reason, art is ruthless and alien to sympathy unless

---

[94] Yevgeni Anichkov, *Vesennyaya obryadovaya pesnya na Zapade i u slavyan* [Ritual Spring Song in the West and among the Slavs], 1903-5.

the feeling of sympathy has been employed as material for construction. But even in this case, it needs to be studied from the point of view of composition, just as you would if you were trying to understand how a car works—by examining the drive belt as a mechanical detail, and certainly not by looking at it from the point of view of a vegetarian.

And Sterne is also unsympathetic. Let me demonstrate how. Mr. Shandy's son, Bobby, dies at precisely the moment when his father is deciding whether to spend a windfall on his son's education abroad or whether to spend it on improving his estate.

> . . . my uncle *Toby* hummed over the letter.
>
> —— —— —— —— —— —— —— ——
> —— —— —— —— —— —— —— ——
> —— —— —— —— —— —— ——
> —— —— —— —— —— —— ——
> —— —— —— —— —— —— —he's
> gone! said my uncle *Toby*——Where——Who? cried my father.——My nephew, said my uncle *Toby*.——What—without leave——without money—without governor? cried my father in amazement. No:——he is dead, my dear brother, quoth my uncle *Toby*. (Volume V, Chapter 2)

Sterne uses death here to create a "misunderstanding"—a quite simple and common construction, in which two interlocutors talk about two different things but think that they are talking about the same thing. Here is an example of such a construction in Gogol's *The Government Inspector* (the first conversation between the Mayor and Khlestakov):

Mayor: Please forgive the intrusion.
Khlestakov: Please don't worry.
Mayor: It is my duty, as mayor of this town, to ensure that all visitors and people of quality suffer no inconvenience.
Khlestakov: [*stammering a little at first, but speaking loudly by the end of his speech*]

What could I do? It's not my fault. I'll pay up, honest I will. They'll send money from home. [*Bobchinsky peeps around the door.*] It's the landlord who's more to blame. Serves meat as tough as old boots—and as for the soup! The devil only knows what he tipped in it. I had to chuck it out of the window . . . He's been starving me for days now . . . And the tea's quite peculiar—it reeks of fish! And why should I? . . . I mean to say . . . I ask you!

Mayor: [*frightened*] Forgive me, but it's not my fault, really— it's not. There's always top-quality meat at the market, supplied by sober and honest butchers from Kholmogory. I've no idea where he could have got that meat from. But if things are not to your liking, may I suggest you accompany me to other accommodation?

Khlestakov: Oh no! I won't go! I know what you mean by other accommodation! You mean the gaol! What right have you, how can you have the nerve . . . I hold a government post in St. Petersburg [*becomes heated*] I . . . I . . . I . . .

Mayor: [*aside*] Good Lord! He's in a terrible temper! He knows everything! Those confounded shopkeepers must have blabbed.

Khlestakov: [*growing bolder*] You can fetch the entire constabulary—I won't budge! I'll go straight to the Minister! [*Thumps his fist on the table.*] Who do you think you are? Tell me!

Mayor: [*standing to attention and shaking all over*] Have mercy, don't ruin me! I've a wife and little ones . . . Don't ruin me . . .

Khlestakov: I won't go! Really! What's it to do with me—just because you have a wife and children I have to go to prison! Very nice! [*Bobchinsky peers around the door and hides in fright.*] Thank you very much, but I'm not going!

Mayor: [*trembling*] It was my inexperience, sheer inexperience, honestly. All through inexperience. And my wretched salary. Please judge for yourself, sir. An official's pay isn't even enough for tea and sugar. And if I did take a few bribes—well, they were simply trifles—something for the table, a piece of cloth for a suit. And as for that story about the sergeant's widow—the one who keeps a stall at the market and whom I'm supposed to have had flogged—I swear it's all malicious gossip, pure slander cooked up by those who wish me harm, the kind of people who wouldn't hesitate to do away with me.

Khlestakov: So what! What the hell's that got to do with me? On the other hand—why are you telling me all this, about enemies and that sergeant's widow? A sergeant's widow is one thing, but don't you dare flog *me*! What a nerve! I ask you! Yes, I'll pay my bill, I'll pay up, but I don't have any money right now. That's why I'm stuck here—because I'm broke. (Act II, Scene 8)

Here is another example of a common misunderstanding, from Griboedov's *The Misfortune of Being Clever* (the conversation between Zagoretsky and the deaf Grandmother Countess):

Zagoretsky: No. It's about Chatsky; it's a sad tale . . .
Grandmother Countess: What? Chatsky had to go to gaol?
Zagoretsky: When he was in the mountains his head was hurt, and, owing to that, he's lost his reason.
Grandmother Countess: What? He's turned Turk and joined the freemasons? (Act III, Scene 19)[95]

We see the same device (with the same motivation of deafness) in the Russian folk-play *Tsar Maximilian*, but here it is used to initiate a series of puns that digress from the main plot and ultimately weaken it. Tsar Maximilian summons the old gravediggers:

Tsar Maximilian: Go and fetch the old gravediggers.
Messenger Boy: I shall go and fetch the old gravediggers.
(Messenger Boy and the Gravediggers)

---

[95] Aleksandr Griboedov, *The Misfortune of Being Clever*, trans. S. W. Pring (London: David Nutt, 1914).

Messenger Boy: Is anyone at home?

First Gravedigger: What do you want?

Messenger Boy: Old Vaska, the Tsar wants you.

First Gravedigger: Who? What star?

Messenger Boy: Not a star, the Tsar!

First Gravedigger: Tell him nobody's home. It's a holiday. We're out of town.

Messenger Boy: Vasili Ivanovich, the Tsar wants to give you a reward.

First Gravedigger: Sure! I've turned you down and now I'm Vasili Ivanovich. What board are you talking about?

Messenger Boy: Not a board, a reward!

First Gravedigger (to Second Gravedigger): Mokei!

Second Gravedigger: What is it, Patrakei?

First Gravedigger: Let's go see the Tsar.

Second Gravedigger: What for?

First Gravedigger: For a reward.

Second Gravedigger: What board? Why would we need a board?

First Gravedigger: No, not a board, but some kind of a reward!

Second Gravedigger: I thought you said board. Sure, let's go if it's a reward.

First Gravedigger: Let's go then!

Second Gravedigger: But tell me, what kind of a reward?

First Gravedigger: Let's just go. I'll tell you on the way.

Second Gravedigger: No! Tell me now! I won't go if you won't tell me now!

First Gravedigger: Remember how well we fought during the Sevastopol War?

Second Gravedigger: Of course I do!

First Gravedigger: Well, maybe he wants to give us each a bottle of vodka.

Second Gravedigger: Aha-a! Let's get going then.[96]

The device of misunderstanding is canonical in folk theater and it

---

[96] Nikolai Onchukov, *Severnye narodnye dramy* [Northern Folk-Plays], 1911.

sometimes completely supplants the novelistic plot structures of the plays. This has been analyzed by Roman Jakobson and Pyotr Bogatyryov in their work on Russian folk theater.

But Sterne's punning on death does not surprise us as much, or does not surprise us at all, as the puns of Mr. Shandy. For Sterne, the death of Bobby Shandy is chiefly a motivation for unfolding the plot: "Will your worships give me leave to squeeze in a story between these two pages?" (Volume V, Chapter 3). And he inserts here an extract of Servius Sulpicius's consolatory letter to Cicero. This insertion is motivated by the fact that Mr. Shandy delivers it as his own words. It is followed by a selection of classical anecdotes about the dread of death. It is interesting to see what Sterne himself has to say about Mr. Shandy's eloquence:

> My father was as proud of his eloquence as MARCUS TULLIUS CICERO could be for his life, and, for aught I am convinced of to the contrary at present, with as much reason: it was indeed his strength——and his weakness too.——His strength——for he was by nature eloquent,——and his weakness—for he was hourly a dupe to it; and provided an occasion in life would but permit him to shew his talents, or say either a wise thing, a witty, or a shrewd one——(bating the case of a systematick misfortune)——he had all he wanted.——A blessing which tied up my father's tongue, and a misfortune which let it loose with a good grace, were pretty equal: sometimes, indeed, the misfortune was the better of the two; for instance, where the pleasure of the harangue was as *ten*, and the pain of the misfortune but as *five*——my father gained half in half, and consequently was as well again off, as if it had never befallen him.

Here Sterne shows with unusual clarity the difference between "happiness" and "unhappiness" taken as an everyday occurrence and as material for art.

It remains for the mother to learn of her son's death. This is accomplished in the following way: Mrs. Shandy stands by the door, eavesdropping, while Sterne decides to construct a parallel action in the kitchen—and, as I have already mentioned, he plays with how long the poor mother has to stand in this uncomfortable pose.

In the meantime, the conversation about the son's death is progressing in the study, and it has already turned into a stringing together of different themes, ranging from a discourse on death in general to the paths of dissemination of ancient scholarship, all the way to Socrates's oration before his judges:

> . . . though my mother was a woman of no deep reading, yet the abstract of *Socrates*'s oration, which my father was giving my uncle *Toby*, was not altogether new to her.——She listened to it with composed intelligence, and would have done so to the end of the chapter, had not my father plunged (which he had no occasion to have done) into that part of the pleading where the great philosopher reckons up his connections, his alliances, and children; but renounces a security to be so won by working upon the passions of his judges.——"I have friends——I have relations,——I have three desolate children,"——says *Socrates*.——
>
> ——Then, cried my mother, opening the door,——you have one more, Mr. *Shandy*, than I know of.
>
> By heaven! I have one less,——said my father, getting up and walking out of the room.

One of the most important devices of development in Sterne is erotic estrangement, which usually appears in the form of euphemism. I have already discussed the origins of this phenomenon in the chapter "Art as Device." In Sterne we find an unusual variety of applications of this device. There are many examples, but a few will suffice to illustrate my point. I will begin with one dealing with the identification of character types:

I am not ignorant that the *Italians* pretend to a mathematical exactness in their designations of one particular sort of character among them, from the *forte* or *piano* of a certain wind-instrument they use,——which they say is infallible.——I dare not mention the name of the instrument in this place;——'tis sufficient we have it amongst us,——but never think of making a drawing by it;——this is ænigmatical, and intended to be so, at least, *ad populum*:——And therefore, I beg, Madam, when you come here, that you read on as fast as you can, and never stop to make any inquiry about it. (Volume I, Chapter 23)

Or here is another:

Now whether it was physically impossible, with half a dozen hands all thrust into the napkin at a time——but that some one chestnut, of more life and rotundity than the rest, must be put in motion——it so fell out, however, that one was actually sent rolling off the table; and as *Phutatorius* sat straddling under——it fell perpendicularly into that particular aperture of *Phutatorius*'s breeches, for which, to the shame and indelicacy of our language be it spoke, there is no chaste word throughout all *Johnson*'s dictionary——let it suffice to say——it was that particular aperture which, in all good societies, the laws of decorum do strictly require, like the temple of *Janus* (in peace at least) to be universally shut up. (Volume IV, Chapter 27)

Two episodes in *Tristram Shandy* are especially characteristic of this kind of erotic estrangement and the wordplay to which it gives rise. They are very similar, but one is simply presented as an episode, while the other unfolds into one of those plotlines that continually interrupt the others throughout the novel. The main one deals with Uncle Toby's wound—a serious injury to the groin. The widow, who is in love with Uncle Toby and wants to marry him, doesn't know whether or not he is a eunuch, and, at the same time, cannot bring herself to ask. This is a terrible impediment to their romance:

> ———there is not a greater difference between a single-horse chair and madam *Pompadour's vis-a-vis*; than betwixt a single amour, and an amour thus nobly doubled, and going upon all four, prancing throughout a grand drama . . . (Volume III, Chapter 24)

—says Sterne of Uncle Toby. The romance is constantly cut short and then re-emerges again in the form of allusions. Finally, the allusions grow thicker (at some point in Chapter 34 of Volume VI), and this is where the motif of the journey intrudes. By the end of the seventh volume, this new motif seems to have been exhausted:

> ———I danced it along through *Narbonne, Carcasson*, and *Castle Naudairy*, till at last I danced myself into *Perdrillo's* pavillion, where pulling out a paper of black lines, that I might go on straight forwards, without digression or parenthesis, in my uncle *Toby's* amours——— (Volume VII, Chapter 43)

And so, the wound in the groin and the impossibility of asking about the details of the injury function as impediments to the romance of Uncle Toby and Widow Wadman. I will quote a few passages to show how Sterne impedes the action.

After a ceremonious promise to continue the story of Uncle Toby's amorous adventures without digression, Sterne holds up the action with multiple nested digressions, which are linked to each other by the repeated phrase: "It is with LOVE as with CUCKOLDOM" (Volume VIII, Chapters 2, 4).

Then come the love metaphors—love as a "furr'd cap" or a "pye," followed by a long account about Widow Wadman's attacks on Uncle Toby. But this account is also interrupted by a long, "endless tale" told by Trim called "The Story of the King of

Bohemia and His Seven Castles." This tale is similar to the one Sancho Panza tells Don Quixote on the night of the adventure with the fulling mill, when he ties Rocinante's legs together. Uncle Toby repeatedly interrupts the narrative with technical military and stylistic remarks. It is the same device that I have analyzed in *Don Quixote*. Just like any "endless tale," it is based on recognition of the deferment device, and therefore must be interrupted by a listener. In this particular instance, its function is to defer the main action of the novel. Trim soon abandons the story of the King of Bohemia and takes up the story of his own love affair; finally, Widow Wadman reappears on the scene. Here the motif of the wound also returns:

> I am terribly afraid, said widow *Wadman*, in case I should marry him, *Bridget*——that the poor captain will not enjoy his health, with the monstrous wound upon his groin——
>
> It may not, Madam, be so very large, replied *Bridget*, as you think——and I believe, besides, added she——that 'tis dried up——
>
> ——I could like to know——merely for his sake, said Mrs. *Wadman*——
>
> ——We'll know and long and the broad of it, in ten days——answered Mrs. *Bridget*, for whilst the captain is paying his addresses to you——I'm confident Mr. *Trim* will be for making love to me——and I'll let him as much as he will—— added *Bridget*——to get it all out of him—— (Volume VIII, Chapter 28)

Once again, Sterne inserts new material here, this time in the form of a *realized* metaphor, which is a rather common Sternean device. He takes the metaphor of the "hobby-horse" (meaning a whim) literally and speaks of it as a real, physical horse; then he does the opposite, turning the real "ass" (donkey) into a metaphor (referring to the body). Perhaps the origin of this metaphor is found in the famous expression of St. Francis of Assisi—he used to call his body "my brother the ass." Sterne further develops the metaphor of the "ass" and constructs therefrom a situation based on a misunderstanding.

Mr. Shandy asks Uncle Toby: "Well! dear brother *Toby* . . . and how goes it with your ASSE?" (Volume VIII, Chapter 32). Toby thinks that he is euphemistically referring to his backside. A detail of the further development is interesting. Mr. Shandy's speech addressed to Uncle Toby is nothing other than a parody of Don Quixote's speech to Sancho Panza regarding governorship. I will not insert parallel excerpts from both speeches here, especially since Widow Wadman awaits us. Uncle Toby and Trim are going to see her. Mr. Shandy and his wife are also on their way; they are following them with their eyes and talking about the upcoming marriage. Here, again, Sterne throws in the motif of the impotent husband who sleeps with his wife only on the first Sunday of every month. The motif that was introduced at the beginning of the novel reappears:

Unless she should happen to have a child——said my mother——

——But she must persuade my brother *Toby* first to get her one—

——To be sure, Mr. *Shandy*, quoth my mother.

——Though if it comes to persuasion——said my father——Lord have mercy upon them.

Amen: said my mother, *piano.*

Amen: cried my father, *fortissimè.*

Amen: said my mother again——but with such a sighing cadence of personal pity at the end of it, as discomfited every fibre about my father——he instantly took out his almanack; but before he could untie it, *Yorick's* congregation coming out of church, became a full answer to one half of his business with it——and my mother telling him it was a sacrament day—— left him as little in doubt, as to the other part——He put his almanack into his pocket.

The first Lord of the Treasury thinking of *ways and means*, could not have returned home with a more embarrassed look. (Volume IX, Chapter 11)

I have only permitted myself this quotation because I want to show how the inserted material in Sterne is not just merely brought in on the side, but really is woven into one of the novel's various compositional lines.

The narrative reverts to its digressions and the motif of knots reappears. Finally, the wound motif comes to the fore: it appears, as is typical of Sterne, from the middle:

CHAP. XX.
_____ *
* *
* *
* *.
  *
* *
* *
* * * * * * ____

——You shall see the very place, Madam; said my uncle *Toby*.

Mrs. *Wadman* blush'd——look'd towards the door—— turn'd pale——blush'd slightly again——recover'd her natural colour——blush'd worse than ever; which, for the sake of the unlearned reader, I translate thus——

"L—d ! I cannot look at it——
What would the world say if I look'd at it?
I should drop down, if I look'd at it——
I wish I could look at it——
There can be no sin in looking at it.
——*I will look at it.*" (Volume IX, Chapter 20)

But something quite different happens.

Uncle Toby thinks that the widow is interested in the

geographical place where he was wounded, not the region of the actual wound on his body. The subject of the conversation is unclear to the reader too. The motivation of this shift in the plot is to impede the action.

And so, Trim brings to the disappointed widow a map of Namur (where Uncle Toby was wounded). The wordplay continues; this time it is the author who takes up the theme in his digressions. Then comes the well-known temporal transposition: the omitted "Eighteenth Chapter" and "Chapter the Nineteenth" appear immediately after Chapter 25. The action picks up from Chapter 26:

> It was just as natural for Mrs. *Wadman*, whose first husband was all his time afflicted with a Sciatica, to wish to know how far from the hip to the groin; and how far she was likely to suffer more or less in her feelings, in the one case than in the other.
>
> She had accordingly read *Drake*'s anatomy from one end to the other. She had peeped into *Wharton* upon the brain, and borrowed* Graaf upon the bones and muscles; but could make nothing of it.
>
> She had reason'd likewise from her own powers——laid down theorems——drawn consequences, and come to no conclusion.
>
> To clear up all, she had twice asked Doctor *Slop*, "if poor captain *Shandy* was ever likely to recover of his wound——?"
>
> ——He is recovered, Doctor *Slop* would say——
>
> What! quite?
>
> ——Quite: madam——
>
> But what do you mean by a recovery? Mrs. *Wadman* would say.
>
> Doctor *Slop* was the worst man alive at definitions; . . .
>
> * This must be a mistake in Mr. *Shandy*; for *Graaf* wrote upon the pancreatick juice, and the parts of generation.

So Mrs. Wadman interrogates Captain Shandy himself about the wound:

> "——Was it without remission?—
> "——Was it more tolerable in bed?
> "——Could he lie on both sides alike with it?
> "——Was he able to mount a horse? (Volume IX, Chapter 26)

Finally, the matter is resolved in the following way. Trim speaks about Captain Shandy's wound with Bridget, the widow's maid:

> ——and in this cursed trench, Mrs. *Bridget,* quoth the Corporal, taking her by the hand, did he receive the wound which crush'd him so miserably *here*——In pronouncing which he slightly press'd the back of her hand towards the part he felt for——and let it fall.
>
> We thought, Mr. *Trim,* it had been more in the middle—— said Mrs. *Bridget*——
>
> That would have undone us for ever——said the Corporal.
>
> ——And left my poor mistress undone too, said *Bridget.*
>
> The Corporal made no reply to the repartee, but by giving Mrs. *Bridget* a kiss.
>
> Come—come—said *Bridget*—holding the palm of her left hand parallel to the plane of the horizon, and sliding the fingers of the other over it, in a way which could not have been done, had there been the least wart or protuberance——'Tis every syllable of it false, cried the Corporal, before she had half finished the sentence—— (Volume IX, Chapter 28)

It is interesting to compare this hand symbolism with the erotic euphemisms in the novel.

Let me make a small, preliminary observation here. For the characters of this novel, this is simply a manner of decorous speech, whereas for Sterne it becomes material for artistic construction by means of estrangement. Curiously, this hand symbolism can also be found in the masculine folklore of "dirty" jokes, where, as you know, there are no rules, except for the rule of speaking as indecorously as possible. Here too we find euphemistic material, and hand symbolism in particular, although employed as a device of estrangement.

Let us return to Sterne. I am compelled to quote yet another passage—nearly an entire chapter, which fortunately is rather short:

> ——'TWAS nothing,——I did not lose two drops of blood by it——'twas not worth calling in a surgeon, had he lived next door to us . . . !——The chamber-maid had left no ******* *** under the bed:——Cannot you contrive, master, quoth *Susannah*, lifting up the sash with one hand, as she spoke, and helping me up into the window-seat with the other,—— cannot you manage, my dear, for a single time, to **** *** ** *** ******?
>
> I was five years old.——*Susannah* did not consider that nothing was well hung in our family,——so slap came the sash down like lightning upon us;——Nothing is left,—— cried *Susannah*,——nothing is left—for me, but to run my country.—— (Volume V, Chapter 17)

She runs to Uncle Toby's house, who is to blame for the mishap, as his servant Trim had taken the leaden weights from the nursery window: "and as the sash pullies, when the lead was gone, were of no kind of use, he had taken them away also, to make a couple of wheels for one of their carriages."

Again, we have the usual Sternean device: the effects appear before the causes. The description of the cause in this case occupies two pages. The incident is related with the help of hand symbolism:

> *Trim*, by the help of his forefinger, laid flat upon the table, and the edge of his hand striking a-cross it at right angles, made

a shift to tell his story so, that priests and virgins might have listened to it;——and the story being told,——the dialogue went on as follows. (Volume V, Chapter 20)

The episode unfolds through everyone's interpretations of the incident, digressions, discussions about the digressions, and so on.

It is interesting that Mr. Shandy, having learned about the incident, runs to his son . . . with a book in his hand, and begins a conversation on the subject of circumcision. It is also worth noting that Sterne is parodying here the motivation of inset passages:

> ——was *Obadiah* enabled to give him a particular account of it, just as it had happened.——I thought as much, said my father, tucking up his night-gown;——and so walked up stairs.
>
> One would imagine from this——(though for my own part I somewhat question it)——that my father, before that time, had actually wrote that remarkable character in the *Tristrapædia*, which to me is the most original and entertaining one in the whole book;——and that is the *chapter upon sash-windows*, with a bitter *Philippick* at the end of it, upon the forgetfulness of chamber-maids.——I have but two reasons for thinking otherwise.
>
> First, had the matter been taken into consideration, before the event happened, my father certainly would have nailed up the sash window for good an' all;——which, considering with what difficulty he composed books,——he might have done with ten times less trouble, than he could have wrote the chapter: this argument I foresee holds good against his writing a chapter, even after the event; but 'tis obviated under the second reason, which I have the honour to offer to the world in support of my opinion, that my father did not write the chapter upon sash-windows and chamber-pots, at the time supposed,——and it is this.
>
> ——That, in order to render the *Tristrapædia* complete,——I wrote the chapter myself. (Volume V, Chapter 26)

I don't have the slightest inclination of studying Sterne's novel to the very end, as I am not interested in Sterne per se, but in the theory of plot. Let me say a few words now about the abundance of quotations. I certainly could have made fuller use of the material introduced in each quotation, for there is hardly a device that appears anywhere in its pure form, but this would have turned my work into something like an interlinear gloss with grammatical annotations. I would have butchered the material in such a way as to make it impossible for the reader to understand it.

I have been following the course of the novel in my analysis only to show its "non-sequentiality" as a whole. What is characteristic here is precisely the unusual ordering of even the most common, traditional elements.

To conclude, in addition to proving that Sterne knew what he was doing and deliberately accentuated and violated the conventional plot scheme, I introduce his very own diagrams of *Tristram Shandy's* storyline:

I am now beginning to get fairly into my work; and by the help of a vegetable diet, with a few of the cold seeds, I make no doubt but I shall be able to go on with my uncle *Toby's* story, and my own, in a tolerable straight line. Now,

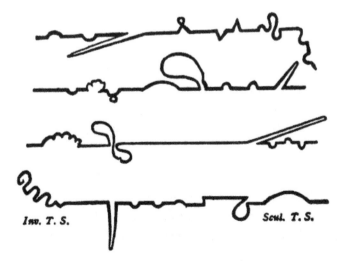

These were the four lines I moved in through my first, second, third, and fourth volumes.———In the fifth volume I have been very good,———the precise line I have described in it being this:

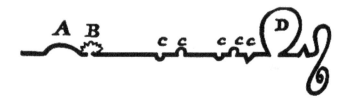

By which it appears, that except at the curve, marked A. where I took a trip to *Navarre*,———and the indented curve B. which is the short airing when I was there with the Lady *Baussiere* and her page,———I have not taken the least frisk of a digression, till *John de la Casse*'s devils led me the round you see marked D.—for as for *c c c c* they are nothing but parentheses, and the common *ins* and *outs* incident to the lives of the greatest ministers of state; and when compared with what men have done,———or with my own transgressions at the letters A B D———they vanish into nothing. (Volume VI, Chapter 40)

Sterne's diagrams are quite accurate, but they do not take into account the interruption of the motifs.

———

The concept of *plot* (*syuzhet*) is too often confused with the description of events—which I propose provisionally to call the *storyline* (*fabula*).

The storyline, in fact, is only the material used to construct the plot.

Hence, the plot of *Eugene Onegin* is not the romance between the hero and Tatyana Larina, but the "plotting" of this storyline, by way of several interrupting digressions. One ingenious artist (Vladimir Milashevsky) has proposed to illustrate *Eugene Onegin* mainly through its digressions (the "little feet," for example)—and from a compositional point of view, this approach appears to be quite relevant.

Forms of art are explained by their own artistic laws and not by motivations of everyday life. By slowing down the action of the novel—not by way of introducing rivals, for example, but simply by transposing the constituent parts—the artist reveals to us the aesthetic laws that underlie these two compositional devices.

It is commonly argued that *Tristram Shandy* is not a novel; for those who claim this, only opera is music, while a symphony is disorder.

Tristram Shandy is the most typical novel of world literature.

ORNAMENTAL PROSE

Andrei Bely

I.

The various aspects of a literary form are more likely to clash with each other than peacefully coexist. When one device becomes obsolete it gives rise to the development of another.

The well-known progression in literary history—from epic, to lyric, to drama—is not so much a succession of origination as a succession of canonization and displacement.

The philosophical worldview of the writer is his working hypothesis. Or, to be more precise, the writer's consciousness is determined by the existence of literary form. Writers' crises coincide with crises of genres. The writer is completely immersed in his craft.

The writer cannot produce a work of art when an external ideology, unsupported by the technical prerequisites of craftsmanship, invades the realm of writing.

This is what happened with Andrei Bely when he set out to create his anthroposophical "epopee." It is indeed very difficult to create an aesthetic parallel to something that is imbued with a non-aesthetic worldview. A work of art bends or straightens the line in accordance with its own laws.

Sometimes even the author himself cannot say what he has created.

In "The Twelve," Blok began with couplet singers and street talk and finished the piece by appending the image of Christ at the end. For many, Christ was unacceptable, but for Blok it was a word rich in content. He too was somewhat baffled by the ending of the poem, but he always insisted that it was inevitable. The poem has a posterior epigraph, as it were; it is resolved unexpectedly in the end. "I don't like the ending of 'The Twelve' either," said Blok. "I wanted a different ending. I was astonished at myself after finishing it: Why Christ, after all? Does it really have to be Christ? But the more I looked at it, the clearer I saw Christ. And then I jotted down in my notebook: 'Unfortunately, it has to be Christ. Unfortunately, it has to be Christ and none other.'"[97]

Is this an ideological Christ?

Here is an excerpt from Blok's letter to Yuri Annenkov (August 12, 1918):

> Concerning Christ: he is not a small, crooked dog limping behind the procession, who meekly carries the flag and then leaves. The image of "Christ carrying a flag" is both Christ and not Christ at the same time. You know that when a flag whips in the wind, we inevitably imagine someone great, someone who attends and relates to it (doesn't just hold it, or carry it, but—I don't know how to say it).

This means that we can understand the theme of Christ in the following way. There is a wind. The wind rips the canvas banners. The wind calls forth the flag, and the flag calls forth someone great, someone "attending and relating to it," and then Christ appears.

Of course, there is no denying that he is "Christ and none other," according to the poet's stock of imagery, but he has been

---

[97] Kornei Chukovsky, "The Last Days of Blok." *Zapiski mechtatelei* [Notes of Dreamers], Issue 6, 1922.

called forth by the compositional imagery of the wind and the flag.

It is hard to write things parallel to something else, whatever it may be, because art is not the shadow of a cause, but the cause itself—the very thing. That's why a work of art is a bad accompanist.

One of the peculiar features of Anthroposophy is its theory that phenomena exist on multiple planes. For example, a group of five Anthroposophists headed by Rudolf Steiner is not just a group, but is also a mystical rose. This rose corresponds in all its parts to the structure of a real rose. And so the world appears to be multi-planed and self-replicating. The world, according to Anthroposophists, resembles a series of shadows cast by a single object placed before multiple sources of light.

Andrei Bely's task then was to construct such a multi-planed structure, based on the teachings of Anthroposophy. "Swarm" and "form" in *Kotik Letaev*, the crucifixion serving as a background grid in *The Transgression of Nikolai Letaev*[98]—all of these are geared toward this anthroposophic project.

Bely's works were (partly) successful in and of themselves, but in anthroposophical terms they failed. *Kotik Letaev* required a secondary motivation for connecting the two planes of "swarm" and "form"—the world is linked with consciousness through linguistic means and motivated by a child's consciousness. The material transcended the anthroposophic intent, which led to the intensification and fortification of the metaphorical axis.

And so, instead of multi-planed anthroposophic prose, we get ornamental prose. The link between the two planes became too complicated and Bely had to introduce "realistic solutions" (see my earlier discussion of "Lion"). He even began to treat the conflict between the two planes in a humorous way.

In the example that I will cite below, where Auntie Dotty (who is at the same time Eternity) is depicted, or rather concretized,

---

[98] Shklovsky is referring to the original title of *The Christened Chinaman*, which first appeared in 1921 in the journal *Zapiski mechtatelei* [Notes of Dreamers], Issue 4. See Andrei Bely, *The Christened Chinaman*, trans. Thomas R. Beyer Jr. (Tenafly, NJ: Hermitage, 1991). [—Trans.]

with a carpet beater in her hand, eternity turns out to have a beater too. Here the author does not conceptualize eternity, nor does he symbolize it, but rather transfers its attributes from one axis to another and employs this device to establish a semantic disparity. In the battle between Anthroposophy and the device called forth by it, the device swallows up the theory. Bely's ornamental prose flowed easily into the other channels of ornamental prose (Leskov, Remizov), which had been called into life by different intentions.

Andrei Bely is the most interesting writer of our time. All of contemporary Russian prose bears his traces. If Bely is smoke, Pilnyak is the shadow of that smoke.

Andrei Bely has written many books, all of them very different. He is the man who authored *The Silver Dove, Petersburg, Kotik Letaev*—the beginning of his *Epopee*. I don't think that he himself knows what this "epopee" is. He has written that *Symphonies, Petersburg, The Silver Dove*, and *Notes of an Eccentric* are "different medallions of the same grand story."[99] He has also said that *Notes of an Eccentric* is merely a preface to the epopee and that he—Andrei Bely—wishes "to write like a boot-maker." Having renounced the novel, he expects his readers to ask: "Just what exactly are you offering us? This is neither a story nor even a diary, but disconnected bits of recollections and 'jumps.'"

However, we shouldn't overestimate the validity of the evidence produced by writers concerning themselves. Often writers speak not so much about their craft, but about the ideological line of thought to which they would like to adhere. For example, in discussing his literary influences, a writer will often point not to his teacher but to some other writer—someone whom he resembles the least. For example, Pilnyak dedicates his work not to Andrei Bely, but to Aleksei Remizov.

---

[99] In *Zapiski mechtatelei* [Notes of Dreamers], Issue 1, a literary journal published by a group of Symbolists headed by Andrei Bely. Only six issues were published between 1919-22 during the years of its existence. [—Trans.]

II.

It is beautiful in Dresden, comrades.

There is a high mountain with cherry trees that bloom each spring. The fields of Saxony stretch out below. They are as blue as the forest scenery on a theater stage during the day, when there is sunlight. Forest scenery is painted blue instead of green. And the blue fields of Germany are also blue in the spring air. Or rather blue, but corrected to green in one's memory. And lower down, pushing off from the mountain's sandstone wall, the Elbe River rushes on toward Hamburg, dull as a butter knife.

And so, on that mountain (be sure to look it up, if you are ever in Dresden—it's called Cherry Mountain, or maybe Deer Mountain), there is a garden. Every tree in this garden rests against a form fashioned from iron rods. The tree is firmly bound to this form by its branches. The forms depict the contours of a woman in a skirt or a saluting soldier in a visorless cap. And the tree also salutes, as it is attached to the iron form. One might scream in horror at the mere sight of this garden. The saluting tree sometimes reminds me of Andrei Bely, who like a blooming cherry tree has been bound to Anthroposophy. Bely is obliged to write about Rudolf Steiner, to rip off his own mask, and to find all the anthroposophic colors in Blok.

He has to pull Blok to the iron trellis too. But Blok was a free man. He first wrote poems quoting Vladimir Solovyov, but then went on to write *The Puppet Show* in which he took an ironic view of his own mysticism.

For Blok, mysticism and "dawns," gypsy songs and vaudeville couplets—all of these were material for art.

Bely reproaches him for his betrayal and laments the fact that he, Bely, a stranger to Anthroposophy at the time, was unable to show Blok how to live and write.

And yet, at the same time, Bely was writing his very ironic *Symphonies*. And even as we speak, he is adapting some parts of

Petersburg for a vaudeville show.

Lev Trotsky said somewhere that when engaging in polemics one ought to maintain "the pathos of distance."[100] He should know: he has been polemicizing for quite a long time.

An artist must maintain the pathos of distance and not allow himself to be tied down. He must adopt an ironic attitude toward his material and not let it get to him. Just as in boxing or fencing.

I see the cause of Bely's current failure in his non-ironic exclamations about Rudolf Steiner. I heard that the Johannesbau—whose columns were being erected by Bely himself—was burned to the ground, and that the Jesuits are to blame. They are also saying that Steiner is rebuilding a new Johannesbau made of cast concrete. If it were up to me, I would roll some ten poods of dynamite into the basement of this building, cover it with stones, run a Bickford fuse from it and show Steiner how to make a hole in the place where the building stood. Because a writer should never be yoked to a trellis and forced to salute.

But let Steiner live and let him have his Johannesbau—art doesn't admit any binds, and Andrei Bely only wasted his time in Dornach.

If he was able to recover his health in Dornach, so be it!

The art of the novel dismissed the attempts of Anthroposophy. Bely's work represents Anthroposophy's attempt to swallow up the writer's craft. But instead it was the writer's craft that swallowed up Anthroposophy and now grows on it as if it were dung.

Subjectively, Andrei Bely wants to rip off the mask. He wants to break from the device, to renounce form, and, at the same

---

[100] Trotsky was probably referencing Nietzsche's concept elaborated in *Beyond Good and Evil:* "Without the *pathos of distance* such as develops from the incarnate differences of classes, from the ruling caste's constant looking out and looking down on subjects and instruments and from its equally constant exercise of obedience and command, its holding down and holding at a distance, that other, more mysterious pathos could not have developed either, that longing for an ever-increasing widening of distance within the soul itself, the formation of ever higher, rarer, more remote, tenser, more comprehensive states, in short precisely the elevation of the type 'man,' the continual 'self-overcoming of man,' to take a moral formula in a supra-moral sense" (Part IX, Aphorism 257). See Friedrich Nietzsche, *Beyond Good and Evil: Prelude to a Philosophy of the Future*, trans. R. J. Hollingdale (New York: Penguin, 2003). [—Trans.]

time, write his *Epopee*. Objectively, he is compelled to renounce his *Notes of an Eccentric* and return, as he puts it, to the novelistic form.

Still, we shouldn't fall for theatrical exposés. It is common to wear greasepaint beneath the mask.

Bely certainly didn't write his *Notes of an Eccentric* like a boot-maker. On the contrary, he even did

    things

        like

            this,

            supposedly

        to

    depict

the German mine that was going to hit the side of the ship on which he was traveling back home. Boot-makers don't write such things.

Notes of an Eccentric is one of Bely's most complex works. While arranging the text of this "boot-maker" who wrote in angles, columns, and zigzagging patterns, the typesetters said they had never encountered such difficulties and demanded overtime pay.

Notes of an Eccentric has a complex structure: it is based on an autobiographical account with temporal transpositions and oriented along comparative lines—the first axis, that of the pun, is connected to a metaphoric axis.

For example, it turns out that Andrei Bely never crossed "the border of Switzerland" but only "the border of Self."

> The railcars were rapping, they were running across France, the wind was blowing in through the window, my head was bobbing up and down, bumping against the boards. The railcars were jostling. The flashes of the electric lamps leaped in and out with a white brilliance. The diurnal consciousness fell to pieces: the border of consciousness shifted. I had crossed the border. The border of consciousness.

The metaphoric axis is confirmed as existing prior to the "realistic axis."

Sometimes this is motivated through the traditional novelistic device of the dream—the old servant of the novel. It comes in two forms: *dream = presentiment* and *dream = prediction*, and often prepares the reader for a certain insight into a future event. Occasionally, the dream may simply be used to motivate the introduction of fantastic elements.

I will not bother with examples—look them up in Dostoevsky.

There is no point in obsessing over an artist's biography: he writes, and then he looks for motivations. And one should bother with psychoanalysis least of all. Psychoanalysis studies the psychological traumas of just *one* person, whereas writing isn't done by just *one* person—a piece of writing is the product of an epoch, the product of a collective.

But let us try to formulate what we can see in Bely's works of the last six or seven years.

These works are autobiographical, or rather, they are written as autobiographies. The progression of the plot is rudimentary; in fact, one could say there is no plot at all. There is only one storyline: a person lives, matures, and grows old.

Bely has constructed a multilayered structure using metaphoric axes on the basis of this storyline. These axes—let's imagine them as vertical houses—are interconnected by suspension bridges. As the storyline moves along, it serves as a pretext for the creation of new metaphoric axes, which, as soon as they emerge, are connected with the already existing ones. This is the framework of *Notes of an Eccentric, Kotik Letaev,* and *The Transgression of Nikolai Letaev.*

The excursions from the main axis are done somewhat differently in *Recollections of Blok.*

The fragment titled "Arbat," which was published in *Novaya Rossiya,* is constructed in a simpler way. Bely's typical feature can be seen here in the way he treats the imagery: he first standardizes the images, and then employs them as basic terms and concepts.

Bely was most consistent in his construction of the two axes in *Kotik Letaev*.

III.

Kotik Letaev was finished in 1917 and was evidently meant to become part of the *Epopee* (Bely's memoirs). As Bely continues to write, the memoiristic foundation of his *Epopee* becomes even stronger.

Recollections of Blok is constructed as a pure memoir. Bely's anthroposophic rationalizations have been confined to specific chapters in which he dissects quotations from Blok along with all the devices of his work on the "Church Fathers." "Arbat" is also pure memoir.

Bely's memoirs differ from those of, say, Anatoli Koni by their treatment of imagery. Even in the passages where Bely is completely absorbed in Anthroposophy, the task he undertakes does not lead him to the creation of an anthroposophic work, but only to a particular construction of imagery.

There is almost no plot in *Kotik Letaev*—the whole setup is geared toward the image. Thus, the autobiographical works of Bely stand in sharp contrast to, for example, Dickens's most autobiographical novel, *David Copperfield*. In the latter we see a definite plot; there are two mysteries—the mystery of David's great-aunt (that her husband is still alive) and the mystery of Uriah Heep (the forging of documents). Emma's fate is foretold through premonitions. *David Copperfield* is a plotted novel. Of course, *Kotik Letaev* and *The Transgression of Nikolai Letaev* also have novelistic features—aspects of a traditional plot structure. But a literary form can certainly outlive itself, just as the customs of the British Parliament have outlived themselves. They have a Chancellor of the Exchequer who sits on a leather bag lined with fur, the explanation of which can only be found in an encyclopedia.

Kotik Letaev is a story about a boy; it actually begins before his birth, although it is told in the first person. In his defense, Bely has placed an epigraph from Tolstoy's *War and Peace*:

> "You know," Natasha said in a whisper, . . . "I think that when you remember and remember and remember, you remember back to what it was like before you were on this earth."

The recollections of this "time before birth" are given in the following manner. Bely presents a series of images, and each image ends with a point of departure and a place of contact with the storyline. The formation of consciousness is given as a delirium of growth:

> All thoughts are like whirlpools: the ocean beats in each one; and it pours into the body—like a cosmic tempest; childhood thought arising resembles a comet; now it falls into the body; and—its tail turns bloody; and—it pours out in rains of bloody carbuncles: into the ocean of sensations; and in between body and thought, in a whirlpool of water and fire, someone has catapulted the baby; and—the baby is frightened.
> . . . .
>   —"Help . . ."
>   —"No strength . . ."
>   —"Save me . . ."
> . . . .
>   —"It's growth, madame."
> . . . .
>   This is—the first event of being; remembering holds it firmly; and precisely describes it; if it is such (and it is)—
>   —*prebody* life is exposed at one of its edges . . . in the fact of memory. (Part I, "We Arose in the Seas")

The device of "elucidation" (see below) is only outlined in this excerpt. Let me quote further from the middle of the chapter "Burning As If on Fire" (Part I). The motivation for the imagery here is provided by delirium.

—At first there were no images, but there was a place for them in the pendule ahead; very soon they opened up: my nursery room; the hole was healing over from behind, turning—into a stove mouth (the stove mouth is—a remembering of something old and long since disappeared: the wind howls in the stovepipe about pretemporal consciousness); . . . An extremely long reptile, Uncle Vasya, used to crawl out at me from behind: snake-legged, mustached, he was then cut into pieces; one piece of him used to drop in on us for dinner, and later I encountered another: on the cover of a very useful booklet, *Extinct Monsters*; it is called a "*dinosaur*"; they say—they have died out; I still encountered them: in the first moments of consciousness. . . .

. . . .

All this was etched into me by the voice of my mother:
—"He is burning as if on fire!"
They later told me that I was continually sick: with dysentery, with scarlet fever, and with measles: *at exactly that time . . .*

And here is the image of "Lion," whom Bely saw one day in Dog Square:

Among the strangest deceptions mistily glinting at me, a very strange one appears before me: before me looms a maned lion's snout; the time to shout had come; everything is kind of sandy yellow; from there the ragged fur calmly looks at me; and—the snout: there is a shout:
—"Lion's coming . . ." (Part I, "The Lion")

First Bely elucidates the inexperience with sand:

—(Later   I used to see a yellow sand circle—between the Arbat and Dog Square . . .

Then, in the next chapter he elucidates the episode with "the lion":

it turns out that "the lion" was a St. Bernard nicknamed "Lion" who used to run around in the square. The author discovers this twenty years later:

> After twenty years my bit of strange dreams had become reality . . .—
>
> —(maybe the labyrinth of our rooms is reality; and—reality is a snake-legged monster: the reptile *Uncle Vasya*; maybe: the incidents with the old woman are arguments with Afrosinya the cook; the hurricanes of the red world are the stove in the kitchen; the whirling torches are sparks; I don't know: it could be . . .) (Part I, "After Twenty Years—After Thirty-Two Years")

Soon thereafter, however, in the chapter "All the Same," Bely rejects the solution of Lion's mystery: "In reality: there was no dog of any kind. There were exclamations:—'Lion's—coming!' And—the lion came."

Further on, he affirms the reality of the fantastic imagery of "the *old woman* and the rooms."

This game should not surprise us; in works that engage with the fantastic, it is common to leave behind one unsolved detail that re-solves the already solved mystery, as it were.

Similarly, in Turgenev's *Klara Milich*, the hero is cured of his nocturnal visions, which are attributed to an obvious case of delirium. Yet, on his deathbed, he is holding a lock of hair in his hand, and the mystery of this lock is never solved.

It is important for a writer to create the possibility of multiple interpretations in his work—the possibility of "ambiguity," for which Blok was criticized. So, in order to maintain this ambiguity, the fantasticality of the work is at one point affirmed and at another point denied.

Bely came to this device by way of Anthroposophy. And yet, the correct order of the appearance of Anna Pavlovna Scherer's salon in *War and Peace* perhaps plays the same role of affirmation of another understanding of war and peace (in lower-case letters) than the one suggested by the author. Tolstoy came to this by way of his morality. But each writer has his own approach to a certain device. It is very much like romances between people: one man loves a woman for her blue eyes, while another man loves a woman for her gray eyes. The result is the same—there is no shortage of children on this earth.

The world comes into being for Kotik Letaev. Dreams, which until then had been infinities, now adhere like wallpaper to the walls of his room. "Auntie Dotty" takes shape out of the sounds "*ti-te-ta-ta-to-tu*" (Part I, "Rooms").

Later she "taps melodically along a sonorous white row of cold-ish little sticks——'to to'——be so Aun-tie Dot-ty-ish . . ." (Part II, "Auntie Dotty").

Then Auntie Dotty appears as the refraction of a sound-movement.

That is how things are assembled out of sounds.

The real storyline is indicated only by a dotted line. People and things are reconnected again through the sound-movement.

If Auntie Dotty is "a melodic sound-movement," Kotik's father, Professor Letaev, is "a *rumble-movement*"—he is connected to Auntie Dotty by sound.

Meanwhile, Auntie Dotty stratifies. Her stratification had begun earlier, in the first part of the book:

Auntie Dotty was melting—

—she hadn't completely taken shape yet: hadn't been embodied, hadn't become actual, and she would appear as a kind of mist, wordlessly: among the slipcovers and the mirrors; for me Auntie Dotty depended: on the slipcovers and mirrors, among which—

—she would take shape in majestic sternness and the calm-est void, extending herself out with a carpet beater raised in her hand, with a related reflection in the mirrors, with a relatedly pensive gaze: emaciated, mute, tall, pale, shifting—a relative,

Auntie Dotty; or rather: Evdokiya Egorovna . . . Eternity. (Part I, "Eternity in Slipcovers")

The boy's relative thus turns out to be Eternity. A few sentences later Bely separates the word from the image and ends with the following wordplay: "Eternity is related to me."

Auntie Dotty continues to stratify, and also turns out to be like "the fall of droplets in a washbasin"; at the same time, she is what Hegel refers to as "bad infinity" (Part II, "Auntie Dotty").

IV.

It is my view that in creating a literary work, especially a long one, the author never follows the original plan.

The author will set out to do a certain thing, but the technique employed in the work will restructure it completely.

The unity of a literary work is probably a myth, or at least that's how it appears to me—someone who has written semi-belletristic works and seen a great deal of how others write.

Poetry easily and conveniently accommodates existing and found materials. This is how Pushkin inserted the different parts into *Eugene Onegin*.

A monolithic literary work is conceivably possible as an isolated case. It seems to me that Bely conceptualized the device of "the image coming into being" in the process of writing. This is how he did it. At first, he simply added a note at the end of each chapter stating that Kotik had been ill, or growing up throughout the duration of the chapter. Then later he concretized the device by introducing the concepts of "swarm" and "form."

Objectively, "swarm" is an axis of metaphors; "form" is an object in the axis that has been fixed by the storyline.

Subjectively, "swarm" is the coming into being of the world; "form" is the world that has come into being. "Swarm" always precedes "form."

"Swarm" is primarily motivated by Kotik Letaev's consciousness as an infant, his illness, and so on. This, however, is treated
by Bely as a "false" motivation. The true motivation, for Bely, is
Anthroposophy.

Cause = the appearance of "swarm," the loosening of the plot
structure, and the shift of focus onto the image. Effect = the
appearance of the so-called Ornamentalists.

To a large extent, contemporary Russian prose is ornamental in
character—i.e. imagery dominates the plot. Some Ornamentalists,
like Zamyatin and Pilnyak, are under the direct influence of Andrei
Bely, others are under the influence of Zamyatin and Pilnyak, and
still others, like Vsevolod Ivanov, are not under anyone's influence.
It was not dependence or influence, however, that created the
Ornamentalists, but rather the general feeling that the old form
was no longer working.

Social demand and worldview are useful for the artist as incen-
tives for changing the form, which is later artistically conceptualized in the process of work.

And now, let us return to Bely's "swarm" and "form":

My first moments are swarms; and "swarm, swarm,—everything swarms" is my first philosophy; I swarmed in swarms; I
made circles—afterward: with the old woman; the circle and
the sphere are the first shapes: con-swarmings in the swarm. . . .
      The con-swarmed became a form for me: circling in the
swarms I circled out a hole with a boundary—
                —a pipe—
                        —along which I ran back and
forth. (Part II, "Swarm—Form")

Papa "becomes," he comes into being, the bull-headed man trans-
forms into Doctor Dorionov, and Auntie Dotty emerges out of a
sound-movement.

Things emerge out of words, and sometimes "swarm" is presented as a pun motivated by a child's perception. For example:

My mama maintained with emphasis:
—"Ezheshekhinsky . . ."
—"What about him?"
—"His business went up in smoke."
This was also reconfirmed by someone else's voice:
—"Ezheshekhinsky is going through fire and brimstone."
(Part II, "Swarm—Form")

The misfortunes of Ezheshekhinsky—whose business had gone up the chimney, and who is still floating around up there to this day—provoke Kotik Letaev's first reflection on the reversals of fate. He explains further in Part III, "Self-Consciousness": "Explanation is the remembering of consonances; understanding is their dance; formation is knowing how to fly on words; the consonance of a word is a siren."

Here, as elsewhere in Andrei Bely, the word "formation" (obrazovanie) is used ambiguously, referencing its two meanings: 1) the process of forming, and 2) the acquisition of knowledge.[101]

Bely is astounded by the sound of the word "Kremlin":

Krem-lin—what's that? I had eaten *crème brûlée* already; it is luscious; they served it in a mold—with juttings; in Savostyanov's bakery they showed me the Kremlin: it is the little juttings of rosy, sugar-candy towers; and it is clear to me that—

—*kre* is a crenellation of juttings (of a *kre-mlin, crè-me, cre-nellation*), and—*m, ml* is—malleability, lusciousness: and then from the window of the back stairs . . . —they then showed me: against the blue distance of the sky—the Kremlin towers: rosy, crenellated, luscious:—" (Part III, "Self-Consciousness")

---

[101] Tracing the etymology of the words used by Bely, Gerald Janecek provides an alternative translation of the word *obrazovanie* in his introduction to *Kotik Letaev*: "[T]he word *obrazovenie*, usually just 'education' or 'formation' regains a direct connection with *obraz* (image, icon) and therefore serves as the crux of a conflict within the child and between his parents" (xvi). Janecek translates *obrazovenie* as "imaging," however, I have reverted to "formation," as it seems closer to the scope of Shklovsky's analysis. [—Trans.]

Sometimes Bely employs a realized metaphor or an expression taken in its literal meaning:

> —"Valerian Valerianovich Bleshchensky . . ."
> —"What about him?"
> —"He is burning up from drunkenness."
> And Valerian Valerianovich Bleshchensky stands before me . . . —afire. . . .
> Valerian Valerianovich Bleshchensky all the same is a log: he is a wooden doll; the wooden doll in the hairdresser Pashkov's window . . . (Part III, "Valerian Valerianovich Bleshchensky Is Burning Up from Drunkenness")

"Swarm" dominates the first two chapters of *Kotik Letaev*; it establishes the axes of imagery. The author then turns to a more story-based narration. There are no new images in this narrative; each character—Papa, Nanny, Doctor Pfeffer—has his or her own set of images. Kotik's habits such as squinting (looking at his nose), the sensation after eating semolina porridge, and even sitting on his special armchair—all have their own sets of imagery. These events (the events of "form") are merely the hooks to which "swarm" is affixed. Each new detail becomes part of "swarm" and is then recycled throughout the work.

"Swarm" accompanies the new detail as a lining, reaffirmed by the series of repeating moments.

> I know how to squint (to look at my little nose); the patterns would move from their places: . . . (Part II, "The Ancient Secret")

> From my little bed I look: at the bouquets on the wallpaper; I know how to squint; and the walls are removed: they fly across onto my nose; . . . (Part III, "Kotik Letaev's Day")

> I know how to squint (to look at my own nose); and right

away the walls are removed—they stick to my nose; . . . (Part V, "From My Little Bed")

Squinting is not just a game, but also a way of displacing things, a subversion of "form," a transition, and a return to "swarm." At times the connection between "swarm" and "form" is intentionally paradoxical: a child on a potty chair is "an age-old Orphist," the semolina porridge has deceived him, he has "discovered the worlds of ancient reptiles," and he sees "the metamorphoses of the universe" (Part II, "The Philosopher").

Bely cares about the second motivation of his work (the first being Anthroposophy), but he fails to uphold its verisimilitude. His little boy sees (in great detail) the inner structure of the human skull, its semicircular canals, and constructs axes that don't realize the metaphor, but rather de-reify the word.

However, the general structure of *Kotik Letaev* allows for only one dominant to define the work. This anthroposophic work, written at the very height of Bely's obsession with Anthroposophy, evolved more and more into an autobiography.

V.

The Transgression of Nikolai Letaev is a continuation and partial duplication of *Kotik Letaev*. If we follow the storyline, the beginning of one work seems to overlap with the end of the other. From this standpoint *Nikolai Letaev* is the sequel to *Kotik Letaev*. Andrei Bely himself has a rather ambivalent view of the work.

According to Bely, *Nikolai Letaev* is spiritual milk—"food for catechumens." But don't take writers at their word; their psychology has nothing to do with the work and should be considered as no more than an appendix to it. A writer might often renounce poetry in a poem, or novels in a novel. Even in cinema, a hero might say on screen (and I have seen it myself): "How beautiful! It's just like in the movies." The assertion, the exaggeration, and the renunciation of an illusion are all devices of art. Of course, objec-tively, *Nikolai Letaev* seems to have replaced *Notes of an Eccentric* and (partly) displaced *Kotik Letaev* in terms of the author's inner struggle. But it certainly isn't a favor to catechumens.

In its structure, *Nikolai Letaev* resembles a memoir—it is richer in events. Constructed independently of their son, it is now the father and mother who dominate the stage. "Swarm" has been de-swarmed. It is perhaps because of this that the language has changed; the imaginal impediments have mostly been supplanted by idiomatic impediments. The object of estrangement is no lon-ger the image, but the word.

Let me quote two excerpts to prove my point (regarding den-sity)—they are both from the chapter "Granny, Auntie, Uncle":

> —and beyond the glass-panes—there, where the mist, a pewter overhang, fell with a flutter of snowflakes, welded into little drops,—a sprinkle-rain began to fall: a blinking! Already from the gutter-drainpipes the melted snow tumbles down: . . .

> Yes and he womanizes indecently and grins all over and shows his "galaks" (these, I know, are his gums: that is what Granny calls them), he cackles-gackles, begins coughing, lets out a word on the fly; . . .[102]

Bely is well aware of the "dictionariness" of his language. For example, he writes:

> From Granny's words was revealed to me:
>   "He is—a bouser!"
>   And what is a "bouser"? You'll find it in Dahl's dictionary, but try to find it in your little head!

---

[102] Andrei Bely, *The Christened Chinaman*, trans. Thomas R. Beyer, Jr. (Tenafly, NJ: Hermitage, 1991). All subsequent quotations from *The Christened Chinaman* are taken from this translation and revised by Shushan Avagyan.

It is curious here just how seriously the author takes the word—he almost gives it away!

Kotik is being crucified, since the quarrel between his parents is rendered in cosmic proportions. The word is nevertheless marked, because—as if in a play of craftsmanship—it is meant to be serious. And here no miracles need to be shown.

"Swarm" is gone—the world has come into being, yet, as an artist, Bely needs the world to come into another state of being in order to maintain the disparity of things. This otherness of the world is presented in *Nikolai Letaev* as a general phenomenon.

The father's character has expanded to become that of a Socrates or Moses, while the quarrel between the parents is an eternal one. The tragedy of the characters lies in their struggle "for something uniquely their own," which at first appears to be a joke, but then turns out to be something quite fundamental. Bugaev (Bely's father) is presented as an ordinary and comical man, and his character is lacking in "this—one's own," which creates an incongruity with his Socratic-Confucian axis.

Meanwhile, the phrase "this—one's own" is uttered by the uncultivated German nanny, Henrietta Martynovna, in reference to a certain German man.

This nonsensical phrase becomes the sign of a mysterious meaning. It actually has no meaning—the mystery in it fails to hold its ground, although it is applied to Kotik's parents, to Afrosim (who tends to be transformed into "Immortality"), and—to complete the axis and further expand the mystery—to the two griffins at the entrance of a neighboring house.

Mechanically applied to an axis or concept by means of the griffins, the phrase becomes linked to traditional mysteries. Here the mystery is given as nonsense or as ambiguity—in the purely verbal sense of ambiguity for which Blok was reproached (and Bely reproached him, too)—the kind of ambiguity that is perhaps necessary for art, but which does not lead to Anthroposophy.

The repeated images and epithets threaded throughout the

work had been made canonical in *Kotik Letaev*. In *Nikolai Letaev* these images and epithets are simply appended to the protagonists and follow them like an entourage. Often an image is repeated and comically realized, while undergoing changes by way of puns, as in this passage:

> Uncle Vasya has: a cockade, a hearty job, a medal; he—had been recommended for a medal; but—he cackles; and—coughs; for five years he has been pounding the doorstep of the Revenue Department.
> And—with what? It's simple—if done with a piece of felt, but not so simple—if done with a stone . . .
> —How? Thrice bent over?

Then the metaphor is realized—Uncle Vasya is made to bend over thrice, "his head between his legs," and "with his teeth he drags his own handkerchiefs—out of his coattail!" To concretize the metaphor even further, Bely arranges this whole passage in a narrow column in the middle of the page. The column breaks at an angle, bending over thrice.

Uncle Vasya's rebellion and heavy drinking is depicted through a negation of this second axis—by negating the realized image:

> And Mama plays:—
> —taken off, borne off; the events of life fluttered in the beinglessness of sounds; again there came during the years someone tall: that's—Uncle; he stood up on the skinny stilts: on his legs; he is withdrawing from us—forever along the whitening roofs: he is withdrawing to the heavens; and he starts to bang out to us from the heavens:—"Yes I am tired of bending over thrice: it's enough!"
> "I am tired of pounding the doorstep of the Revenue Department!"
> "Here is—the felt, here are—the stones: let others pound it."

"I am tired of trades: a trade is not a useful thing! . ."
"I am withdrawing from you!"

I deliberately kept this excerpt long in order to show the relationship between the images: the mother's piano playing is connected to her "roulade" axis, while the last expression sums up the Uncle Vasya theme.

The piano playing is further developed in the form of a little girl walking on sounds—this little girl is the hero's mother, but later she turns into "Understanding."

In the conventional novel, the connection between the objects of the storyline axis was usually placed in the foreground. If the hero was accompanied, it was usually by an object, and sometimes the object played a role—it served as one of the connecting threads of the plot.

In Andrei Bely, however, connections are achieved not through objects but through images. The *Epopee* is a project of major scope.

VI.

Recollections of Blok is not really part of the *Epopee*, but it stands close to it. Presumably, it is material for the *Epopee*.

The work unfolds through both a development of separate episodes and the introduction of chapters devoted to Bely's anthroposophic interpretation of Blok. These chapters consist of nothing but quotations that are fragmentary and out of context, and that fail to take into account the changes in a word's meaning depending on its use in a poem. In these chapters Bely explains, for example, Blok's evolution with regards to the changes in the frequently occurring colors in his poems. His approach seems to be logical, but it is wrong. The works of a poet should never be taken as a series of personal confessions confirmed by a solemn oath. Even a writer as self-revealing as Andrei Bely cannot truly reveal himself. What seems like a personal utterance to Bely turns out to be a new literary genre.

One should believe even less in the *documentality* of poets' confessions and in the seriousness of such confessional worldviews.

The worldview of a poet—a professional poet—is uniquely refracted by the fact that it serves as material for the construction of poems.

For that reason, a poet's beliefs are full of irony; they are part of a game. The boundaries between the serious and the humorous are blurred in a poet partly because the humorous form, being the least canonical and at the same time the most dependent on the perception of semantic disparities, prepares new forms for serious art. The Formalists (Osip Brik, Boris Eichenbaum, Yuri Tynjanov) have frequently analyzed the connection between Mayakovsky's form and the forms of the writers from the journal *Satirikon*, as well as between Nekrasov's verse and the verses of the Russian vaudeville. Examples from Andrei Bely are less known. His *Symphonies* is a semi-humorous work—i.e. a more serious conceptualization of this work appeared later, and now it seems that new Russian literature would be impossible without *Symphonies*. Even those who scold Bely are unconsciously under his stylistic influence. Bely himself once told me about the "humoristic" (I can't recall the exact word he used) intent of his *Symphonies*, and he had the look of a man who had suddenly discovered an amazingly interesting picture in the 1893 issue of *Niva*.

Apart from the inserted anthroposophic articles with quotations about the symbolism of lilac and gold, *Recollections of Blok* is filled with echoes of Blok's quarrels with Bely. These quarrels appear to be very real, and should not be wholly ascribed to a mere matter of style. They need to be explained. In the past, a writer would never have written about such things (Lvov-Rogachevsky thinks that the writers of the past were better for this reason). The choice of facts is in the hands of the writer. For example, Chekhov never published his own notebooks during his lifetime, and yet they are interesting to us in their own right. Now Gorky is publishing his own notebooks, and Chekhov's stories seem boring to us.

There is a folk tale about a peasant and a bear. They worked together and shared the harvest equally: one got the roots of the crop, while the other got the stems and leaves (and vice versa). In reality, the peasant was trying to outsmart the bear—he sowed rye and gave the roots to the bear, then he sowed turnips and gave the bear the stems and leaves. Literature also has its own roots and stems, and the focus of the literary moment is constantly shifting. Now they are sowing turnips, and memoir literature—the "raw material" of writers' notebooks—is the crop above the ground.

In *Recollections*, Blok's quarrel with Bely (except for certain moments unknown to us and not elucidated in the book) is described in such a way that it appears that Bely was always a Dresden tree, whereas Blok never was. True, there was a coalition between Blok, Bely, Blok's wife Lyubov Dmitrievna, and S. M. Solovyov that aspired to install a "Mamacy" (as opposed to the Papacy) in Rome. But the charter of this coalition was meant to be a joke. It is also true that Bely considered the wedding of Blok and Lyubov Dmitrievna to be an epochal event, and the quarrel was about whether Lyubov Dmitrievna was Beatrice or Sophia. Meanwhile, the formation of this coalition, which Bely analyzes through his anthroposophic lens, was a conscious act of parody. The gatherings were always interrupted by jokes, improvisations, and comic imitations:

> We could have used Apollo's golden carpet; we fooled around, mimicking ourselves and how we would have appeared to the uninitiated. S. M. would usually start the buffoonery, and we would appear in these parodies as the followers of the "Blok sect." The contours of the sect were sought by a punctilious professor of culture from the twenty-second century; S. M. concocted a name for him: academic philosopher Lapan, who raised the most difficult question of whether a sect like ours had ever existed.[103]

---

[103] Andrei Bely, *Vospominaniya o Bloke* [Recollections of Blok], 1922.

Thus, the philosophical side of this circle existed merely as a quasi-parody. In the book (not in real life), Blok's quarrel with Bely is depicted as Blok's departure from Lapan's commandments. For the Bely of 1922, Lapan was truth itself.

Bely viewed the writing of *The Puppet Show* (and Blok's ironic, punning treatment of mysticism) as a betrayal. Blok was much freer in his use of artistic material (until the writing of "The Twelve"). He couldn't stand Bely's friends (Ellis, for example) and the whole thing with Anthroposophy. And Bely, tearing himself out of the work, tragically reproaches fate:

> Later—I told Blok: Anthroposophy had opened for me what had been closed to us during those years, but it was already too late; A. A. had been scorched, because he stood before the Gates longer than anyone else.

A few sentences later, Bely writes: "We gave ourselves to the ray of light, we reached out and grabbed it like children, but the light turned out to be a blaze; it burned us. . . . *Blok* is asleep now, while I limp along the belated paths of salvation."

Bely's use of every word as a reference to the "Infinite" might appear to the contemporary reader as the fashion of 1901. It could also be read as a new conceptualization of "swarm," but when it is done so loosely, it is unbearable. It is awfully hard to learn on every single line that the human being (*chelovek*) = the brow of the century (*chelo veka*).

There is a far more interesting compositional device that Bely employs throughout his *Recollections of Blok*. Things are presented from two different perspectives—Bely's and Blok's. This is especially effective in the passage where Bely, after describing his first meeting with A. A., immediately gives a second description, as Blok "would have described the scene."

Compositionally speaking, Bely also renews the device of the streaming image and employs it most effectively in the chapters on D. S. Merezhkovsky. This is where he describes Merezhkovsky's famous "pompon" slippers and Pirozhkov (the publisher with whom D. S. is negotiating). Pirozhkov is first described, then consolidated as a character. Bely mentions him a few more times and suddenly turns him into an image: "D. S. came by, he was very, very amiable and endearing, and almost courtly: it was as if *Pirozhkov* had stopped by." However, the work is far from being finished. Bely keeps trying to create "landscapes of fantasy, heard quietly from behind the word," but he has succeeded only in writing memoirs, the most tolerable parts of which are the humorous pages with a hint of caricature.

I don't know how exactly "Arbat" relates to *Recollections*. It seems to be the continuation of the latter, but it has a very different tone and is clearly oriented toward the documentary genre. "Arbat" does not simply turn into a memoir; it is conceived throughout as an artistic composition. The proper names are used to create an impeded form. The work seems to have been written in a dialect, but with a concrete motivation behind it. Moreover, it proceeds in periods that span no more than two pages; the periods, replete with "references to facts," turn into streaming images.

The backdrop of the work is presented through the conception of Arbat Street and everything that goes on there as a microcosm of the universe.

So, "Vygodchikov's light" refers to the light in the store owned by Vygodchikov; seeing the light, Bugaev[104] as a child utters his first word: "Fire." But "Vygodchikovs light" is, at the same time, "light in general,"[105] while the proper names in "Arbat" are nothing but Bely's idiosyncratic replacement of the streaming images.

The old argument that led to a split among the Symbolists resembled the division of a particular race into long-headed and short-headed people. The argument evolved around the question of whether or not Symbolism was only a method of art.

---

[104] Andrei Bely's real name was Boris Bugaev. [—Trans.]

[105] Shklovsky is probably playing here with another sense of the word *svet* = world/society, which is suggestive of Bely's "coming into being" in "Vygodchikov's world/society." Vygodchikov, according to Bely, was a colonial trader on Arbat Street. [—Trans.]

Andrei Bely showed throughout life that Symbolism was *not only* a method of art.

The argument, it seems, has come to an end. There is hardly anything of Anthroposophy in Bely's last work. Anthroposophy has played out its role in literature; it created a unique double-planed structure and a new way of relating to the image.

I think it was Henri Poincaré who said that mathematicians razed the thick forests through which they had reached their formulation. Bely's forests are also being razed. His prose today is by no means simpler than his previous work, but the new form is wholly conceptualized in aesthetic terms. It will become part of the new Russian prose.

Bely's failed attempt to live parallel to Anthroposophy is his personal tragedy. Sometimes human culture needs such ancillary tragedies. They are as necessary as the separation of characters for slowing down the action in a novel.

LITERATURE WITHOUT PLOT

I.

There is a section in Goethe's *Wilhelm Meister* entitled "Confessions of a Beautiful Soul." The heroine of these confessions says that she used to view a work of art in the same way as letters in a book: "Good printing gives pleasure: but who reads a book for the quality of the printing?"[106]

Both she and Goethe knew that one who speaks this way understands nothing about art. And yet, such an attitude is as common among the contemporary scholars of art as slanted eyes among the Chinese.

If this view has already been ridiculed in music and is considered to be provincial in the fine arts, it is very much alive in the literary world and manifests itself in all its various hues.

When studying a literary work and looking at its so-called form as a kind of a shroud that has to be penetrated, the contemporary theorist of literature is like someone who jumps over a horse while trying to mount it.

A literary work is pure form; it is neither an object nor material, but a relationship of materials. And, like any relationship, it too is zero-dimensional. Which is why the scale of the work is irrelevant,

---

[106] Johann Wolfgang von Goethe, *Goethe's Collected Works, Volume 9: Wilhelm Meister's Apprenticeship*, trans. Eric A. Blackall and Victor Lange (Princeton University Press, 1995).

the arithmetical value of its numerator and denominator does not matter. What matters is the relationship between them. Comic or tragic works, well-known or small-scale works—the juxtaposition of one world to another world is equal to the juxtaposition of a cat to a stone.

And that is precisely why art is harmless, self-contained, and non-domineering. The history of literature moves along a discontinuous, fractured line. If we lined up all those literary saints who have been canonized, let's say, in Russia from the seventeenth to the twentieth century, we still wouldn't get a continuous line along which we could trace the history of literary form. What Pushkin writes about Derzhavin is neither witty nor true. Nekrasov does clearly not descend from the tradition of Pushkin. Among prose writers, Tolstoy obviously does not issue from Turgenev or Gogol, and Chekhov certainly does not derive from Tolstoy. It is not because of the chronological intervals between the names cited that these ruptures occur.

No, the fact is that the heritage passed down from one literary school to the next is not from father to son, but from uncle to nephew. Let us first unpack the formula. Each literary epoch has more than one literary school. They exist simultaneously in literature, while one of these schools represents the canonical crest. The others exist outside of the canon, in obscurity; such as in Pushkin's period, for example, when the tradition of Derzhavin existed in the poetry of Kyukhelbeker and Griboedov alongside other traditions such as the Russian vaudeville and the pure adventure novel of Bulgarin.

Pushkin's tradition was not continued after him, as is typically the case with geniuses who have no exceptionally gifted children.

But in the meantime, new literary forms emerge out of the lower stratum of art and replace the old ones, which have lost their palpability in the same way as grammatical constructions in speech are depleted of their artistic elements, becoming merely instrumental and imperceptible. The younger generation

jumps into the seat of the older generation, and vaudeville writer
Belopyatkin becomes Nekrasov (Osip Brik's study), Tolstoy, a
direct descendent of the eighteenth century, creates a new novel
(Boris Eichenbaum's work), Blok makes canonical the themes and
rhythms of the so-called "gypsy romance," while Chekhov introduces the satirical journal *Budilnik* (Alarm Clock) into Russian
literature. Dostoevsky elevates the devices of the tabloid novel to a
literary norm. Every new literary school is a revolution, somewhat
akin to the emergence of a new class.

But, of course, this is only an analogy. The defeated "line" is
not destroyed, nor does it cease to exist. It is only pushed down
from the crest; it lays fallow and may be resurrected again, an
eternal aspirant to the throne. The matter is complicated by the
fact that the new hegemon is usually not the pure restorer of the
previous form, but a more intricate synthesis of the features of
other, younger schools, as well as the features inherited from its
predecessor on the throne that have now become ancillary.

Let us now turn to Vasili Rozanov for new digressions.

In my note on Rozanov I touched upon only three of his latest
books: *Solitaria* and the two volumes of *Fallen Leaves* (the first
and second "bundles").[107]

Intimate to the point of obscenity, these works reflect the soul
of their author. But I will endeavor to prove that the soul of a literary work is none other than its structure, its form. Or, using my
formula: "The content (also the soul) of a literary work is equal
to the sum of its stylistic devices," I turn to a quote from *Fallen
Leaves* (Bundle I):

> Everyone imagines that the soul is a being. But suppose it is
> music?
> And they look for its "properties" (the properties of an

---

[107] The first version of this article was published in the newspaper *Zhizn' Iskusstva* (The Life of Art)
in 1921 under the title "Theme, Imagery, and Plot in Rozanov." During that same year Shklovsky
expanded and published it as a small book titled *Rozanov: From the Book* Plot as a Phenomenon of Style.
Later it was included, with some changes, in the first two editions of *On the Theory of Prose*. [—Trans.]

object). And how come it has everything but *form*? . . .
(*Over morning coffee*)[108]

The soul of a work of art is like a form, like a geometric relationship of masses. The choice of material for a work of art is
carried out also through formal signs. It is often material that has
significant, palpable dimensions. Every epoch has its own index,
its list of themes forbidden due to obsolescence. Tolstoy's index,
for example, includes themes of a romanticized Caucasus and
moonlight.

In most cases, it is the typical interdiction against "romantic
themes." In Chekhov, however, we see something quite different.
In a vignette from his earlier years entitled "Elements Most Often
Found in Novels, Short Stories, Etc.," he offers a list of stereotypes:

A rich uncle, open-minded or conservative, depending on circumstances. His death would be better for our hero than his
constant demands.

An aunt in the town of Tambov.

A doctor with an anxious face, giving hope in a crisis; often
he will have a bald pate and a walking stick with a knob. . . .

A dacha outside Moscow and an impounded estate in the
south.[109]

As you can see, the interdiction here is against certain conventional, everyday "situations." The interdiction is put in place not
because of a shortage of doctors who declare that the crisis has
passed, but because this situation has become a cliché. It is possible
to renew a cliché by stressing its conventionality; the success lies
in playing with banality. But that seldom happens. Let me give
an example from Heine:

---

[108] Vasili Rozanov, *Fallen Leaves* in *The Apocalypse of Our Time and Other Writings*, trans. Robert Payne
and Nikita Romanoff (New York: Praeger Publishers, 1977). All subsequent quotations from *Fallen
Leaves* are taken from this translation and revised by Shushan Avagyan.

[109] Anton Chekhov, *The Undiscovered Chekhov: Thirty-Eight New Stories*, trans. Peter Constantine (New
York: Severn Stories Press, 1998).

Die Rose, die Lilie, die Taube, die Sonne,
Die liebt' ich einst alle in Liebeswonne.
(Further on, he plays with rhymes: *Kleine—Feine—Reine—Eine*.)

But the forbidden themes continue to exist outside the literary canon in the same way that the erotic anecdote has always existed and still exists today, or in the way that repressed desires exist in the psyche, revealing themselves occasionally and unexpectedly in dreams. The theme of domesticity, the domestic relation to things, the marital bed, was never or almost never elevated to the "high society" of literature; yet it existed elsewhere, for example in letters. So, for example, Tolstoy wrote to his wife (November 10, 1864): "I kiss you in the nursery, behind the screens, in your gray housecoat." In another letter he wrote:

So, Seryozha puts his face on the linoleum and cries "Agu"? That I have to see. You surprised me when you explained that you are sleeping on the floor; but Lyubov Aleksandrovna said that's how she sleeps, too, and then I understood. I both like and don't like it when you imitate her. I would have liked you to be as essentially good as she.

The day after tomorrow, I'll be standing on that same linoleum in the nursery, embracing you, my slender, swift, dear wife. (December 10, 1864)

But as time passed, Tolstoy's material and technique faded and succumbed to cliché. Being a genius, Tolstoy didn't have any disciples. And without any announcement, without making new lists of forbidden themes, his creativity was placed in the repository. What happened next is what happens in marital life, according to Rozanov, when a couple ceases to feel that they are different:

The cogs (difference) have become worn and blunted, and no longer mesh with each other. And the *shaft* stops, the *work* has stopped: because the *machine*, as the *adjustment* and *harmony* of "opposites," has disappeared.

This love, which has died naturally, *can never* again be renewed . . .

Therefore, before its (final) conclusion, *betrayals* arise, as the last hope of love: Nothing so *separates* (creates a *difference* between) lovers as the betrayal of one by the other. The last *not yet worn-down cog* shoots up and catches on the opposite cog. (*Fallen Leaves*, Bundle I)

The succession of literary schools is perceived as just such a betrayal in literature.

It is a well-known fact that the greatest works of literature (I refer here only to prose) do not fit within a given genre. Indeed, it is difficult to determine what *Dead Souls* represents or to classify it under a particular genre. *War and Peace* and *Tristram Shandy*, with a nearly total absence of a frame story, may be called novels merely because they violate the very laws of the novel. The purity of a genre—for example, the genre of pseudo-classical tragedy—is understood only in contrast to a genre that has not yet been made canonical. But it may be that the canon of the novel is parodied and subverted more often than any other genre.

In keeping with the canon of the eighteenth-century novel, I shall now permit myself a digression.

Speaking of digressions. There is a chapter in Fielding's *Joseph Andrews* that is inserted immediately after the description of a fight. The chapter describes a discourse between a poet and an actor and bears the title "Of no other Use in this History but to divert the Reader."

Digressions generally have three functions. First, they allow the insertion of new material into the novel. So, for example, the speeches of Don Quixote allowed Cervantes to insert into the novel a variety of critical, philosophical, and other types of material. The second function of digressions is much more significant: that is, the deferment or deceleration of the action. This device is widely used by Sterne. The premise of the Sternean device is that a single plot motif unfolds either through an exposition of characters or through the introduction of a new theme (that's how the story of the protagonist's great aunt and her coachman is introduced in *Tristram Shandy*).

Toying with the reader's patience, the author repeatedly reminds him of the abandoned protagonist, yet doesn't return to him even after the digression, and the reminders serve only to renew the reader's anticipation.

In a novel with parallel intrigues, such as Hugo's *Les Misérables* or Dostoevsky's novels, a digression is achieved by interrupting one action with another.

The third function of digressions is to create a contrast. Fielding explains:

> And here we shall of Necessity be led to open a new Vein of Knowledge, which, if it hath been discovered, hath not, to our Remembrance, been wrought on by any antient or modern Writer. This Vein is no other than that of Contrast, which runs through all the Works of the Creation, and may probably have a large Share in constituting in us the Idea of all Beauty, as well natural as artificial: For what demonstrates the Beauty and Excellence of any thing but its Reverse? Thus the Beauty of Day, and that of Summer, is set off by the Horrors of Night and Winter. And, I believe, if it was possible for a Man to have seen only the two former, he would have a very imperfect Idea of their Beauty. (Book V, Chapter 1)[110]

I think that this quotation sufficiently clarifies the third function of digressions—i.e. to create contrasts.

When Heine was assembling a book, he selected his chapters with great care, deliberately changing their consecutive order for the creation of such contrasts.

---

[110] Henry Fielding, *The History of Tom Jones, a Foundling* (Oxford: Clarendon Press, 1974).

II.

I now return to Rozanov.

The three books by him examined here represent a completely new genre, an extreme act of betrayal. These books include full-length literary articles that are broken up and that are interjected with one another, a biography of Rozanov, scenes from his life, picture postcards, and so on.

These books are not completely formless—we see a certain consistency in the way that they have been designed.

To me, these books represent a new genre that comes closest to the parody novel, featuring a loose frame story (the main plot), yet without a comic dimension.

Rozanov's books were a heroic attempt to get away from literature, "to speak without words, without form," and they turned out to be remarkable, because they gave birth to a new literature, a new form.

Rozanov introduced new "kitchen" themes into literature. Domestic themes had been introduced before; Charlotte slicing bread in *The Sorrows of Young Werther* was for its time a revolutionary phenomenon, as was the name Tatyana in *Eugene Onegin*; but the familial, the quilt, the kitchen and its smells (without satiric overtones), had never existed in literature before.

Rozanov introduced these themes without reservation, as in the following series of fragments:

> My housekeeping expense book is worth as much as Turgenev's letters to Madame Viardot. It is *something else*, but it is just as much the axis of the world and essentially just as poetical.
>
> What great efforts! economies! fear of overstepping "the limits!" and satisfaction when "on the first of the month" one has made ends meet. (*Fallen Leaves*, Bundle I)

And elsewhere: "I love tea; I love to put a patch on my cigarette (where the paper is torn). I love my wife, my garden (in the country)" (*Fallen Leaves*, Bundle I).

Or else, he introduced kitchen themes as tender memories:

> . . . I still shake out the tobacco from cigarette butts. I don't do
> it always, only if half of it is unsmoked. No: sometimes even
> less. "Everything must be put to use."
>
> I earn 12,000 rubles a year, so I am not in any need. Why
> do I do it?
>
> The old slovenly way I have with my hands (childhood) . . .
> and perhaps from tender memories of boyhood.
>
> Why do I love my boyhood so much? My tortured, shame-
> ful boyhood. (*Fallen Leaves*, Bundle II)

Among the newly created things, a new image of the poet emerges:

> Wide open protruding eyes, licking my lips—that's *me*.
> Not pretty?
> So what! (*Fallen Leaves*, Bundle II).

And elsewhere:

> My soul is woven together from dirt, tenderness, and sadness.
> Or:
> It is like gold fish, "playing in the sun," but placed in an
> aquarium filled with dung-water.
>
> And they are not suffocating there. Quite the contrary. . . . It
> does not sound like truth. And yet *it is so*. (*Solitaria*)[111]

Why did Rozanov introduce new themes? Not because he was
special, although he was a genius, and therefore special. The laws
of the dialectical self-generation of new forms and the attraction
of new materials had left a void after the death of the old forms.
The soul of the artist sought new themes.

---

[111] Vasili Rozanov, *Solitaria*, trans. S. S. Koteliansky (Westport: Greenwood Press, 1979). All subsequent
quotations from *Solitaria* are taken from this translation and revised by Shushan Avagyan.

And he found them. A whole range of themes, themes of every-day life and family.

Objects periodically rebel. In Leskov, for instance, it was the rebellion of the "great, mighty, truthful" Russian language, as well as the abandoned Baroque language of the petty bourgeoisie and impoverished gentry. Rozanov's rebellion was much grander. The objects that surrounded him demanded halos. Rozanov gave them halos and glorified their existence.

> Certainly it has never happened before, and it is unthinkable that it should ever happen again—when my tears are running down my face and my soul is torn apart, I feel they are flowing like literature, like music, "waiting to be written down," and I feel this with the unerring ear of a listener. And it was only because of this that I recorded it (*Solitaria*—the little girl at the railway station; the fan). (*Fallen Leaves*, Bundle II)

Here are the two passages mentioned by Rozanov in parentheses:

> If you fail to give something, there is anguish in the soul. Even if you fail to give a present.
>
> (*About a little girl at the railway station in Kiev, to whom I wanted to make the present of a pencil; but I hesitated, and she and her grandmother went on.*)
>
> The little girl came back and I gave her the pencil. She had never seen one like it, and I could hardly explain to her what a "wonderful thing" it was. How happy she was, and I too. (*Solitaria*)

> Distractingly, but not loudly, the ventilator hums in the pas-sage; I (almost) cried: "Just to hear it I want to live longer, and above all 'my Friend' must live longer." Then came the idea: "Won't she ('my Friend') hear the ventilator in the other world?" And a longing for immortality seized me so keenly by the hair that I nearly dropped down on the floor. (*Solitaria*)

This concreteness of Rozanov's horror is a literary device.

Let me call attention to a *graphical* detail in order to demonstrate Rozanov's conscious use of domesticity as a literary device. Perhaps you remember the family photo-cards glued to the pages of Bundles I and II of *Fallen Leaves*. These photo-cards leave a bizarre impression on the viewer. If we look at them closely, we will see why: the photo-cards are printed without a border, as is normally done in books with illustrations. The gray background of the card comes to the very edge of the page. There are no captions or inscriptions accompanying the card. All of these together create the impression that we are not looking at an illustration, but at a real photograph glued or inserted into the book. This mode of reproduction was a conscious choice, because only certain *family* photographs were reproduced in this way in *Fallen Leaves*, while other illustrations were printed with margins.

Admittedly, the photograph depicting the writer's children is printed with margins, but the caption beneath it is quite peculiar: "Mama and Tanya (standing by her knees) in the small front garden on Pavlovskaya Street in St. Petersburg (the Petersburg Side). Next to them is the Nesvetevich boy, a neighbor. Yefimov House, No. 2."

The distinctive thing about this caption is the mention of the address (in the manner of a precise police report), which also appears to be a definite stylistic device.

My words about the domesticity of Rozanov should by no means be understood as implying that he was actually confessing—i.e. pouring out his soul. He was using the confessional tone as a literary device.

III.

In *The Dark Image, Moonlight Men*, and *The Family Question in Russia*, Rozanov had appeared as a publicist, as a person who attacked, and as an enemy of Christ.

Such were his political views. Although it is true that he wrote as a black journalist in one newspaper and as a red in another. But he did so under two different names, and each thread of articles was strong-willed and catalytic, and demanded its own special movement. The existence of these two threads in one soul was known only to him and represented a purely biographical fact.

Everything changed abruptly in Rozanov's last three books—or more accurately: it was transformed completely.

"Yes" and "no" exist simultaneously on the same page in these works—the purely biographical fact is raised to the level of a stylistic fact. "Black" Rozanov and "red" Rozanov create an artistic contrast in the same way as "profane" Rozanov contrasts with "divine" Rozanov. His "prophetic" voice also changed, losing its proclamatory effect and becoming domestic, going nowhere.

> Prophecy in my case has no reference to Russians,—but is my domestic circumstance, and it refers *only to myself* (having no significance or influence; it is a detail of my biography). December 14, 1911. (*Solitaria*)

This is where (out of literary necessity) "I do not want to" comes from—the absence of Rozanov's will to action. Values have turned into artistic material; good and evil have become the numerator and denominator of a fraction, the dimension of which is zero.

I want to cite a few examples from the text to show what I mean by Rozanov's "I do not want to":

> No interest at all in self-realization, a lack of all external energy, of the will to live. I am the most un-self-realizing man. (*Solitaria*)

> Do I wish to play a role? Not the slightest (desire). (*Fallen Leaves*, Bundle I)

> Do I wish my doctrine to be widely known?

No.

A great agitation would arise, and I love peace so much . . . and the sunset, and the quiet evening pealing of bells. (*Solitaria*)

I could have filled the world with clouds of purple smoke . . . But I do not want to.
(*Moonlight Men—to be precise, March 22, 1912*)
And everything would have been burned . . . But I do not want to.
   Let my grave be peaceful and "all by itself."
(*At the same time as above*)
(*Fallen Leaves*, Bundle II)

The only thing that is doubtlessly clear here, the only thing that he wants to do—is "to write down!"

Every movement of the soul in me is accompanied by *utterance*. And every utterance I want without fail to *write down*. It is an instinct. Was it not from such an instinct that (written) literature was born? (*Solitaria*)

All of these statements of "I do not want to" appear in a special book—a book that equates itself with the Holy Scripture. The alphabetical index to Solitaria and Fallen Leaves (Bundles I and II) is compiled according to Symphony, a collection of passages from the Old and New Testaments, arranged in alphabetical order:

Abraham was called by God. In my case God was called by me. . . . (*Solitaria*)
And I couldn't wipe out the petty merchant from my soul. (*Fallen Leaves*, Bundle II)
Autonomy of the university. (*Fallen Leaves*, Bundle II)

I have endeavored to show that these "three books" by Rozanov constitute a literary work. I have also highlighted the nature of one of his predominant themes—the theme of everyday life, the hymn of private life. This theme is not given in its purest form, but used to create contrasts.

The great Rozanov—gripped by fire, like a blazing firebrand, writing the Holy Scripture—likes to smoke after bathing and writes a chapter on "1 Ruble and 50 Kopeks."[112] This is where we enter the domain of the complex literary device.

See—so elegantly naked,
She's happy being sad.

—writes Anna Akhmatova in her poem "Statue in Tsarskoe Selo."[113]

What is important in Akhmatova's fragment is the contrast between the words "happy" and "sad" and between "elegantly" and "naked" (not elegantly dressed, mind you, but elegantly naked).

Mayakovsky has whole works constructed using the same device, such as the poem that begins with "Four words, heavy as a blow":

If I were
    as small
        as the Great Ocean . . .

And in the next stanza:

Oh, to be poor!
Like a multimillionaire![114]

---

[112] *Fallen Leaves,* Bundle I. This chapter has been omitted from the Robert Payne and Nikita Romanoff translation. [—Trans.]

[113] Anna Akhmatova, "Statue in Tsarskoe Selo" in *Russian Poets,* trans. D. M. Thomas (New York: Alfred A. Knopf, 2009).

[114] Vladimir Mayakovsky, "To His Beloved Self, the Author Dedicates These Lines" in *The Bedbug and Selected Poetry,* trans. Max Hayward and George Reavey (Cleveland: Meridian Books, 1966).

What we have here is an oxymoron. It can have multiple applications.

The title of one of Dostoevsky's short stories, "An Honest Thief," is an oxymoron, but the *content* of the story itself is also an oxymoron that has been *extended into the plot of the story.*

Thus we arrive at the concept of oxymoronic plot. According to Aristotle (and I am not citing his *Poetics* as the Holy Scripture):

> But when the tragic incident occurs between those who are near or dear to one another—if, for example, a brother kills, or intends to kill, a brother, a son his father, a mother her son, a son his mother, or any other deed of the kind is done—these are the situations to be looked for by the poet. (Chapter 14)

The oxymoron here is based on *the opposition between kinship and enmity.*

There are many oxymoronic plots; for example, the story of the tailor who kills the giant, David and Goliath, the frog and the elephant. The plot here provides the justification—the motivation—and at the same time serves to extend the oxymoron. This is precisely how the oxymoron is used by Dostoevsky ("a justification of life")—Marmeladov's prophecy about the drunkards at the final judgment.

Rozanov's creative work and universal statements set against the background of "1 Ruble and 50 Kopeks" and his reasoning on how to close dampers on the stove—are one of the most remarkable examples of an oxymoron.

The effect is enhanced by yet another device. The contrasts are based not only on the change in themes, but also on *the incongruity between a thought or experience and its setting.* There are two main types of literary landscape: a landscape that coincides with the main action, and a landscape that contrasts with it.

Examples of coinciding landscapes can be found among the Romantics. A good example of a conflicting landscape is the description of nature in Lermontov's poem "Valerik" or Tolstoy's description of the sky over Austerlitz. Gogol's landscape (in his later works) is a slightly different phenomenon: Plyushkin's garden does not conflict with Plyushkin directly, but it is part of the lyrical—elevated—aspect of the work, and this lyrical thread as a whole is juxtaposed against the satirical. Moreover, Gogol's landscapes are *phonetic*—i.e. they serve as a motivation for phonetic constructions.

Rozanov's landscapes are of the second, *conflicting* type. I am talking about the parentheticals that appear at the end of fragments, explaining where or in what circumstances the fragment was written.

Some fragments were written in the bathroom; thoughts about prostitution crossed his mind as he was walking behind Suvorin's coffin; he conceived the article on Gogol in the garden when his stomach was aching; and so on. Many of the fragments were "written" in a cab or else were ascribed by Rozanov to such a time.

Rozanov explains in a postscript:

> The place and setting in which these ideas came to me are always indicated (absolutely exactly) for the sake of refuting the fundamental doctrine of sensationalism: "*Nihil est in intellectu quod non fuerit in sensu.*" All my life I have observed that what takes place *in the intellect* is in complete discord with *what is experienced through the senses.* That, in general, *the life of the soul* and *the flow of sensations* come into contact, repel each other, react against each other, coincide, flow in parallel lines, but only to a *certain* extent. In fact, *the life of the soul* flows through another channel, *its own independent* channel, and, more importantly, it has another *source*, another *impetus.*
>
> Whence does it come?
>
> From God and from birth.
>
> The *non-coincidence* of one's inner and outer life is, of course, known to everyone. But in my case, from my *earliest years* (from my thirteenth or fourteenth year) that non-coincidence was so astonishing (and often distressing, and with

regard to my "work" and "career," so utterly harmful and destructive) that I was constantly amazed by the phenomenon (the *degree* of it). As I have written here, "everything without exception that struck or surprised me," as well as "what I like" or "don't like at all," I have also put this down. In which I have not made one iota of alteration about "the nature of things" (the time and the setting of these notes).

This belongs to the *intellect*. Yet these notes of time and setting also serve a moral purpose; and I shall speak about this at some later time. (*Fallen Leaves*, Bundle I)

The postscript comes *after* the list of errata. It is typical of Rozanov to set the material in unusual places.

What interests me here is the author's orientation toward the contradiction between the place of action and the action itself. His emphasis on the "veracity" of the place is not as interesting as how he selected where to give the parenthetical indicating the place of action (since not all fragments are located). The claim of the documentality of the text is a common literary device, which appears as often in Rozanov as in Prévost's *Manon Lescaut* and is more often expressed in such comments as, "If this were a novel, the hero would have said such and such, but since I am not writing a novel . . . ," after which the novel resumes. Let's compare this to Mayakovsky:

That—
is impossible to say in verse.
The groomed tongue of the poet
can't lick the blazing pans![115]

—and yet the poem continues.

These kinds of claims about departing from literature usually serve as motivations for introducing a new literary device.

---

[115] From Mayakovsky's poem "War and the World" (1916). Probably quoting from memory, Shklovsky has misquoted the last line, replacing Mayakovsky's *goryashchie zharovni* (burning ovens) with *ognennye skovorody* (blazing pans). [—Trans.]

IV.

Now I will try briefly to outline the plot schemes of *Solitaria* and Bundles I and II of *Fallen Leaves*.

They consist of several themes. The main ones are: 1) the Friend (referring to his wife), 2) cosmic sexuality, 3) newspaper articles about the opposition and the Revolution, 4) literature, with fully developed articles on Gogol, 5) biography, 6) Positivism, 7) the Jewry, 8) a long inset installment of letters.

Such a profusion of themes is not unique. We are familiar with novels that have four and even five times as many intrigues. And the device of plot subversion by means of inset themes that echo each other had already been used by Sterne, who mobilized a number of concurrent themes.

Of the three books, *Solitaria* is the most complete in itself.

New themes are introduced in the following way. We are first given a fragment of a situation, the appearance of which is not explained, and we don't understand what we have before us. Then comes the unfolding—we are first given the riddle, as it were, then the solution. The theme of the "Friend" (Rozanov's wife) is very typical of this pattern. First comes a simple mention, then various hints lead us into the midst of things. The person is given in increments, piece by piece, as it were, appearing as an acquaintance, and only much later are the fragments connected, at which point we have a coherent biography of Rozanov's wife. Bekhterev's faulty diagnosis also first appears through the mere mention of Doctor Karpinsky's name:

> Why didn't I call Karpinsky?
>> Why didn't I call Karpinsky?
>> Why didn't I call Karpinsky? (Fallen Leaves, Bundle I)

Later we get an explanation regarding the story of the wrong diagnosis, which failed to take into account the "pupillary reflex."

The same thing with Byzov. His name comes first and then he is developed into an image. This prepares the ground for the new theme, so that it is not introduced out of the void, as in a collection of aphorisms. Rozanov weaves in the new theme gradually, and the character or situation *runs throughout the plot*.

These echoing themes make up the threads which, by appearing and disappearing, weave the fabric of the plot. In developing the second part of *Don Quixote*, Cervantes employs the names of people mentioned in the first part of the book—for example, Sancho's neighbor Ricote the Morisco.

There are curious accumulations of fragments that fall under the rubric of certain themes; for example, the theme of literature contains a fully developed article on Gogol. In other words, this theme contains a complete piece in addition to the fragments. Similarly, at the end of Bundle II, the hints and fragments of Rozanov's counterrevolutionary ideas are concentrated in a full-fledged article. It is written in the tone of a newspaper article and is unexpectedly contrasted with the cosmic ending of the book about the Earth's breast.

Generally speaking, in Rozanov the fragments follow one after the other according to the principle of contrasting themes and planes. For example, the plane of everyday life alternates with the cosmic plane, and, more specifically, the theme of the wife alternates with the theme of the Egyptian god Apis.

As we can see, Rozanov's "three books" represent a compositional unity typical of novels, but without the connective aspect of motivation. Let me explain what I mean by this. A fairly common device in novels is the interpolation of poems, as we see in Cervantes, *The Arabian Nights*, Ann Radcliffe, and occasionally Maxim Gorky. These poems represent specific material that is somehow related to the prose of the work. Authors use different kinds of motivations to introduce them into the main text; they can be in the form of epigraphs or of poems written by the main or inset characters. The latter is an example of a plot motivation, while the former bares the device. In essence, they are the same. We know, for example, that Pushkin's "The Upas Tree" and "There Lived a Poor Knight" could have served as epigraphs to the different chapters of Dostoevsky's *The Idiot*; however, we encounter them in the body of the work, read by the characters themselves. In Mark Twain's *Pudd'nhead Wilson*, we find the main character's aphorisms presented as epigraphs to chapters. Similarly, in Vladimir Solovyov's *Three Conversations* it is stressed that the verse on pan-Mongolism that serves as the epigraph was written by the author himself (it is revealed through the lady's question and the gentleman's answer).

Likewise, the use of kinship as a means of connecting characters is sometimes completely arbitrary and poorly substantiated, as is the case with Werther's patrimony in *The Sorrows of Young Werther* or Mignon's family history in *Wilhelm Meister's Apprenticeship*, where it merely serves to motivate the construction of the novel— the compositional juxtaposition of characters. At times the motivation is too convoluted, such as a dream; at other times it is playful. Remizov often makes use of the dream motivation. The shifts in the plot and the mistaking of the history of a cat with that of a man in Hoffmann's *Tomcat Murr* is motivated by the fact that the cat had been writing on his master's papers.

Solitaria and *Fallen Leaves* may thus be qualified as novels without a motivation.

And so, thematically, these novels are characterized by their making new literary themes canonical, and compositionally, by their baring of the device.

V.

Let us examine the sources of the new themes and the new tone in Rozanov. In the foreground, as I have already mentioned, stand letters. The emphasis on letters first appears in individual recommendations:

Instead of the "trash" of the latest magazine fiction, which should be thrown away, they should publish . . .

Well, let them publish *real work*: science, colloquies, philosophy.

But now and then—and let it be in book form—they should publish a trunkful of old letters. Tsvetkov and Gershenzon would be able to fish a great deal out of them. Many readers would "enjoy them with absorbed attention," and also some serious people . . . (*Fallen Leaves*, Bundle I)

Rozanov even tried to incorporate the raw material of letters into literature by publishing the letters of his schoolmate in Bundle II. This thread of letters is the longest by far and spans forty pages.

The second source is the newspaper, since, despite the intimacy of Rozanov's writing, his works include whole newspaper articles. His very approach to politics is journalistic. These short feuilleton pieces, with their typical device of extending a particular fact into a general, universal fact, are presented by the author as ready-made articles.

But the most important feature pointing to Rozanov's dependence on the newspaper is the fact that half of his book is comprised of journalistic material.

It is possible that the abruptness of transitions, the absence of motivation for the connection of the separate parts, first appeared in Rozanov as a journalistic technique and was adopted as a stylistic device only later. Apart from the canonization of the newspaper form, it is interesting to note how aware Rozanov is of his position as the successor of a minor line of Russian literature.

While Leskov's genealogy goes back to Vladimir Dahl and Aleksandr Veltman, Rozanov's genealogy is much more complex.

Above all, he makes a complete break from the official tradition of Russian journalism and renounces the legacy of the 1870s. And yet at the same time, Rozanov is an acutely literary man; in his three books he cites one hundred and twenty-three writers, but he is constantly drawn to the young and unknown writers like Rtsy,

Shperk, and Govorukha-Otrok. He even says that fame interests him mainly for the chance to make these obscure writers famous:

> Compared with Rtsy and Shperk, how extensively has my literary activity unfolded itself, what a number of books I have published. . . . But throughout my life no reviews in the press, no dithyrambs (in the press) gave me that quiet pride as the friendship and (I felt it) the respect (and also love from Shperk) of these three men.
>
> But what a destiny is that of a literary man: why are they so unknown, rejected, forgotten?
>
> Shperk, as though anticipating his fate, used to say: "Have you read Gruber (I think)? You haven't? I am awfully keen on finding something by him. I am generally fascinated by unknown writers, by those who remained unnoticed. What sort of men were they? I am so delighted when I find in them an idea unusual and before its time." How simple, profound, and true it is! (*Solitaria*)

Rozanov undoubtedly associated himself with this minor line of literature, as the very title of his book *Fallen Leaves* echoes Rtsy's *The Fall of the Leaves*.

Rozanov was the Pushkin of this literary line. He too was the last of his school (according to Stasov and Rozanov himself). Rozanov refers to Pushkin in his essay "An Eternally Sad Duel" (1898):

> Pushkin's connection with the literature that succeeded him is generally problematic. There is a feature in Pushkin that is hardly ever noticed—by the structure of his spirit, Pushkin's work looks to the past, not the future. The great harmony of his heart and the experience of his mind, clearly visible in his earlier works, come from the fact that he essentially represents the culmination of a great intellectual and spiritual movement beginning with Peter the Great and ending with himself . . .

In his brilliant *Notes on Pushkin*, Nikolai Strakhov shows through an analysis of the texture of Pushkin's verse that he never had a "new form," and attributes this to the poet's modesty and "humility"—his unwillingness to be original on the level of form.

Pushkin was building anew. There was no need to subvert a canon in Russia, since no strong canon existed in the first place, which was a well-known fact in his time and in the period immediately before him. Sterne was not perceived as a writer who was subverting and complicating conventional plot structures, and Karamzin "imitated" Sterne by writing works with immaturely simple structures. *Sterne was understood in Russia only thematically*, while the German Romantics integrated his principles of composition—that is, rhymed with what was supposed to appear independent in it.

Rozanov became the canonizer of the younger line at a time when the older line was still in power. He was rebellion itself.

It is interesting that Rozanov did not raise every feature of this preceding line of art, which had a seemingly pitiful, non-canonical role before him, to a certain artistic height. Rozanov borrowed from everywhere. He even introduced slang words used by thieves:

"I have not disturbed your Excellency, because I wanted to catch them red-handed."

I really like this folklore.

I think there is something artistic in the language of thieves and policemen. (*Fallen Leaves*, Bundle II)[116]

Rozanov was fascinated with made-up words such as "Brandelyas" (*Solitaria*).[117] He finally introduced the theme of the detective novel, speaking in great detail and affectionately about the "Pinkertons," and he used this material in *Moonlight Men* and renewed it again in *Fallen Leaves*.

---

[116] This passage has been omitted from the Robert Payne and Nikita Romanoff translation. [—Trans.]

[117] Omitted from the S. S. Koteliansky translation. Rozanov uses the word "Brandelyas" for its pure sound: "The good thing in this sound is that it doesn't express anything, doesn't mean anything. And due to this very quality, it is particularly applicable to writers." [—Trans.]

There are terribly interesting and precious details. In one small book the matter concerns "the first thief of Italy." The author evidently brought his manuscript to the publisher, but the latter, finding the title "The King of Thieves" not enticing or interesting enough for the purpose of sale, crossed out the title and wrote over it his (publisher's) title "The Queen of Thieves." And so I am reading and waiting in anticipation, wondering when the queen of thieves will appear. It turns out that there is no queen of thieves in the book. It is only about "a gentleman thief." (*Fallen Leaves*, Bundle II)[118]

Here the publisher's trick is perceived as an artistic detail.

There are many notes on Sherlock Holmes, especially in Bundle II.

"Children, it is harmful for you to read Sherlock Holmes."

And having confiscated the lot, I am now secretly absorbed in the books.

Each book has forty-eight pages. The stations on the trip between Severskaya and St. Petersburg fly by as in a dream. I also sin "before going to sleep" even until the past three in the morning. Awful stories. (*Fallen Leaves*, Bundle I)

Again, as you can see, the theme here is only named, but not developed. It is further developed in Bundle II, where whole episodes are given in their ideational conception. There is an episode in Bundle I that is very characteristic of Rozanov's technique, wherein Sherlock Holmes is merely hinted at and the whole intention behind this is to intensify the material and estrange the question of marriage. Let me quote a passage:

Evil separator, evil separator. Witch. Witch. Witch. And you dare to bless the marriage?

(*on the English Church; a domestic story involving Sherlock*

---

[118] Omitted from the Robert Payne and Nikita Romanoff translation. [—Trans.]

Holmes: "The Blue Tattoo" and "In Underground Vienna."[119] *The "bride" had to return to the criminal, who killed her husband, who had left her a long time ago and had settled in America, and took possession of his personal documents. He also happens to resemble the dead husband. The criminal is forced to give up his whisky and the aristocratic lady must become his wife, according to Church law) (Fallen Leaves,* Bundle I)

Pay attention to the device here, the ideas are not important. "Ideas can be all kinds of things" (*Fallen Leaves*, Bundle II).

But not all of the material has undergone a transformation, as I have already mentioned. Part of it has remained unmodified. The elements that have not been revised in Rozanov's books can be called Nadsonian. For example, the following semi-poems:

Still, dark nights,
    The terror of crime,
    The anguish of loneliness,
    Tears of despair, of fear, and of the sweat of labor.
    Here thou art, religion . . .
Help to the drooping,
Help to the tired,
Faith of the sick.
Here are thy roots, religion,
Eternal, miraculous roots.
(*Correcting the proofs of an article*) (*Solitaria*)

Or here is another example:

Dim little star, pale little star,
    Alone, you burn before me.
Ill and trembling,
    Soon you will be extinguished forever. (*Fallen Leaves*, Bundle II)

---

[119] Most likely pseudotranslations that were extremely popular at the beginning of the twentieth century in Russia and were sold as collections supposedly written by Arthur Conan Doyle. [—Trans.]

And the same can be found in prose:

"What do you love?"
    "I love my dreams at night," I shall whisper to the wind I meet. (*Solitaria*)

These themes and compositions are perceived as banal. Evidently the time for their resurrection has not yet come. They are not in such "bad taste" to merit improvement.

Here everything depends on the change of perspective, on the presentation of the object anew and its juxtaposition against new material, a new background. Rozanov's images are also organized in this way.

VI.

The image-trope takes shape when something is given an uncommon designation—i.e. when something is called by an unusual name. The purpose of this device is to shift the object onto a new semantic axis, a row of concepts that belong to another order. For example, the stars are called eyes, or a girl is called a gray duck; the image is usually extended by a description of the substituted object.

The image can be compared with the syncretic epithet that defines, for example, auditory concepts by means of visual concepts, and vice versa. For example, "crimson ringing" or "shining sounds." This device was often employed by the Romantics.

There is no confusion at work here, despite the mixing of auditory notions with visual ones: the device simply removes an object from its standard category and places it on a new axis. It is interesting to examine Rozanov's imagery from this point of view. He perceives this phenomenon by quoting Shperk:

I also remember his aphorism about children: "Children differ from us in that they apprehend everything with a power of realism which is unknown to grown-up people. To us a 'chair' is a detail of 'furniture.' But a child does not know the category 'furniture'; and to him a 'chair' is huge and alive in a way it can't be to us. That is why children *enjoy things* much more than we do." (*Solitaria*)

That is precisely what a writer does when he violates the category by snatching the chair out of the furniture.

SKETCH AND ANECDOTE

Ancient Greece did not produce any theory of the novel, but it did give us both novels and novelistic schemes, some of which are still alive to this day. However, little respect was paid to this centuries-old genre; the novel was never theorized. And in Russian literature as well, the novel and the tale have been left untouched by theory for a long time; perhaps the only theory of the novel available to us can be found in translator's prefaces.

Plotless prose is in the same position today. It has grown in importance and historical significance—nearly all the works of the Russian encyclopedists, essayists, and publicists, as well as the whole gamut of writings by the so-called belletrists, belong to the genre of plotless prose.

But this genre exists without a genealogy, and though its aesthetic part is quantitatively greater than the entire novelistic realm, it nevertheless calls for new discoveries.

Plot is a lock pick, not a key. Plot schemes correspond rather loosely to the material of everyday life that they formulate. Plot distorts the material through the very fact of selection, which may be carried out on the basis of quite arbitrary criteria. This is particularly noticeable in the history of ancient Greek literature, where the themes concentrated on the conflicts of a few families. The formal reasons for this kind of concentration had already been pointed out by Aristotle. The anecdotes about our contemporaries

I am about to recount originate from the depths of the centuries.

When Count von Rantzau died, the newspaper *Izvestiya* published an article about his famous riposte to the claim that he was supposedly the descendant of an illegitimate line of the Bourbons. Here is the scheme of his response: *It wasn't my mother, but my father who was acquainted with the Bourbons.* In other words, he was implying that it was the Bourbons who were the illegitimate relatives. This scheme is the exact repetition of the elegant conversation in which the immortal George, the English Lord, engaged in the house of "Elizabeth's mother."[120]

The anecdotes that we tell each other are of a similarly noble origin. The anecdotes recorded by Pushkin were later published as "Anecdotes about Malorussians," while the famous anecdote about the Jew who committed himself to teaching the elephant how to talk—hoping that either the elephant or the shah would die, otherwise he himself would have to die—was recorded, but without the Jew, by Andrei Bolotov as having been told to Catherine the Great.

A plot scheme with a resolution is a rarity—it is an accidental ailment of the material. Its contact with the material usually occurs only at one point. Such a resolution is as rare as a fan-tailed goldfish with telescope eyes.

Sometimes a historical fact has no footing whatsoever and consists of an anecdote.

For example, there is a story by Tolstoy entitled "What For?" about a Polish officer who escapes from Siberia in a coffin that is supposed to carry the bones of his children. Tolstoy scholars point to Sergei Maksimov's *Siberia and Penal Labor* as the source of this story. And indeed, on page 356 of Maksimov's book you will find an account of the story and the name of the person—Migurskaya, a woman—to whom it actually happened. But here too there is a reference indicating that the factual details of the account can

---

[120] A reference to Matvei Komarov's novel *Povest' o priklyuchenii anglijskovo milorda Georga* [A Tale about the Adventure of the English Lord George], 1782. [—Trans.]

be found in Vladimir Dahl's story titled "The Incredible in the Credible, and the Credible in the Incredible."

Such stories do exist. The incident concerning the Polish officer can be found on page 94 of the second volume of the collected works of Dahl (it was previously published in *Patriotic Notes* in 1846). The scheme is the same as in Tolstoy: a Cossack betrays the couple, but the hero doesn't have a name, and the conversation ends with: "You are saying that you witnessed the incident . . ." This is remarkable not only because of the strangeness of the incident, but also because it involves the realization of someone else's intention. Have you read the little book by Kotzebue titled *The Most Remarkable Year of My Life*? In the second volume Kotzebue tells the same anecdote in the form of a hypothetical story—a dream of escape: how his wife, who was visiting him, was supposed to take him back with her.

I intended to have made a partition in my large room, and in one of the outward corners to have placed a great clothes-press. After such preparations, I should have lived two months with my family, to all appearance easy and contented. After that time I intended to affect a progressive decay of health, and at last a derangement of mind. This deception should have continued for another two months. I should then have placed my furred cloak and cap, some dark evening, upon the bank of the Tobol, near the spot where the ice is broken for the purpose of drawing water. This being done, I should have returned quietly home and hidden myself in the clothes-press, which should be so contrived as to admit air.

Having succeeded thus far, my wife would have spread an alarm; search would have been made after me; my clothes would have been found, and everyone one would have concluded that I had thrown myself into the river: a letter in my own hand-writing would have announced my design of putting an end to my existence; my wife would then have appeared the victim of despair; she would have kept her bed the whole day, and at night, would have furnished me with sustenance. Report would have been made of this accident at Tobolsk, and from thence to Petersburgh, where it would have been thrown aside, and I should have been forgotten. Some time after this my wife was to have appeared to recover; she was then to ask for a passport to Livonia, which, in the common course of things, would not have been refused her. She would then have procured a large sledge-kibick, in which a man may lie at full length, and which, indeed, would have been the only carriage in which such an enterprise could have been executed. (Volume II)[121]

There is no mention of the coffin in Kotzebue's story; it has not yet been fully developed. But the details, like escaping specifically in the winter, or the furred cloak by the riverbank, are already in place. So what we have in front of us is not the literary reworking of a non-literary fact (Tolstoy), but rather the synchronization of a literary invention (Kotzebue) with a certain locality and name, the recording of this legend, and the beginning of its literary life.

This is a very typical case. If we look through the records of criminal cases, we will see that it is always the same incidents that end up undergoing a literary reworking. For example, I know an eighteenth-century anecdote about a jeweler who is taken to a psychiatrist. The jeweler thinks that the psychiatrist is a buyer, while the psychiatrist thinks that the jeweler is a patient who constantly raves about diamonds. The plot plays a distorting role in both the selection and arrangement of the material. Moreover, existing facts are ascribed to a character from a different context for the creation of a type, distorting the material even further.

Presently the inertial function of plot has been fully revealed, and the deformation of the material has reached its extreme limits. Class struggle no longer appears to us only as the typical struggle

---

[121] Augustus von Kotzebue, *The Most Remarkable Year of the Life of Augustus von Kotzebue, Containing an Account of His Exile into Siberia, and of the Other Extraordinary Events Which Happened to Him in Russia*, trans. Benjamin Beresford (London: Richard Phillips, 1802).

within a family, although, generally speaking, the family today is more often than not homogenous in terms of class.

The scheme of the "story of two brothers"—now motivated as "white and red" instead of "good and evil"—perpetuates the rather worn anecdote about Cain.

But we can't simply get rid of plot, especially not the kind of plot that has a storyline and is based on the circular construction of the hero's fate. The hero functions as a small "x" on a photograph, or as a wood chip floating down the river—he simplifies the mechanism by focusing our attention. In cinematography, for instance, we know that a film with a plot uses its material more intensively than a newsreel. Of course, we could also say the opposite—that the plot squeezes out the material.

The question now is: What should replace plot in prose? The most elementary replacement would be the method of shifting the point of narration—spatially in journey narratives, or temporally in memoirs. Here we have a pure interest in the material joined with the conventional technique of moving from fact to fact.

We should point out, of course, that memoirs are also subject to the distorting influence of the devices of art. The beginning of Bolotov's memoirs is obviously colored by *Gil Blas*, while Vinsky's memoirs, which make direct reference to Shandyism, are colored by Sterne, whose strong influence can also be felt in Zhikharev's memoirs.

The contemporary feuilleton is an attempt to integrate material not through a protagonist, but through a narrator. This is a de-novelization of the material. The feuilletonist employs his method by shifting the object to another plane not by means of plot techniques, but by comparing large-scale objects with small-scale objects, making them intersect in a single word, or recounting an incident that took place in the West and comparing it with an incident that happened here in Russia.

The feuilletonist does what an ideal editor ought to do—of course, not only an ideal editor, but also a real one. When we say that the novel will be displaced by the newspaper, we are not talking about individual articles. The journal represents a certain literary form that goes back to the early days of English journalism, when the authorship of the editor was clearly felt. Today the journal has shed its literary form and this is especially true of the thick journals. However, we may observe some organic features in the newspaper, provided that it is not overburdened with informational or regulatory material. A newspaper such as *Krasnaya Gazeta* (The Red Gazette), especially in its beginnings, can certainly be qualified as having a literary form, wherein the general direction and tangibility of the newspaper can be felt not only in the articles, but also between them. Even when writing a book, it is generally easier for a writer of documentary prose to work with fragments than with whole pieces. Today, unfortunately, the sketch writer simply colors his material with belletristic details—for example, when describing something he inserts the color of the sky. But this is useless, especially when the color of the sky is conveyed by rote, from memory, without any real, scientific understanding of what clouds are and what they designate. The good sketch writer, however, has his own standard of comparison. So, for example, Ivan Goncharov described the exotic against the subtly expressed but palpable background of the natural scenery and everyday life of ordinary Russia. This discovery of a special point of view that shifts the material and allows the reader to rearrange it anew is a much more organic device for the sketch writer than using comparisons that rarely hit their mark.

The literary development of the factual must not move toward a convergence with high literature, but rather toward a divergence from it—and one of the most important conditions is the struggle against the traditional anecdote, which in its rudiments carries all the properties and all the vices of the old aesthetic method.

APPENDIX I

(to page 34)

Broder Christiansen writes in his Philosophy of Art:

I will single out only one group of non-sensual forms, the most important, in my opinion—*differential sensations* or *sensations of difference* (*Differenzempfindung*). Whenever we experience something as a *deviation* from the habitual, from the normal, from the established canon, we undergo an emotional impression of a special kind, which is not very different from the emotional elements aroused by sensual forms, the only difference being that it creates a perception of dissimilarity with its "antecedents," i.e. something inaccessible to sensual perception. This is a realm of inexhaustible variety because these differential sensations differ qualitatively from each other in terms of their point of departure, their forcefulness, and their line of divergence. . . .

Why can't we fully perceive the lyric poetry of a foreign nation even when we have learned that nation's language? We hear the play of consonance, apprehend the succession of rhymes and feel the rhythm, understand the meaning of the words and grasp the images, comparisons, and content. We are able to take in all the sensual forms, all the objects. So what is missing? Differential sensations—the minutest deviations from the habitual in the choice of expressions, in the combinations of words, in the arrangement and inflections of phrases—these can be perceived only by someone who lives in the element of a given language, who, due to a living consciousness of the normal, is immediately struck by any deviation therefrom, which is akin to sensory irritation. However, the domain of the normal in language extends far beyond this. Every language possesses its own characteristic degree of abstraction and imagery. The repetition of known sound combinations and certain types of comparison belong to the realm of the habitual, and any deviation therefrom is felt forcefully only by a person who stands closest to that language. And thus, every change in expression, imagery, lexical combination strikes him sensually. . . .

This, in turn, creates the possibility of double and reverse differentials. A certain degree of variance from the ordinary can become a point of departure and a gauge for divergence, so that any return to the habitual is experienced as a divergence. . . .

This idea, in essence, appears in one of Nietzsche's aphorisms on "Prose and Poetry": one only writes good prose "*in view of poetry*" (Book II, 92).[122] For prose is uninterrupted, polite warfare with poetry: all its attractions depend on the fact that it constantly evades and contradicts poetry. If poetry is impossible when it cannot distance itself from common prose, then good prose, in turn, must keep itself at a certain distance from poetry.

Anything that may serve as a canon may become the point of departure for active differential sensations. In poetry, it is the geometrically frozen system of rhythm: words submit to this rhythm, but not without certain nuances, not without contradictions that weaken the severity of the meter. Every word insists on its own syllabic stress and length, thereby expanding or contracting the space allotted to it in the verse line. This is how we feel minute deviations from the rigid demands of the system. There is also the opposition of meaning and verse: the

---

[122] Friedrich Nietzsche, *Joyful Wisdom*, trans. Thomas Common (New York: Frederick Ungar, 1960).

verse line demands the emphasis of certain syllables on which the main stress falls, while the sense of the text transfers the accent unnoticeably onto other syllables. Then there is the delimitation of each line of verse from its neighboring lines. The link, demanded by the sense, leaps over these intervals, not always allowing a pause, which is necessary at the end of each line, and carries it over, possibly even to the middle of the next line. We register a continual violation of the basic rhyme scheme due to the stresses and pauses demanded by the sense. These distinctions bring life to the structure of lines, while the scheme functions, besides its formal rhythmic impressions, as a gauge for divergence and thus serves as a basis for differential impressions. The same goes for music: the mathematical conception of beat has to be felt as a background in order for the live stream of sound to stand out, and this is attained through an aggregate of the most subtle nuances of difference.[123]

---

[123] Broder Christiansen, *Die Philosophie der Kunst* [The Philosophy of Art], 1909 (translated into Russian in 1911).

APPENDIX II

(to page 51)

See Shein, 16 (Mogilev governorate): The sparrow demands that the blade of grass rock her baby to sleep and the blade of grass refuses, etc.; Federowski, 11, 4; Rudchenko, 1–2 (Poltava governorate); tale no. 2 in Moszynska, 37 (Kiev governorate); Weryho, 5: The sparrow demands that the blade of grass rock her like a cradle—no mention of the baby sparrow, 47: no mention of the goat with the nuts. The continuation of tale no. 46 in Afanasyev: The she-goat goes after the nuts, the he-goat sets the wolves on her. The wolves refuse to chase her, and the he-goat calls the bears to chase the wolves, and so on. Erlenvein, 11 (Tula governorate); Bessonov, 139; Afansyev, 27; Romanov, 3, 8 (Mogilev governorate); Romanov, 3, 8, additional version (Mogilev governorate). Shein, 15 (Mogilev governorate), the same, not in the form of a song, but in the form of a theatrical dialogue: "I will set the wolf on you.—Wolf, go eat the she-goat." "I won't go." Also see Bessonov, 136: "She-goat, where have you been?" "I was watching the horses." "Where are the horses?" "They are in the forest." "And where is your soul?" "It went up to heaven." Romanov's collection (Mogilev governorate): The grandfather sends the mouse to eat the *sochivo*.[124] The mouse refuses to eat it, and so on. In the illustrated

---

[124] A special Russian Orthodox Christmas Eve dish made from scalded wheat grains, poppy seeds, and honey. [—Trans.]

weekly *Voskresny dosug* (Sunday Leisure), Issue 19, 1871: The hen lays golden eggs, the mouse steals them, and the old woman kills the mouse. There is a clatter in the street, the Volga floods, and the hen drowns in the Volga. (This version seemed strange to A. Smirnov). Both this version, where the Volga floods because of the death of the mouse, and the tale "The Rooster and the Hen" are strange in the way that they link their steps. Why does the sea need the tusk of the wild boar? The storyteller simply didn't succeed in linking up these steps. He just placed them side by side without any logical connection. They were brought together due to the principle of filling in the pattern.

The tale about the rooster (or the hen) that choked on a grain. Federowski, 11, 6: The hen chokes on a bean, the rooster runs to the sea for water. Afanasyev, 34 (Arkhangelsk governorate): The rooster dies. Onchukov, 227 (Arkhangelsk governorate); Manzhura, 5 (Yekaterinoslav governorate); Romanov, 33 (Mogilev governorate): The rooster is saved and comes back to life. See also Sadovnikov, 49 (Samara governorate); Onchukov, 215 (Olonets governorate); the journal *Zhivaya starina* (Living Antiquity), no. 3, 1895—a Malorussian tale with detailed listings; Ivanitsky, 30 (Vologda governorate); Weryho, 16 (Belarusian tales).

The tale about the hen and the rooster (blaming each other). Afanasyev, 33 (Tambov governorate): The rooster and the hen go out to pick walnuts. The rooster injures the hen's eye with a walnut: "Rooster, why did you injure the hen's eye?" "The walnut tree ripped my pants," and so on. From *A Collection of Materials Describing the Terrain and Tribes of the Caucasus*, Vol. XV, 19; the pedagogical journal *Uchitel* (Teacher), Issue 23, 1862 (Kharkov governorate): The hen lays an egg, the mouse breaks it, and all hell breaks loose. Afanasyev 35: The hen lays an egg, the mouse breaks it; the old man and the old woman weep. They tell the communion wafer baker and she breaks all the wafers. They tell the deacon and he breaks all the church bells. They tell the priest and he tears up all the holy books. Chubinsky, 11, 24 (Poltava governorate); poetic rendition—Grachenko, 1, 156 (Kharkov governorate); Sadovnikov, 50 (Samara governorate); tale no. 1 in Moszynska, 36 (Kiev governorate); *Uchitel* (Teacher), Issue 23, 1862, a rather weak poetic rendition (Kharkov governorate); Onchukov, 216 (Olonets governorate): The hen is startled, taken aback by the collapse of the firewood. She shouts to the rooster: "The sky has fallen down!" and so on. The ending is the same as in the tale "The Animals in the Pit." The tale "Kolobok" follows the same pattern of "accumulation" where the storyteller maintains the repetition of all previous steps. Rudchenko, 11 (Poltava governorate); Onchukov, 133 (Olonets governorate); Avdeev, 2, 63 (Perm governorate); Bessonov, 129: A random insertion about Kolobok. Shein, 6 (Vitebsk governorate); Romanov, 3, 21 (Mogilev governorate): The versions are mainly given according to the directory of themes from Russian tales by A. Smirnov (Academy of Sciences, Department of Russian Language and Literature, Vol. XVI, 1911).

This type is similar to tales that involve an exchange. For example, the first tale in Afanasyev: the fox exchanges a rolling pin for a goose, the goose for a turkey, and the turkey for a bride. The same device is used in the Western European fairy tale reworked by Hans Christian Andersen and titled "What the Old Man Does Is Always Right." The exchange of goods is enlivened with a humorous conceptualization of a gradual *decrease* in the value of the bartered goods.

For the purpose of comparison, here is an excerpt from Solomon Beilin's book entitled *Traveling or Universal Tales and Legends in Ancient Rabbinical Literature* (1907), where the author cites tales of the type a < b < c < d in the sense of a geometric progression.

In the twelfth fable of the third book of *Panchatantra*, "The Mouse Who Became a Girl," as well as the seventh story of the eighth chapter of *Kalila and Dimna* (about the recluse and the mouse) we read the following:

A recluse whose piety and devotion were such that his prayers found acceptance in the regions above, sitting in calm repose at the door of his cell, noticed that a kite, when flying along, had dropped a young mouse. Hurrying to secure the poor little creature, he carried it within, and, thinking that perhaps it might not be a welcome gift in his home, he prayed that the creature might become a girl. When his intercessions were answered, he handed her over to one of his disciples. In due course, after a lapse of years, the time arrived for the girl to be married, whereupon he bade her select whom she would. She not unnaturally was desirous of choosing a husband of exalted station, a happy possessor of might, majesty, dominion, and power. The devotee suggested that the sun in the heavens would meet her wishes; but the latter refused, on the ground that a cloud was more powerful, inasmuch as it at times completely screened him from sight. The cloud was equally unwilling, since it could be dissipated by the wind, to whom it must yield obedience. The wind in turn writhed with shame, inasmuch as it possessed no power against a mountain. Once again the recluse met with refusal, in so far that it was pointed out that simple tiny mice made homes in the sides of the largest hill, which was quite unable to eject them. Thus disappointed on all sides, no hope remained but to change the damsel back to her original shape as a mouse, so she could become the bride of the all-powerful creature, which could riddle a mighty hill, and pierce the sides of a lofty mountain.[125]

The moral of the fable: Nature and innate properties never change.

In the Romanian tale "The Mouse Always Returns to Its Hole," the wind asserts that the oak is stronger than the mouse, because the latter withstands the strong winds and violent storms. But the wind also says that the oak will soon fall to the ground, since the mice have dug holes near its roots. So the wind advises the mouse to return to its hole where it will find the strongest creature on earth.[126]

---

[125] *Tales Within Tales,* trans. Janice Dohm and Arthur N. Wollaston (London: John Murray, 1909).

[126] Aleksandr Yatsimirsky, trans. *Sobranie Rumynskikh skazok i legend* [A Collection of Romanian Tales and Legends], 1902.

We read the following in the Midrash Rabbah (edited circa third to fifth centuries): When Terah found out about the heretical ideas and reckless actions of his son Abraham (that Abraham had intentionally and provocatively smashed popular idols, spitefully and pointedly mocked the ancient faith, and was preaching some new teaching of "the one God"), he delivered him to Nimrod: "Let us worship the fire!" Nimrod proposed. "Let us rather worship water, which extinguishes the fire," replied Abraham. "Then let us worship water!" "Let us rather worship the clouds which bear the water." "Then let us worship the clouds!" "Let us rather worship the winds which disperse the clouds." "Then let us worship the wind!" "Let us rather worship human beings, who withstand the wind." "You are just bandying words," he exclaimed; "We will worship nought but the fire. Behold, I will cast you into it, and let your God whom you adore come and save you from it" (Book I, 38:13).[127]

In the Babylonian Talmud (Baba Bathra) we find the following instruction about the mighty and beneficial power of deeds of kindness (justice, charity, etc.) containing a similar but more detailed parallelism (an order, so to speak) listing the physical and spiritual forces of nature overpowering one another: "Rabbi Judah says: Great is charity, in that it brings the redemption nearer, as it says, Thus saith the Lord, Keep ye judgment and do righteousness [zedakah], for my salvation is near to come and my righteousness to be revealed (Jer. XL, 3; spoken by Nebuzaradan to Jeremiah). He also used to say: Ten strong things have been created in the world. The rock is hard, but the iron cleaves it. The iron is hard, but the fire softens it. The fire is hard, but the water quenches it. The water is strong, but the clouds bear it. The clouds are strong, but the wind scatters them. The wind is strong, but the body bears it. The body is strong, but fright crushes it. Fright is strong, but wine banishes it. Wine is strong, but sleep works it off. Death is

---

[127] *The Babylonian Talmud: Midrash Rabba*, ed. Isidore Epstein, trans. H. Freedman (London: Soncino Press, 1961).

stronger than all, and charity saves from death, as it is written, righteousness [*zedakah*] delivereth from death" (Folio 10a).[128]

A similar stepped parallelism can be found in Midrash Kohelet, but with a different elucidation or conclusion; here it is carried out as a satire on "the wicked wives." The idea of the satire is the following: one element overpowers the other; one is mightier (fiercer) than the other, and yet there is nothing worse than a wicked (spiteful) woman. She is more terrifying than anything else in the world; she is even worse than death itself.

According to Rabbi Judah (Kohelet, 7:46), there are fourteen things, each worse than the one before: the abyss is almighty, but the earth conquers it; the earth is powerful, but the hills stand supreme over it; the mountain is strong, but iron cleaves it; iron is hard, but fire penetrates it; fire is all-devouring, but water extinguishes it; water is mighty, but the clouds suffer it; the clouds are heavy, but the wind scatters them; the wind is fierce, but a wall resists it; the wall is solid, but man can tear it down; man is tough, but trouble can shake him; trouble is injurious, but wine can tame it; wine is controlling, but sleep can make it pass away; sleep is unshakable, but illness can unsettle it; illness is bad, but the angel of death carries off the soul. But a wicked wife is worse than all of these.

There is an analogous Ethiopian parable, according to which "iron is strong, but fire is stronger; and yet, water is stronger than fire; the sun is stronger than water; the cloud is stronger than the sun; the earth is stronger that the cloud; man is stronger than the earth; grief is stronger than man; wine is stronger than grief; sleep is stronger than wine, but the strongest of all is woman."[129]

Spiteful or comical commentary on "wicked wives" like that of the Midrash can also be found in old Slavonic texts that were transferred into oral folklore in the form of folk riddles and jokes:

If the temple burns, what will extinguish the fire?—Water.

---

[128] *The Babylonian Talmud: Tractate Baba Bathra*, ed. Isidore Epstein, trans. Maurice Simon and Israel Slotki (London: Soncino Press, 1961).

[129] Fyodor Buslaev, *Stranstvuyushchie povesti i rasskazy* [Traveling Tales and Stories], 1874.

What is greater than water?—The wind. What is greater than the wind?—The mountain (because it withstands the wind). What is greater than the mountain?—Man (because he digs through the mountain). What is more vicious than man?— Drunkenness (because it numbs the hands and legs). What is more vicious than drunkenness?—Sleep. What is more vicious than sleep?—The wife.[130]

The song "Barelach villin nicht falln" (The Pears Don't Want to Fall) is a favorite among Lithuanian Jewish children.

The song "Chad Gadya" (One Little Goat) is even more popular—still to this day—among Central and Eastern European Jews or the so-called Ashkenazim (Jews of German extraction), and has even made its way into the Passover Haggadah (texts read during the first two evenings of the Passover in commemoration of the Jewish exodus from Egypt).

These folk songs involve both animate and inanimate objects that fight and overpower each other.

The content of the first song—with the exception of a few minor changes—is the same as the content of the following German folk tale: The Lord created the pear tree that it may bear fruit, but the tree refused to bear fruit, and the pears in turn did not want to fall (from the tree). Then the Lord sent the young lad (Jockel) to harvest (pick) the ripe pears from the tree, but Jockel, in turn, didn't want to go and pick the pears, as the pears didn't want to fall (into his hands). So the Lord sent a dog to bite Jockel for his disobedience, but the dog refused to go. The Lord sent a stick to motivate the dog, but the stick refused to beat the dog. Then the Lord sent fire to burn the stick, water to extinguish the fire, an ox to drink up the water, a butcher to slaughter the ox, and finally the angel of death to slay the butcher. But all is in vain: they refuse to obey. But when the Lord Himself fetches the angel of death, things change and everyone becomes obedient. The

---

[130] Ivan Khudyakov, *Velikorusskie zagadki* [Velikorussian Riddles], 1864. Also see Aleksandr Pypin, *Istoriya drevnerusskoy literatury* [The History of Old Russian Literature], 1902.

angel of death agrees to kill the butcher if the latter disobeys. The butcher promises to slaughter the ox, the ox is willing to drink up the water, and so on. And all this ends with the lad going to pick the pears, and the pears fall willingly into his hands from the tree.

There is a similar song among the Slovenes (Fyodor Buslaev): They send a dog to bring the lad Yurka home, but the dog refuses to go fetch him. They send a stick, but the stick refuses to beat the dog. They send fire to burn the stick, water to extinguish the fire, oxen to drink up the water, a butcher to slaughter the oxen, a witch to cast a spell on the butcher—but all is in vain. Finally they send the devil after the witch, who casts a spell on the butcher, who goes to slaughter the oxen, who go to drink up the water, which goes to extinguish the fire, which goes to burn the stick, which goes to beat the dog. The dog goes after Yurka and the latter returns home.

There is also a similar song sung by Russian children, according to Buslaev: A goat goes to gather some nuts and doesn't come home. They send wolves after the goat, but the wolves refuse to go. Then they send men after the wolves, and so on. Nothing works, nobody obeys. They finally send geese after the worms:

> The geese go to peck at the worms,
> The worms go to sharpen the knife,
> The knife goes to kill the oxen,
> The oxen go to drink the water,
> The water goes to extinguish the fire,
> The fire goes to burn the stone,
> The stone goes to hone the axe,
> The axe goes to fell the trees,
> The trees go to beat the bear,
> The bear goes to scare the men,
> The men go to drive out the wolves,
> The wolves go to chase the goat—
> Here comes the goat with the nuts.

"Chad Gadya" and the other songs and tales mentioned above all involve a chain of objects and characters that overpower each other in a struggle for dominance. The chain leads to God, who is always the victor.

The difference between this liturgical song and other similar children's tales is in the relationship between the characters and their actions. In the Passover song, the characters act voluntarily, of their own accord—some of them motivated by an evil will, while others out of their own sense of justice—rather than being forced, as in the rest.

Here is the content of the song "Chad Gadya": The little goat bought by the singer's father for two *zuzim* was ripped to pieces by a (wild, ferocious) cat. In punishment, the dog bit the cat, the mother beat the dog with a stick, the fire burned the stick, the water extinguished the fire, the ox drank the water, the slaughterer (shochet) killed the ox, the angel of death came and slew the slaughterer, and finally the Holy One came and smote the angel of death.

In this song, the relationship between the author and his subject-matter is incorrect, as he pays attention to something insignificant: how the various semantic content is applied to the given device. One might think that the moral appended at the end of the song has as little to do with the song as the tears shed by its audience. It is well known that composers often adapted their chorales for humoristic couplets and the public was highly entertained by the wit and joy of the music that seemed to them religious in its very essence when heard in church (Eduard Hanslick).

The most important thing here is the device of deferment. The purpose of this device is to construct a palpable, perceivable work. A prosaic perception of this device induces an impatience among the listeners and a desire to cut it short. Such an attitude can often be seen among the gentlemen collectors of folk tales who readily omit the deferrals and repetitions. The creators of folk tales were aware of such a perception and even played with it. This is what "endless tales" are based on. Sancho Panza tells a similar tale about "goats being ferried across a river" to his master in *Don Quixote* (Book I, Chapter 20).

APPENDIX III

(to page 67)

From the preface of Ferdinand Brunetière's *Manual of the History of French Literature*:

> . . . I have not omitted to note those other influences on which it is the habit to lay weight, the influence of race or the influence of environment; however, as I hold that of all the influences which make themselves felt in the history of a literature, the principal is that of *works on works*, I have made it my special concern to trace this influence and to follow its continuous action. We wish to be different from those who have preceded us in history: this design is the origin and determining cause of changes in taste as of literary revolutions; there is nothing metaphysical about it. The Pleiad of the sixteenth century wished to do "something different" from the school of Clément Marot. Racine in his *Andromaque* wished to do "something different" from Corneille in his *Petharite*; and Diderot in his *Père de Famille* wished to do "something different" from Molière in his Tartuffe. The Romanticists of our own time wished to do "something different" from the Classicists.[131] It is for this reason that I have not concerned

---

[131] There have also been writers who have wished to do "the same thing" as their predecessors. I am well aware of the fact! But in the history of literature and of art, they are precisely the writers who do not count.

myself with the other influences, except in so far as the succession of periods is not sufficiently explained by the influence of works on works. The useless multiplication of causes is to be avoided, and under the pretext that literature is the expression of society, the history of literature must not be confounded with that of manners. They are quite distinct.[132]

---

[132] Ferdinand Brunetière, *Manual of the History of French Literature*, trans. Ralph Derechef (London: T. Fisher Unwin, 1898).

AFTERWORD: DESTINATIONS

Lyn Hejinian

In what may be the most aesthetically invigorating chapter of *On the Theory of Prose*—itself, as readers of this volume will certainly agree, a magnificently tantalizing book—Viktor Shklovsky remarks, "The history of literature moves along a discontinuous, fractured line. If we lined up all those literary saints who have been canonized, let's say, in Russia from the seventeenth to the twentieth century, we still wouldn't get a continuous line along which we could trace the history of literary form." Viktor Shklovsky's writings—both their substantive content (the ideas he elaborates) and their complex narrative structures (replete with interpolations and interruptions—leaping, dashing, burrowing, and plunging like a rabbit chased by a predator *and* a bobcat chasing its prey)—have *directly* influenced many North American literary writers and *indirectly* (or vicariously) influenced even more.

The title of the chapter from which I've just quoted is, as we find it here in Shushan Avagyan's wonderful translation, "Literature Without Plot." Its first publication in English, in a translation by Richard Sheldon, occurred in 1982, where, under the title "Plotless Literature," it inaugurated *Poetics Journal*, being given pride of place as the first essay in the journal's first issue. Barrett Watten and I, as the founding co-editors of *Poetics Journal*, wanted to begin the work of publishing a journal dedicated to the discovery and exploration of issues emerging from new aesthetic practices by acknowledging the fundamental contributions made by Viktor Shklovsky (and of Russian Formalism more generally) to the very possibility of imagining *poetics* as itself an aesthetic practice.

And it was very much poetics, not stylistics, that engaged Shklovsky's attention.

The difference is a profound one, and it can perhaps be best located in the distinction between elements of style and technique. Elements of style come from outside the work and are applied to create some effect, pleasing perhaps but not fundamental. Technique, on the other hand, is manifest in a work's specific devices (rhymes, parallelisms, parataxis, juxtapositions, deceleration, estrangement, etc.) and the thinking that propels them is structural; technique is formal, in an architectural sense, but also formative. At their best, elements of style provide delight and excitement, but technique provides the very purport of the work—its raison d'être and, therefore, its meaning. They are not technical but methodological. They are, to use Shklovskian terminology, *motivated*. And it is with the emphasis on motivation that a number of North American writers made a turn to poetics, not as a substitute for their poetry or literary prose but as an integral part of it.

Perhaps most committed to this turn was the group of poets and prose writers associated with what is now known as Language writing, a movement that was first emerging in the mid-1970s, just as English language editions of Viktor Shklovsky's principle works were appearing in rapid succession.[1] In the course of making the turn to poetics, they also shifted the context in which Russian Formalism had previously been read, away from New Criticism's insistence on the separation of works of literature from life and toward what, in an important but radical re-understanding of Formalism's central precepts, could become a social aesthetic.

Carla Harryman's association with Language writing is long-standing; from its inception, she has been a prominent presence in its social formations and in the aesthetic activism for which it is well known. But, prior to that association, she began her literary activities as a fiction writer, studying with Ronald Sukenick in the days just prior to the founding, in 1974, of the Fiction Collective. It was under Sukenick's tutelage that Harryman first read Shklovsky, during a period in which she was beginning to formulate her challenge to conventional narrative structures. And it was not long before she virtually abandoned story, and turned instead to the literary investigation of the *situation*. In so doing, she could focus attention not only on the narratives that get produced through actions and agents but also, and primarily, on production and agency itself. I will return to her work. For now I want only to note that one trajectory of Shklovsky's influence on North American writing can be traced through the kinds of experimental fiction that Sukenick and the Fiction Collective were developing.

Among poets, however, credit for much of the most cogent initial understanding of Shklovsky's work for North American literary thinkers must be given to Barrett Watten, one of the original and still one of the most significant of the Language writers. Watten brought Russian Formalism into the public conversation with a talk titled "Russian Formalism & the Present," presented on March 18, 1979 as one in an ongoing series of "Talks" initiated and curated from 1977 to 1981 by Bob Perelman, another of the Language writers.[2] In that talk, Watten takes up a key Russian Formalist concept, which proposes that the literariness of a literary work is to be found at work principally through its devices. Speaking of his own interests, which he aligns here with those of Shklovsky, he says, "[M]y criterion of interest has been, in general, that a given work comes to an identity with its particular technique. How it comes into being is the same as what it is."[3]

Watten's model, then—like that of the Russian Formalists

whose notions Watten is describing—is dynamic; technique mobilizes processes. One of these processes, of course, is *ostranenie* (estrangement or defamiliarization), a term that Viktor Shklovsky coined and a device about which he wrote on numerous occasions, including here in *On the Theory of Prose*:

> And so in order to restore the sensation of life, in order to feel things—to make the stone stony—we have something called art. The purpose of art is to convey the sensation of an object as something visible, not as something recognizable. The devices of art—*ostranenie,* or the "estrangement" of objects, and the impeded form—magnify the difficulty and length of perception, because the process of perception in art is an end in itself and must be prolonged. *Art is a means of experiencing the making of an object; the finished object is not important in art.*

It is not just the reinvigoration of everyday life and of perception even at the level of the quotidian that devices of defamiliarization achieve, however. Certainly the prolongation and intensification of the aesthetic is of critical importance to a lived life, but of equal importance are the semantics of occasion—the reasons, rational or not, that configure a moment such that it becomes an event. As Watten in "Russian Formalism & the Present" turns his attention to poetry of the essay's immediate present (spring, 1979), he points to a technique that is virtually the signature of Shklovsky's work, the use of radical, and sometimes (as in Watten's own work, even jolting) juxtapositions. These can cause sudden shifts of focus, open new pathways for attention, propel new trajectories of thought and affect, as well as construct astute parallelisms. These parallelisms function to facilitate ongoing processes of semantic shifting, which in turn produce changing possibilities and renovated opportunities for meaning. The message is clear: we are not stuck.

Here Watten's address is to the social potential of literary technique—which is to say of literariness itself, which ceases to exist—literariness vanishes—when the work is no longer constructing meaning. It may do so again, of course—the literariness of Alexander Pope or Henry Wadsworth Longfellow, for example, comes and goes.

Even prior to Barrett Watten's 1979 poet's talk in San Francisco, information about Russian Formalism was becoming available. Victor Erlich's seminal study, *Russian Formalism: History-Doctrine*, first came out in 1955, and a revised second edition came out ten years later in 1965 (both from Mouton Publishers in The Hague). There were subsequent reprintings, and my own, much underlined, copy is from 1980; I probably purchased it in the wake of Watten's talk. Several other volumes played an important role in shifting the literary conversation of the period: *Russian Formalist Criticism: Four Essays* (trans. Lee T. Lemon and Marion J. Reis; Univ. of Nebraska Press, 1965), *Russian Formalist Theory and its Poetic Ambience* (Krystyna Pomorska; Mouton Publishers, 1968), *Readings in Russian Poetics: Formalist and Structuralist Views* (eds. Ladislav Matejka and Krystyna Pomorska; MIT Press, 1971), and *The Futurists, the Formalists, and the Marxist Critique* (ed. Christopher Pike; trans. Christopher Pike and Joe Andrew; InkLinks, 1979). This last volume includes an essay by one of Shklovsky's closest literary friends, Yuri Tynjanov. Tynjanov writes:

> Verse is transformed speech; it is human speech which has outgrown itself. The word in verse has a thousand unexpected nuances of meaning, verse gives a new measure to the word. New verse is new vision.[4]

In May 1979, two months after he gave his "Russian Formalism & the Present" talk, Watten's *Plasma / Paralleles / "X"* was published. In the trio of works that comprise the chapbook, we can see him working out, and extending the possibilities of, some of the devices that most interested Shklovsky: those mentioned above, along with techniques of displacement and renaming (for example, through lexical shifts or synecdochic substitutions), the dialectical coexistence of rupture and linkage, and an affective energy for which we lack terminology but which is intensely experienced. In "Paralleles" (whose very title calls attention to the poem's most obvious formal device), much of that energy is emitted by the logical quandaries—the struggle for meaning—that the parallelisms construct. The workings of causation seem persistently present, but connecting particular causes to specific effects, or even being assured that such connections are possible, is difficult. Take, for example, this sequence (stanzas 5-7 of the seventy-stanza poem):

> Think of war a distance over flat water. The weekend traffic slows. A telescope points over roofs toward the bay.
>
> Simple facts compete with synthetic carpets. Rot undermines basic floorboards.
>
> Puns, hysteria, and pain are different forms of mental politics. Plugs and sockets "quote" the same.
>
> "I have my motives." Idea plugs into speech.[5]

"Paralleles" is built of sentences, generally with one to three per stanza, although one stanza has four; over half of the stanzas are two sentences long. Radical juxtapositions (and, thus, patent ruptures) are abundant. Excitement is kept high, and, as leaps are taken from one stanza to the next and the next, a sequence of short-circuits and redirections are brought into play. Narratives— or situational (and, perhaps, situationist) trajectories—proceed, but resolution is eschewed. Perhaps it is deemed impossible, but my guess is that Watten would regard resolution as being, in the current world, fated to bring suffering rather than satisfaction. It is, after all, a world in which one *can* "Think of war a distance over flat water." In the current historical moment, alas, it is placidity, not peace, that prevails, thanks precisely to the falsification (the false consciousness) that the distance taken by the perceiver from those suffering war produces. Indeed, that distance is the false consciousness. And it is such a consciousness that Watten has devoted his career to combatting.

Barrett Watten is not alone among the Language writers in having engaged from early on with Viktor Shklovsky's *On the Theory of Prose* and other works. Shklovsky's ideas are explicitly addressed in Ron Silliman's widely read essay "The New Sentence" and in his "Migratory Meaning," both of which were originally presented as talks and then published in 1987 in a volume that takes its title from the former.[6] And Kit Robinson titled one of his most audacious works "A Sentimental Journey," after Shklovsky's memoir of that title.[7]

Shklovsky's memoir recounts his experiences of the February Revolution of 1917, the subsequent October Revolution, and the tumultuous period of civil war that followed. During the stormy five or so years of which he writes in his memoir, Shklovsky's "journey" cast him into myriad difficult roles and multiple situations of political or military danger. He was, more or less in order: a soldier in an armored car unit of the Red Army stationed in Petrograd; a member (between the two revolutions) of the Petrograd Soviet; a participant in ongoing heated conversations with the circle of literary and artistic avant-gardists; a soldier on the Austrian front; a member of the Russian occupying army in Persia; co-publisher back in Moscow with Vladimir Mayakovsky and Osip Brik of a journal; a partisan fighting to restore the Constituent Assembly that the Bolsheviks had dismantled (and thus was under threat of arrest as a counter-revolutionary); a demolition man assigned to the Red Army; wounded (a bomb went off in his hands); and a resident again of Petrograd, where he and his wife lived in the House of Arts. The House of Arts was home to a number of writers and artists, and Shklovsky conducted weekly seminars there with the radically experimental prose writers who called themselves the Serapion Brotherhood. The seminars gave him an occasion to elaborate on his literary theories, and to illustrate many of them he turned to the writings of Laurence Sterne. His studies of Sterne's compositional techniques were analytical, but much of what he discovered in Sterne, who himself (in 1768) wrote a book titled *A Sentimental Journey*, plays a central role in the making of Shklovsky's memoir, for which he appropriated Sterne's title.

Kit Robinson discovered Shklovsky's work on his own, around the same time, coincidentally, that Harryman did: "I first discovered Shklovsky at the SF Public Library in 1971–1972, his *Mayakovsky and His Circle* [. . .]. I was quite taken by VS's short paragraph form."[8] It wasn't until almost twenty years later that an English translation of the full text of *On the Theory of Prose* was available, though there are many who argue that it is Shklovsky's most important book. It is, of course, primarily a book of literary theory. But it is also a consciously literary artifact, its devices as much manifesting as discussing the ways in which literary works engage with the dynamics of formation. That said, the paragraphs in this work tend to be longer than is typical in much of Shklovsky's writing, including *Mayakovsky and His Circle* and, to a lesser extent, *A Sentimental Journey*. Throughout his writings, however, regardless of the length of the paragraphs, motifs (including that of rapid and sometimes radical moves from one paragraph to the next) provide the centers of gravity around which the narrative is organized; motifs in their recurrences—unplotted but palpable—provide the works with coherence.

Kit Robinson in his version of "A Sentimental Journey" picks up on this with magnificent intensity. It is one of the two fundamental compositional devices guiding the poem. The other is its staccato, terse (and perhaps nervous or irritable) pace. Just looking at the first of the seventeen pages of the poem, one notes the rapid mobility of attention as the poem registers pedestrians, vehicular traffic, literary issues, wage earning, news media, time and time-clocks, urban sounds, music, and someone or something called

Selby.[9] The poem seems to have almost limitless scope, even as it remains local and present. It inhabits a site of ongoing sensation; eye, ear, brain, spirit are diversely engaged in a world of percussive energy.

Here are a few stanzas from near the beginning of the poem (the eleventh through fifteenth):

Oh shit it's the idiot. Over there. I'll sit here like this. Just look at the sky. Selby's twentieth century, don't explain, places bets (words) here and here and here. A psychologist of the 50s. Despair, killing fucking time. Stop the clock. & Other Diversions. As staccato claxon sounds from Mission Street this moment your reporter and a tip and thanx to the hat in hand line of word, the line, playing out a hand. Time goes both ways, hands you a line. "Where I just came from . . . the fifties." Memory. Oh I'd. So Selby. Simple. Struck dumb by all those periods. He don't stop for nothin.

I want to rip history to shreds.

Think of a boot. Does it fit?

Thickness. I'll sit down.

To this: kids and dogs and a woman leaning in different windows. It's natural here. Humanly possible. Girls and boy are dressed (black and blue and tan and magenta) and turning, over the shoulder, to check each other out.[10]

The poem goes on—176 stanzas of something akin to reportage, written, I would guess, over some period of time. Indeed, the poet seems to be marking time, as a flaneur might. In that sense, the poem may owe something to Baudelaire, and to Walter Benjamin, as well as to Viktor Shklovsky. Robinson's poem, however, is full of agitation, not idleness. And, though occasional memories appear, they don't produce nostalgia nor pack a more emotional punch than do the sight of two men jumpstarting a car or of "Sun on a rock."

Not everything that the poem registers belongs to the visual sphere, but "appear" does seem to be the right term for this work of phenomenological intensity and its affective burden. "A Sentimental Journey" is a poem of sensibility—a word that, in Laurence Sterne's day, was synonymous with sentiment: the human capacity to be profoundly affected by the world. Sentiment or sensibility in the eighteenth century named an aptitude for intensity and recognized it as something of profound value. It is expressed not through lachrymosity or epiphanic truisms but, as Shklovsky so amply demonstrates in his attention to Sterne's work in *On the Theory of Prose*, through ellipsis, juxtaposition, and irony.

"Your first impression upon picking up Sterne's *Tristram Shandy* and starting to read it is one of chaos." What Shklovsky says here of *The Life and Opinions of Tristram Shandy, Gentleman*, could be said of Robinson's "A Sentimental Journey." Whatever narrative might have been possible is short-circuited by digression, distraction, and detail. For the reader, this is a blessing, since it is precisely in violating the form of a travel diary (or corporate report or news item) that Robinson writes his great poem.

"I prefer to distribute narrative rather than deny it." So begins "Toy Boats," which appears as the opening work in Carla Harryman's 1995 collection *There Never Was a Rose Without a Thorn*, but was written and published some years earlier, in *Poetics Journal* 5 (1985) and then in *Animal Instincts* (1989).[11] Speaking recently about her interest in Viktor Shklovsky's work (first from her encounter with *A Sentimental Journey*, which she read in 1971 as a college student working, and subsequently from his other books), Harryman notes, "It is not only his devices in a technical sense [. . .] but also the way he works with memory [. . .] and his approach to genre."[12]

As its opening sentence suggests, "Toy Boats" is about narrative, although it is not only about that. It was written in response to a question sent to potential contributors to a "Symposium on Narrative" that duly appeared in the fifth issue of *Poetics Journal* titled "Non/Narrative." The question asked, "What is the status of narrative in your work?"

Harryman answers in something closely akin to the Aesopian language that is a prominent device in Shklovsky's work, perhaps most obviously in *Zoo, or Letters Not About Love*. There Shklovsky plays with the form of the epistolary novel, and also with the motif of censorship. Not very far in the background lies a prohibition issued by Elsa Triolet, with whom he had fallen in love. Triolet permitted him to write to her but forbade him from speaking about love. There are other prohibitions, some imposed by Shklovsky's delicate political position (he was exiled from the Soviet Union and living in Berlin, lonely and cold and hoping to be allowed to return), and some by a sense of civility—he had reason to strongly dislike a number of literary people but restrained himself, albeit "with difficulty," as he later said.

As he ostensibly avoided various topics, Shklovsky inserted others—substitution is one of *Zoo*'s most prominent devices. But the appearance of the forbidden topics, especially that of love, is a complementary device and equally prominent. "I'm not going to write about love. I'm going to write only about the weather" (*Zoo*, 16). "Writing about love is forbidden, so I'll write about Zinovy Grzhebin, the publisher" (*Zoo*, 27). "Forgive me, Alya, that the word 'love' has again crept so blatantly into my letter. I am tired of writing not about love" (*Zoo*, 83).[13]

Aesopian language is a term that was first used by the great nineteenth-century Russian satirist Mikhail Saltykov-Shchedrin, to describe the various forms of circumlocution available for circumventing censorship or worse. As David K. Danow describes them, "[T]he devices of Aesopian language included the utilization of imagery borrowed from fables, allegorical fairy tale descriptions, the use of periphrasis and pseudonyms, hidden allusions at times coupled with fairly direct references (e.g., to official repression), irony, and various juxtapositions and contrasts."[14]

It is only now, rereading "Toy Boats" and thinking about the abundant social intelligence of Harryman's work more generally, that it occurs to me that one might regard her as a satirist. Ridicule and melancholy are its coefficients, as in this exchange:

> The facts we have come up against are in need of processing.
> I don't have to tell a story to make a point.
> The story is an example of your point. An ugly howling face comes out of nowhere. It is artfully executed.
> You mean a bad boat.
> No, you have provided *that* information. But don't get upset by the disparity. A harmonious relationship produces a tedious vanity and a single repetitive conversation . . .
> (Then the boat sank, leaving behind them pieces of purple debris floating out of the harbor.)[15]

There's an element of burlesque here. The speeches are juxtaposed, but speakers seem to be at cross purposes; images ("ugly howling face," "bad boat") conflict; it comes to a bad end. This isn't funny—but satire isn't necessarily humorous. Its concerns are with power, the public imaginary, and hierarchies of value (or, in the case in point, "a hierarchy of literary values I don't entertain in my work," as Harryman puts it in "Toy Boats").[16]

To describe Harryman as a satirist wouldn't be adequate, nor by any means always true of her work, but certainly she is constantly thinking about social ills, and alert to the ways in which we so often fail even to notice them, much less address them. When anger is present in her work, it is expressed not as diatribe but tonally, so as to register, though not exercise, a right of refusal.

In fact, in my reading of "Toy Boats," refusal is always part of its dynamic dialectical complex; it is a motif that coexists with others that contradict as well as complement it, thus disabling its capacity to suppress. There is almost never a moment in which some kind of critique isn't underway, but it is propelled by desire. "For what?" is the obvious question to ask. For better stories, bearing better possibilities. Perhaps in this particular work, critique takes form as a toy boat bent on travel and bound for faraway ports.

The opening sentence of "Toy Boats" alone achieves a startling convergence of motifs, bringing *distribution* (from the economic sphere), *narrative* (from the literary), and *denial* (from the psycho-social) into a formulation that is both satisfying and unreasonable. Near the end of the piece Harryman speaks of histories, one (but only one) example of narrative: "Histories that have been intercepted en route by questions. The result might be something like a montage of collapsed ideas."[17] As Shklovsky points out in his discussion of "stepped structure," art is not about generalizations or all-encompassing formulas. Harryman's answer to the question posed to her was—is—art. In "Toy Boats" she has created a shifting (or, one might say, bobbing) montage, each element of which is an instance of narrative, and all of which together progresses toward a jumble. That's Harryman's term: "the words fall in place in anticipation of a jumble."[18] There is some whimsy to this statement, but also a profound, albeit implicit, advocacy for the truths to be engaged with through jumbling. This is not to say that Harryman celebrates quandary, however—there are few social critics capable of her level of clarity and of informed action—off the page as well as on it. And there are few whose interventions into Shklovskian form are more deliberate and inventive.

One of the major North American prose writers of the past few decades is Renee Gladman, a writer considerably younger than Harryman and one who has, clearly, carefully read her work. She has also read Viktor Shklovsky: "I've definitely read Shklovsky, most memorably *Third Factory* and [*Zoo,*] *Letters not About Love*. Something happened for me when I read *Factory*. I don't know if it was influence exactly but I noticed in a bodily kind of way something about how his voice felt intimate to me as it was moving through all these different objects, things both close and far away."[19]

Gladman's most recent project is a multifaceted study of what she terms "prose architectures," under which rubric she has written theory (most conspicuously an essay title "The Sentence as a Space for Living"), a graphic study of syntactic structures (superficially closer to Tatlin than to Shklovsky, perhaps), and a trio of inter-related novels.[20] The novels engage in a magnificent, melancholy exploration of the dystopian city-state of Ravicka, or about the architectures of its absence, since Ravicka is progressively disappearing. It is tempting to read the three Ravickian books as an extended fable—of architecture itself, perhaps, except that the architecture of Ravicka is already half-fabulous, its every element raised to prefigure whatever meanings can make their way into the empty spaces architecture provides. In Ravicka they are edifices of connotation and displacement.

> From the sky there was no sign of Ravicka. Yet, I arrived; I met many people. The city was large, yellow, and tender. A cab delivered me. When I walked through the door I expected a crowd, but there was just a man. "Hello," I said. "Hello," he returned then added, "My name is Simon." "Simon, are you the one with whom I am speaking?" I had started my Ravic right then.[21]

So begins the first of the novels, *Event Factory*, whose title, of course, evokes that of Shklovsky's *Third Factory*. The opening of *Event Factory* resembles that of *Third Factory*—not closely, but certainly in its disorienting effects. Shklovsky's is, ostensibly, another of his memoirs and not the first. So he begins, as it were, in medias res, but also in a way that simultaneously signals distance and invites intimacy, establishes absence and declares presence. The opening gambit is titled simply "I Continue" and begins thus:

> I speak in a voice grown hoarse from silence and feuille-
> tons. I'll begin with a piece that has been lying around for a
> long time.
> The way you assemble a film by attaching to the beginning
> either a piece of exposed negative or a strip from another film.
> I am attaching a piece of theoretical work. The way a soldier
> crossing a stream holds his rifle high.[22]

The shift from cinematic editing room to war zone is, if one
reads the second as an equivalent of the first, almost heavy-hand-
edly symbolic. But of what: the courage of the artist or the caution
(though not cowardice) of the soldier? These are contradictory. But
contradiction here is merely another name for paradox. The soldier
and the film editor are both learning the language of abeyance, a
language that is charged with unreleased but palpable meaning,
and the language of that meaning, which is discharged, however
hesitantly, in the fraught structures that bring contradictions into
conjunction.

Shklovsky exercises the principle of selection; it produces paradox. Gladman's narrator searches for the principles whereby selec-
tions might be made. In both cases, something political and therefore psychological (since politics impacts persons) is active, but (of
necessity for Shklovsky and for existential reasons for Gladman)
they are veiled. What veils them is speculation. And it is speculation, not veiling, that is the operative device.

It is used in the service of sentiment again—the interplay of
states of mind alert to stages of sensation. And this is one of the
many techniques by which something of the social enters into
structural aesthetic dynamics and the composition of the literary.
The social here is not conceptual, not even generalizable, and
certainly not universal. It is, indeed, strangely, and paradoxically,
intimate.

But perhaps paradoxes are always found, finally, where intimacy is present. Both depend on parallelism, and on divergences from it.

In a letter to his long-time friend Boris Eichenbaum, Shklovsky wrote:

> Life was long. How much was unclear? So many people passed through.
>
> How dear to us our time is. How dearly we have paid for it. Sometimes at night I think about art.
>
> Mainly about Chekhov. To whom will we leave our knowledge? [. . .]
>
> We will live out our lives, my friend and brother, and maybe on the boggy shore of old age we will still see the evening sun and the wide shadows of inspiration.
>
> Your Viktor[23]

1. *A Sentimental Journey: Memoirs, 1917–1922* (1970); *Zoo, or Letters Not About Love* (1971); *Mayakovsky and His Circle* (1972); and *Third Factory* (1979); *Mayakovsky and His Circle* was edited and translated by Lily Feiler; the other volumes were translated by Richard Sheldon. *Theory of Prose* was not available in book form in English until 1990 (trans. Benjamin Sher; Normal, IL: Dalkey Archive Press).

2. "Russian Formalism & the Present," first published in Bob Perelman, editor, *Hills 6/7*, 1980; republished in Barrett Watten, *Total Syntax* (Carbondale, IL: Southern Illinois University Press, 1985).

3. Watten, *Total Syntax*, 1.

4. Pike, 108.

5. Barrett Watten, *Plasma, Paralleles, "X"* (Berkeley: Tuumba Press, 1979), unpaginated; reprinted in Barrett Watten, *Frame (1971–1990)* (Los Angeles: Sun & Moon Press, 1997), 70.

6. Ron Silliman, *The New Sentence* (New York: Roof Books, 1987).

7. Robinson's "A Sentimental Journey" was first published in *Hills* magazine (Bob Perelman, ed., *Hills* 4, 1981); it is collected in Kit Robinson, *Windows* (Amherst, Mass: Whale Cloth, 1984).

8. Kit Robinson to Lyn Hejinian; email, May 18, 2015.

9. Robinson tells me that it is Hubert Selby, Jr., the author of *Last Exit to Brooklyn*. Kit Robinson to Lyn Hejinian; email, June 1, 2015.

10. Kit Robinson, *Windows*, 49-50.

11. Carla Harryman, *There Never Was a Rose Without a Thorn* (San Francisco: City Lights Books, 1995); Carla Harryman, *Animal Instincts* (Oakland, CA: This, 1989).

12. Carla Harryman to Lyn Hejinian, email, May 18, 2015.

13. Viktor Shklovsky, *Zoo, or Letters Not About Love*, trans. Richard Sheldon (Chicago and Normal, IL: Dalkey Archive Press, 2001).

14. David K. Danow, "Aesopian language," in *Handbook of Russian Literature*, ed. Victor Terras (New Haven and London: Yale University Press, 1985), 9.

15. Harryman, *There Never Was a Rose Without a Thorn*, 5.

16. Ibid.

17. Carla Harryman, *There Never Was a Rose Without a Thorn*, 6.

18. Ibid, 5.

19. Renee Gladman to Lyn Hejinian; email, May 29, 2015.

20. The Sentence as a Space for Living" was presented as the 2014 Leslie Scalapino Lecture in Innovative Poetics at the University of California, Berkeley; the series of "Prose Architecture" drawings remains a work-in-progress; the three Ravickian novels are *Event Factory* (Urbana, IL: Dorothy, a Publishing Project, 2010), *The Ravickians* (Urbana, IL: Dorothy, a Publishing Project, 2011), and *Ana Patova Crosses a Bridge* (Urbana, IL: Dorothy, a Publishing Project, 2013).

21. Renee Gladman, *Event Factory*, 11–12.

22. Viktor Shklovsky, *Third Factory*, trans. Richard Sheldon (Chicago and Normal, IL: Dalkey Archive Press, 2002), 3.

23. From manuscript version of selected letters between Viktor Shklovsky, Boris Eichenbaum, and Yuri Tynjanov edited by Olga Panchenko. Much of the manuscript was published in *Voprosy Literatury* 12 (Moscow, December 1984) but this particular passage was omitted. Translated by Elena Balashova and Lyn Hejinian.

Printed in the USA
CPSIA information can be obtained
at www.ICGtesting.com
JSHW021351210524
63541JS00002B/6